MEET CHARLIE'S "ANGELS"

Lady Jane Wellesley
Lady Sarah Specer
Princess Marie-Astrid of Luxembourg
Tricia Nixon
Laura Jo Watkins of San Diego
Margaret Trudeau
Davina Sheffield
Farrah Fawcett-Majors

These are just a few of the women with whom Prince Charles has been linked in bold print and whispered rumor, in rendezvous that range from private country manor weekends to nude beach frolics. What is it like to go out on a date with a Prince? How far have these romances gone? Who is he likely to choose as his royal mate? You will find the answers in this uncensored, intimate look at —

THE MAN WHO WILL BE KING
H.R.H.

THE MAN WHO WILL BE KING

TIM HEALD & MAYO MOHS

BERKLEY BOOKS, NEW YORK

This Berkley book contains the complete
text of the original hardcover edition.
It has been completely reset in a type face
designed for easy reading, and was printed
from new film.

H.R.H.: THE MAN WHO WILL BE KING

A Berkley Book / published by arrangement with
Arbor House

PRINTING HISTORY
Arbor House edition / August 1979
Berkley edition / July 1980

ISBN: 0-425-04659-1

A BERKLEY BOOK ® TM 757,375
Berkley Books are published by Berkley Publishing Corporation,
200 Madison Avenue, New York, New York 10016.
PRINTED IN THE UNITED STATES OF AMERICA

Contents

AUTHORS' NOTE:

ROYALTY is uniquely sensitive about its image—and the friends and associates of royalty are even more sensitive. We would like to acknowledge the help of those who have assisted us, but most of the persons who have provided us with accurate or intimate details of Prince Charles's life have done so only with the understanding that they would remain anonymous. The wishes of our informants have been respected. Among those who have not sought anonymity, the staff at Buckingham Palace deserve our special thanks. We especially wish to express our debt to John Dauth, who has gone out of his way to provide information and to reassure reluctant sources that there was no Palace opposition to their being interviewed for the purposes of this book. Prince Charles's own policy is not to give exclusive interviews to the author of *any* biography of him; the verbatim quotations attributed to the Prince in this book are taken from the public record. Obviously, then, this is not in any sense an official or authorized biography; but neither Prince Charles nor Buckingham Palace has frowned on our labors, and for this we thank them.

T.V.H.
M.A.M.

London and New York

PROLOGUE

FOR MOST PEOPLE in the Western world life is a matter of choice as well as chance. Indeed, it is a cornerstone of our beliefs that we can make of ourselves what we will. But for Charles Philip Arthur George, twenty-first Prince of Wales, heir to the throne of Her Majesty Queen Elizabeth the Second, there is no such luxury. He was born a prince, and a prince he will remain until the day he dies or becomes a king. A prince is a prince; he cannot become a common man. He cannot become a brain surgeon, or a novelist, or a coal miner or a cab driver, nor can he take on the anonymity enjoyed by his subjects. From the day of his birth in 1948 Prince Charles's life has run on a course planned by committees and consensus.

Charles is defensive about the strictures of his position, as any self-respecting man would be. "I have got a life of my own and I like it," he says. "Perhaps I would like another life more, but this is the one I know." And in a very restricted sense, Charles's life *is* his own—but only as long as he lives in a certain way. For while he may one day rule over the people of Britain and the Commonwealth, he is also, by the paradox of constitutional monarchy, the servant of the people as well as their master. His motto, *Ich Dien*, has been the motto of the

1

Princes of Wales for hundreds of years, and it means "I serve." By virtue of his birth Charles enjoys colossal advantages and privileges scarcely dreamed of by ordinary mortals, but from his birth the Prince has worn shackles which most people would never endure. In the modern world which prides itself on equality of opportunity for all its inhabitants and in a country which, since the end of the Second World War, has moved along the road to socialism with scarcely a hiccough, Prince Charles is the ultimate anachronism.

"I am conscious of being different," he has said. "You don't know—you can't know, can you?—how much different. After all, you only know what it is to be you, though you can study other people and deduce things about how *they* feel, to an extent. But I've been brought up the way I have, and I've had the background I've had, and not many other people have had that. So it makes one different, and makes one feel different."

Not that, on first impression, Charles *looks* different, although he is considered rather handsome, especially by young women. He is five-feet-eleven-inches tall, but seems shorter (even his press secretary is inclined to forget and say that the Prince is five-feet-ten). Charles's chest measures thirty-eight inches and he has a thirty-one-inch waist. His complexion is ruddy and his hair is just beginning to thin at the back and at the corners of the forehead. Like his father, Prince Philip, Charles speaks with a very upper-class British accent, with just a hint of querulousness, but there is nothing effete in the mellifluous baritone of the former student actor. Charles is affable and good-humored, but he expects—and commands—the respect his rank demands. Even some of the Prince's girlfriends call him "Sir," in the fashion of the admirers of Charles's predecessor as Prince of Wales, Edward VIII. Edward's girlfriend Wallis, later his wife, used to call him "David." British society was shocked. "In my day," said one of Edward's earlier flames, "we either called him 'Sir'...or 'Darling.'" Charles apparently prefers "Sir," even in most small informal gatherings, and on meeting the Prince everyone, without exception, is expected to show deference—men by bowing, women by curtseying.

Although he probably has more names and titles than any

man on earth, the future sovereign of Britain signs himself simply "Charles," in a looped, backward-sloping hand. He could (but doesn't) add "P" afterward, for the Latin "Princeps." Charles, on the other hand, has a disarming and leavening sense of the absurd: in November, 1978, while in Yugoslavia for a meeting with Marshal Tito, the Prince signed the visitors' book in a maritime museum and then stared wryly at the single name on the large blank page. "That's odd," he said. "Who on earth will know who it is?"

He has a surname—at least nominally—but there is some uncertainty whether it is Mountbatten-Windsor or simply Windsor; the Queen's pronouncement on the subject was rather ambiguous. Whatever his surname is, Charles will have scant occasion to use it—and for a man who can trace his ancestry back through more than fifteen hundred years and fifty-four generations to Cerdic, King of the West Saxons, such commonplaces as surnames seem irrelevant. Although he has some non-royal blood in his veins, every drop is bluer than blue. Both his parents are direct descendants of Queen Victoria: the Queen is descended through Victoria's son, Edward VII, and Prince Philip through Victoria's daughter Alice. Chances are that Charles will retain his given name all his life, although members of royalty have a disconcerting habit of changing name when they become kings. Charles's grandfather was Albert, or "Bertie," until becoming King George VI, and Charles's great-uncle was always known to the family as "David" until he became King Edward VIII. Charles will probably be King Charles III, but he could conceivably decide to become Philip I, Arthur I or George VII, or even choose perversely to take an entirely different name. For the moment he is styled Prince of Wales and Earl of Chester, Duke of Cornwall and Duke of Rothesay, Earl of Carrick and Baron Renfrew, Lord of the Isles and Great Steward of Scotland. All of these titles carry more cachet than conventional surnames, although none but the Principality of Wales and the Duchy of Cornwall have much more than euphony to commend them.

Cornwall is the key to Charles's fortunes. The Duchy was created in 1337 by King Edward III to provide an independent income for the monarch's eldest son. It now comprises more than 120,000 acres, including much prime farm land, an oysterage, three golf courses (golf is ironically one of the Prince's pet aversions) and much of the South London borough of Kennington, now a densely populated area thick with apartment buildings but once a royal hunting forest. Under law Charles is not required to pay any tax on the quarter-million pounds or so to which inflation and sound management have now raised the annual income of the Duchy. In fact he elects to return half the money to the British treasury; with equal generosity he donated his entire naval salary to the King George Fund for Sailors. Such gestures, of course, however sincere, are not exactly crippling... the Prince also maintains a rakish Aston-Martin DB6 Volante sports car as well as a string of polo ponies and hunters, and he is still authoritatively described as "probably the second richest person in the United Kingdom"—the first being his mother, the Queen.

Wealth makes Charles's life comfortable, but not necessarily easy. His recreations are noticeably spartan and physically demanding, and he takes the *Ich Dien* motto on his three-plumed badge extremely seriously. The motto is also on the gold signet ring Charles always wears on the little finger of his left hand. (Charles has referred to himself as "a ring lunatic. I like all kinds of rings—boxing, telephones, bells, and even the Colgate Ring of Confidence.")

The German motto, like the Duchy of Cornwall, has a romantic but apparently authentic origin, dating back to 1346 and the pivotal battle of Crécy in the Hundred Years War between England and France. The Prince of Wales of that day, a gallant warrior known to history as the Black Prince, won his spurs on the bloody battlefield as a sixteen-year-old boy fighting alongside his father, King Edward III. Among the enemy slain the young victor found the blind King John of Bohemia, who had ordered his knights to lead him into the fray. The Black Prince was so moved by the courage of the fallen king that he adopted his ostrich-plume crest and motto for himself and his successors. Other princes have sometimes seemed to disdain the idea of service, but Charles has a genuine sense of noblesse oblige. "I don't want to be a figurehead," he said firmly at the age of twenty-five. "I want to get things done."

In November, 1978, Charles turned thirty, and he is still chafing to "get things done," worried that he has not yet made a mark on the world. After a trip to South America earlier that same year he observed that people there "think I'm twenty-two or twenty-three years old, not very flattering when you think about it."

Flattering or not, Charles has always seemed young for his age—perhaps a result of being shielded from so many of the rough edges of everyday life. (The Prince is adept at making jokes about his cosseted upbringing; once, during a Cambridge University revue-skit, he came onstage as himself, carrying a large, fully-spread umbrella, and brought down the house with the quip, "I lead a very sheltered life.") Nevertheless, he has an extraordinary number of skills and personal achievements to offset any apparent immaturity. He is, for example, the first heir to the throne to earn a university degree—a bachelor of arts from Trinity College, Cambridge, where he followed a full three-year course, studying archaeology, anthropology and history. Earlier princes studied at Oxford or Cambridge, and sometimes both, but their attendance was perfunctory, their exam results derisory. Charles "swotted" (crammed) for his exams like any earnest undergraduate, enjoying few concessions to his rank and status, and achieved respectable grades despite such time-consuming and unusual distractions as the State opening of Parliament, a royal visit to Japan, a term in Aberystwyth to learn Welsh, and his much publicized investiture as Prince of Wales at Caernarvon Castle. His tutor, Dr. Denis Marrian, commented: "How on earth he did it all, I don't know."

He also learned to fly an airplane, thus emulating his father, who is still inclined to take to the controls of whatever aircraft he happens to be traveling in. In March, 1971, Charles matriculated at the Royal Air Force College at Cranwell and passed through a compressed five-month course that took him from jet trainers to supersonic Phantoms. He was awarded his wings in August of that year and became a member of the Ten Ton

Club—pilots who have flown faster than 1000 miles per hour. At his own request the Prince joined his fellow cadets in a parachute jump into the sea.

During the five years of active service with the Royal Navy Charles won his Navy wings learning to fly helicopters, which some pilots consider the trickiest aircraft of all. The Prince's instructors considered him a natural; one senior officer says Charles was among his most outstanding students. "It was uncanny," the officer recalls. "He had an instinct for helicopters which was second to none. It was a joy to teach him."

Prince Charles combined his expertise with a panache and some bravado, which surprised those who had found Charles shy and reserved in childhood. At a rugby tournament at Twickenham on the outskirts of London in 1977, for example, Prince Charles, the guest of honor, had to leave early, but instead of an unobtrusive exit he went out to the nearby field where his twin-engined red Wessex helicopter was parked and flew in low between the grandstands, hovering in brief farewell to the 60,000 spectators before banking up and away. In the United States he might have been called a "hot pilot."

Despite such inclinations, the award of his RAF wings at Cranwell brought an end to Charles's active Royal Air Force duties. For a man only one step away from the throne, combat duties at supersonic speed were simply considered an unjustifiable risk. Like his great-grandfather, grandfather and father before him, Charles entered the Royal Navy, though here, too, his life was hardly commonplace. His tours of shore duty—routine extended interludes for most career officers—were brief stints intended mainly to supplement the crash course in naval skills he had received as a cadet at the Royal Naval College at Dartmouth. Before he left his first sea duty aboard the guided missile destroyer H.M.S. *Norfolk* Charles had stood engine room watches, assisted in the emergency steering room and shared the bridge watch during a force-ten gale off Sardinia. On the frigate *Minerva* he was assistant gunnery and guided missile officer, and on the *Minerva*'s sister ship *Jupiter*, communications officer, responsible for everything from the ship's signal flags to its cryptography room.

Temporary assignments broadened, so to speak, Charles's nautical horizons. Aboard H.M.S. *Scimitar*, the Royal Navy's fastest torpedo boat, he took the helm in exercises against the *Norfolk*. As assistant navigator on the hydrographic vessel H.M.S. *Fox* he helped float a Swedish bulk carrier grounded on a coral reef in the Caribbean. He also insisted on going through submarine familiarization at the coastal station at Gosport, where training involved a hazardous set of simulated submarine escapes without any breathing apparatus from a deep tank 30, 60 and 100 feet below the surface.

Charles's comments on his exploits reveal a self-deprecating sense of humor. At Resolute Bay in northern Canada he spent twenty minutes in a diving suit exploring near-polar waters that stood at a chilling 28.5 degrees Fahrenheit. On emerging he confessed, "I could not resist pressing the inlet valve on my suit and inflating the suit to capacity. Looking exactly like Mr. Michelin [the bulbous trademark figure of the French tire company] I floated out of my tent and took the assembled press and TV cameramen by complete surprise." Even Queen Victoria's son Edward, that elephantine Prince of Wales, never looked more bloated.

The clowning did not reduce the Navy's opinion of Charles as a sailor-prince. Early in 1976 he was awarded what every young officer seeks and few get: a command of his own. The ship was not spectacular—a wooden-hulled, shallow-draught minehunter named H.M.S. *Bronington*. The *Bronington* rolled about like a cork during the mildest weather and brought on acute seasickness in her royal captain. Not that there was anything shameful in that—Horatio Nelson, Britain's most famous naval commander, was another notoriously seasick sailor. Indeed, after just under a year at the helm of the *Bronington*, Charles had earned a reputation as an adept small-ship skipper and leader, whether on such routine tasks as searching the Firth of Forth for mines left over from World War II, or more up-to-date missions like shadowing Soviet submarines in the English Channel. "I try very hard to be as professional as possible," Charles said. Actually he did more than that. He seemed to be testing himself all the time, proving to himself that he was up to

7

what was required of him and more.

Apart from the military, Charles just seems to thrive on competition and danger. His favorite relaxation—perhaps to the point of obsession—is polo, and he has made himself into a plus-three handicap player, about average for a frequent polo player but, as his polo manager puts it, also one "on the way up." The manager, Major Ronald Ferguson, an ex-calvary officer renowned as Britain's foremost polo expert, believes that "Charles is not a naturally good games player but he's *made* himself into one and acquired a real games sense. He's physically very tough." Whether fearless could develop into foolhardy is a question Charles seems already to have answered. In 1972, at the Thruxton Racetrack in Hampshire with driving champion Graham Hill, Charles climbed into Hill's own Formula Two racer—essentially a gasoline tank on wheels—for a drive around the track. Hill was supposed to follow closely in an Aston-Martin, but Charles, his foot on the accelerator, soon lost him and barely missed spinning out on a turn. In his posthumously published autobiography Hill recalled, "If he crashes, I'll be heir to the bloody Tower." Somehow Charles straightened the car out and brought it in. There is also no evidence that he has ever climbed into anything faster than his 140-mph Aston-Martin since.

The Queen's reaction to that episode is not recorded, but if there is a worry in the Royal Family now that Charles is past thirty, it is less about derring-do than marrying-won't. At twenty-seven Charles remarked that "a good age for a man to get married is around thirty." That seemed safe enough at the time, but now that he is past that milestone Charles shows little sign of settling down. The Royal Family's memories are still fresh of uncle David, the last Prince of Wales, who drifted through his thirties and into his forties before marrying—and then abdicated the throne to wed the twice-divorced American Wallis Warfield Simpson, "the woman I love," as he put it in his dramatic abdication speech. In 1965, when the Queen gave a dinner party for an informal but distinguished assemblage of men who have long advised on the Prince's education and career, she is reported to have said that she feared "an Edward

VII situation." By which she meant she worried that her son would wait throughout his adult life with nothing to do but anticipate his mother's demise and his own succession. Now, however, the more immediate concern would seem to be an "Edward *VIII* situation."

Still, if Charles is reluctant to marry it may be because so many others have for so long been so painfully eager to see him marching down the aisle of Westminster Abbey with a *suitable* bride on his arm. More than twenty years ago a London newspaper first published a list of possible consorts for Charles, and royalty-watchers have been at the game ever since. Most of the possibilities have long since married, and only one of those "little princesses" first cited by *Women's Wear Daily* remains a remote and very controversial contender: Princess Marie-Astrid of Luxembourg, now a vivacious blonde in her early twenties. But any possibility of a match there—once the Queen is said to have favored—may have been botched by premature publicity and the uproar in Parliament about Charles marrying a Roman Catholic.

There is more to popular concern over Charles's future bride than a delight in Court badinage. After the scandalous era of the late Hanoverians when the royal image was tarnished by self-indulgence and sexual extravagance, Queen Victoria and her consort Prince Albert worked hard to mold the royal family life into a model for the nation. Their son, Edward VII, let them down with his roistering behavior, but George V and his son George VI were exemplary in their devotion to family life and established a tradition which has been resolutely maintained by the present Queen Elizabeth and her husband.

In the present Royal Family, Charles is definitely the ace in the pack, or in the words of his great-uncle Lord Mountbatten, "a bloody miracle." The Queen is widely respected, and as the spontaneous celebrations accompanying her Silver Jubilee in 1977 demonstrated, more deeply loved than even some Britons had realized. But she is, by reason of her fifty-three years and her position as head of State, a more remote and austere figure than her relatively youthful, relatively unrestricted son. Charles has also served as something of an antidote to British displeasure with the Queen's headstrong sister Princess Margaret, whose long, painfully public liaison with Roderick "Roddy" Llewellyn, a thirtyish would-be pop singer, sometime-landscape gardener and man-about-town has caused considerable embarrassment. And Charles's sister Anne, a dedicated horsewoman who sometimes seems to prefer horses to people, has not helped the family's popularity lately (at an equestrian event in which she was competing, Anne gave forth with "Shit, shit, shit," precisely timed to coincide with the clicks of a photographer's camera).

Other members of the Royal Family inspire greater affection. Charles's grandmother Elizabeth, the Queen Mother, is, in her late seventies, generally known as "The Queen Mum" and remains unfailingly gracious and outgoing. Despite being royalty only by marriage (her father was a mere earl), she often seems the most regal of the lot. Prince Philip's occasional expletives and bouts of ill-temper now excite little comment; indeed, they are frequently admired as displays of spirit. Charles's younger brother Andrew, age nineteen, is just beginning to emerge as, in Charles's description, "the Robert Redford" of the family—lean, lanky, sexy and even more of a daredevil than Charles. Prince Edward, still a schoolboy at fifteen, seems quieter and more introspective than any of his siblings, and shows an intellectual bent. But at Edward's age Charles gave little hint of the extrovert he was to become.

At times Charles seems almost too good to be true, and in recent years he has enjoyed an unprecedented honeymoon with the public. Even Britain's workers seem to like him. When *Time* magazine ran a cover story on Charles in 1978, a porter and World War II veteran named Jack Diment was quoted as saying, "He's first rate. He's sensible, down to earth—of that there is no doubt. He has got guts. He's a thoroughly good bloke."

When he gets the chance he reads avidly. On his world cruise in H.M.S. *Jupiter* he managed Solzhenitzyn's *Gulag Archipelago*, Cecil Woodham-Smith's *Queen Victoria* and the novels of Thomas Hardy. More recently he has become a devotee of E.F. Schumacher's "small is beautiful" philosophy. Charles even reviews books from time to time; he gave a critical rave to Welsh comedian Harry Secombe's first novel in the humorous magazine *Punch*. The Prince is also something of a musician, who has played piano, trumpet and cello with varying success, and whose listening taste ranges from Berlioz to The Three Degrees.

Recently Charles has been taking on more duties that will increase his influence in the public sphere—president of the United World Colleges, a multi-national, multi-racial educational scheme with schools in the U.K., Canada and Singapore and students from all over the world; creator of his own organization, the Prince's Trust, to create opportunities for some of Britain's underprivileged young people; head of the Royal Anthropological Society; colonel of several army regiments; chairman of the Appeal Fund which marked his mother's Jubilee Celebrations. He travels widely, showing the Union Jack and reminding everyone that the Queen is not just Queen of Great Britain and Northern Ireland but also of Canada, Australia, New Zealand, not to mention Fiji and Papua-New Guinea. His intense enthusiasm for almost everything he does has led some observers to remark that he could slip easily into a comfortable, if energetic, bachelor existence that might last for years. It is difficult to say who is more devastated by such speculation—his mother or his would-be consorts.

For Charles, the future is a question mark. As he begins on the fourth decade of his life, the pressures grow, multiply. If his mother serves out her reign (as everyone expects her to) and if she remains in robust health, then Charles has two or three decades of status quo ahead of him. At thirty Prince Charles knows that his future is likely to be more dangerous and problematical than his past. In an egalitarian world he is one of the last of an endangered species. There are fewer crown princes than whooping cranes or Bengal tigers, and there are plenty of republican poachers who would be glad to have him removed. It doesn't seem too likely, though. He is astonishingly popular, and the British consider they are lucky to have him. His great-uncle, Earl Mountbatten of Burma, disagreed. "It's not luck," he said. "It's a bloody miracle."

This, then, is the story of a young man who manages, despite all the odds, to combine the extraordinary with the ordinary. The authors' researches have taken them from the inside of Buckingham Palace to a wintry hillside above the coal mines of working-class Wales; from aristocrats to artisans; polo players to estate agents. From them they have tried to create a genuine portrait of a unique man—the man who will be King.

CHAPTER ONE

A Day in the Principality

IT WAS A COLD, gray December day in 1978, a day of unrelenting public attention as the Prince progressed the length of his tiny, mountainous principality greeting his subjects wherever he went, making speeches, cracking jokes, waving to the crowds. "Charlie," the people called him, as they stood waiting by the roadside. Seeing him would make their day; to touch him would be true joy.

The day, however, also had its low points. The royal procession ran late all morning and was almost late again at night—Prince Charles nearly missed his train. Still, there was a moment of magic on the mountain in the dusky chill of late afternoon, and an evening of hearty Welsh song and celebration as Charles stepped into the midst of hundreds of wellwishers, then waited as drums rolled, the band began to play and a chorus of strong Welsh voices literally rose to the rafters. "God bless the Prince of Wales!" they sang. "Oh let the prayer re-echo, God Bless the Prince of Wales!" Such a moment in the Club Double Diamond, in the South Wales town of Caerphilly, was distinctly one to savor...

Caerphilly is famous for three things: its mild but delicious cheese, its Norman castle and the Club Double Diamond, a huge barn of a place where eight hundred or so Welshman can eat a three-course dinner, drink a pint or two of ale and listen to some of the biggest names in show business. On the night of December 15, 1978, the hall was packed with men in black ties and tuxedos—famous Welsh rugby players like Gerald Davies, Welsh personalities like writer and broadcaster Wynford Vaughan Thomas, and hordes of anonymous Welshmen, their thick shoulders and battered features proclaiming a long allegiance to their national sport. The women were in long dresses, hair lacquered, shoulders exposed to the flickering spotlights. Outside in the car park the massed Rolls-Royces testified that at least some Welshmen were doing all right. The occasion was charity—£25,000 was raised that night—£600 of it for an autographed Rugby Ball auctioned in the middle of dinner. But the draw, the main attraction, was the presence of stars.

On stage the first star of the evening was all sequined gown and tawny skin: Singer Shirley Bassey, black, beautiful and Welsh, born in Cardiff's tough Tiger Bay waterfront slum, daughter of a Yorkshirewoman and a black merchant seaman from West Africa. She was on home turf; she had been singing for more than a quarter-century, belting out her torch songs and show tunes, first as a teenager in Cardiff workingmen's clubs, later as a voluptuous, brassy-voiced headliner in Las Vegas. An outrageous flick of the hips, an outsize wink, and Miss Bassey greeted the evening's other star, sitting in the place of honor, a red carnation in his buttonhole.

"Your Royal Highness," she intoned, "what's a Princely Prince like you doing in a *joint* like this?" The audience cheered and applauded, partly because they recognized this prelude to "Big Spender," one of Miss Bassey's best known hits, and partly because the affectionate *lèse majesté* of her greeting so exactly matched their own feelings. Later, after the singer had belted her way through a repertoire of her most popular numbers, she announced that she was dedicating her next song to the Prince of Wales. The Prince sat impassively about thirty yards from the stage. "There's something," sang Miss Bassey, "in the way . . . he

14

smiles...." Applause, cheers. "Something in the style...that shows..." Cheers, whistles.

And so on to the climax: a rhythmic soaring, a crescendo from the band; and a provocative bow that had more to do with suggestion than deference. Everyone was on his feet, the Double Diamond alive with cries of "Encore" and "Well done, Shirley," and "Come on Charlie." Seconds later the dapper, faintly embarrassed figure of the heir to Britain's throne was up on stage. "It's kind of you to stand up," he said, diffidently but in a firm, mellow, aristocratic voice. "I much appreciate it. I wish I could do something useful and sing." He didn't sing, though the remark was greeted with still more applause. Instead, he thanked Miss Bassey for "an evening I shall remember for a very long time," and added with a straight face that he was "grateful to whoever it was who released her from jail"—a reference to the singer's recent arrest in confusing circumstances at a London night club. "Amazing," he added, "what you can do on bail." It was a popular line and everyone applauded again, one or two women standing on their chairs for a view, waving their arms and jumping like adolescents at a rock concert.

It was an audience ready and willing to laugh at anything, hanging on every word. When Prince Charles continued in muted, urbane fashion, "I would hope Miss Bassey would come back once more," the din increased. Shirley came back, there was a final song, and then a mounting chorus of "Give her a kiss, Charlie," so insistent that finally the Prince did kiss the Showgirl. A little later *she* kissed *him* and then, in a husky voice, announced, "Gentlemen of the press, you can make of *that* what you want." But within minutes, at about 11:20 P.M., the Prince was off to catch his train, threading his way through the still-applauding guests, out into the cold Welsh air and the waiting Rolls from the Royal Mews at Buckingham Palace. Away rolled the Rolls down the main A470 road to Cardiff and the relative peace and privacy of the private sleeping car which was to carry him to a quiet family weekend in Scotland, and perhaps dreams of the irreverent Shirley.

The day that ended on the railway began there, too, more

than a hundred miles to the south, in the Wiltshire Cathedral town of Salisbury, immortalized in the canvases of 19th-century English painter John Constable. The royal train, not the latest, flashiest royal train but an older model more able to cope with the winding tract to the morning's first stop, the seaside resort Rhyl on the north coast of Wales. Prince Charles had been dining just outside the city at Boscombe Down, the Royal Air Force's Experimental Establishment, where the latest batch of Britain's test pilots had been celebrating the completion of their training. Prince Charles, a qualified pilot, had joined the fête. Shortly before midnight he and his principal secretary, a forty-eight-year-old former RAF squadron leader named David Checketts, and the Prince's personal detective, Chief Inspector Paul Officer, boarded the train. The Prince was still wearing the official best uniform of the Royal Air Force, complete with medals, while his two aides wore plain black tuxedoes and black bow ties. Waiting for them aboard the train was the Prince's press officer, a thirty-one-year-old Australian named John Dauth, on temporary duty from his country's diplomatic service. Dauth had not been at Boscombe, but had made his own way from Buckingham Palace to Salisbury using public transport.

Ten minutes before midnight the train jolted out of Salisbury en route for Wales and the town of Rhyl. For an ordinary traveler a rail journey from Salisbury to Rhyl would be forbiddingly complicated, involving numerous changes of trains and long waits on wintry depot platforms. The royal train, an older model chosen for its ease of handling on the winding Welsh roadbeds, had no such handicaps: it would roll right through to the destination. At 12:30 A.M., with a heavy day of ceremonies ahead of him, the Prince decided it was time for bed. "Goodnight, Your Royal Highness," said the aides. "Goodnight, John. Goodnight, David." (Even at bedtime, even among his closest colleagues, a royal etiquette prevails.)

They breakfasted at eight on the morning of December 15. British trains are famous for their breakfasts, but Prince Charles is a frugal eater who doesn't drink even tea or coffee. He drank a glass of milk while Checketts and Dauth ate breakfast. All three

16

read the morning newspapers, which were full of Lord Snowdon's wedding. Snowdon, whose marriage to Prince Charles's aunt Margaret had recently been dissolved, had taken as his second wife Lucy Lindsay-Hogg, a thirty-seven-year-old TV researcher and divorcée whose name had been linked with Snowdon's since the couple had worked together on a television feature in Australia.

After breakfast, Charles put on his working clothes, assisted by Ian Armstrong, one of his two valets. The outfit was a plain cream shirt, serviceable and highly polished brown shoes, a two-piece suit in the gray check sometimes known as "Prince of Wales Plaid," and the blue, red and white striped tie of the University of Wales, of which Charles is Chancellor. From the breast pocket about a third of a white handkerchief showed. The suit was tailor-made, cut in a peculiarly British style, very long in the jacket, giving an almost skirted look and accentuating the Prince's long torso and correspondingly short legs. The trouser bottoms lay long over his heels in another approved British manner. The Prince's hair, very black and slightly wavy, was brushed back from the forehead and parted on the left, very straight and white enough to land flies on.

As the royal train stopped at the Rhyl platform at 9:35, Prince Charles alighted crisp and immaculate to greet the waiting dignitaries. It was the sort of reception committee Charles has learned to expect—apprehensive, honored, eager to please. Her Majesty's Vice Lord Lieutenant of the County of Clwyd, Colonel J. Ellis Evans, headed the delegation. (He is the Queen's senior representative in the county, but it is largely an honorary office that allows him to shine only on such ceremonial occasions.) With the studied dignity of an Edwardian butler the Vice Lord Lieutenant introduced Charles to the other waiting officials: the High Sheriff of Clwyd, the Clerk to the Lieutenancy, the Mayor of Rhuddlan Borough, the Mayor of Rhyl, the Town Clerk, the Chief Constable and the Divisional Manager of British Rail. . . . The men bowed with a brief bob of head and shoulders; the only woman, the Mayor of Rhyl, executed a perfect curtsey. The ritual was over in three minutes.

The December morning sky hung gray and gloomy as the

17

royal party drove to Rhuddlan Castle, a formidable riverside stronghold built during King Edward I's 13th-century conquest of Wales. The stop was brief; another round of homage from welcoming dignitaries and a brief wade into a crowd of local citizens with whom Charles exchanged some pleasantries. Within minutes the entourage was off again, this time to St. Asaph, a small and ancient town distinguished as the site of Britain's smallest cathedral. Founded in the sixth century by Celtic monks, destroyed and rebuilt many times since, the sturdy little cathedral was to have been a momentary stop on the Prince's royal progress, but its Dean prevailed upon Charles to address the assembled congregation. Charles is far too practiced a performer to be fazed by such irregularities, and only those closest to him (Checketts and Dauth) could have noticed that he was in any way discomfited by the invitation. Charles ceded to the request with good grace—but not without having the last word.... "I'm glad to see that the roof is intact," he observed, smiling and looking upward at the arches over the nave. "Otherwise you would ask me to be chairman of an appeal." He was, of course, right about that.

By the time Charles and his party reached Howells School at Denbigh, his major appearance of the morning, they were twenty minutes behind schedule, less because of the impromptu address at St. Asaph than the size of the roadside crowds encountered along the way. (The Prince believes it is the worst of manners to speed past people who have come to see him.) The visit to Howells, an all-girls school, was more leisurely: a full two hours, time enough to make up the loss. Before the morning was over, Charles had heard the school orchestra play a Hungarian March by Berlioz, watched an excerpt from Jean Anouilh's play *Ring Round the Moon*, toured exhibitions of pottery, weaving and local history and accepted the gift of a Christmas cake. The schoolgirls themselves, most of them barely in their teens, had been entrusted with showing Prince Charles around, a task they performed with such confidence that Charles, perhaps thinking of himself, said later, "Odd how very much more sophisticated and mature girls of that age are than boys."

At fifteen minutes past noon, back on schedule, the

motorcade was on the road to Hawarden Airport, where Charles and his staff boarded a bright red Andover aircraft of the Queen's Flight, a collection of RAF aircraft reserved for royal use. The Andovers in the Flight are meticulously maintained and comfortably equipped—and they are a quarter-century old. But they are also twin-engine prop planes, a joy to fly, especially for an irrepressible pilot like Charles. Instead of relaxing after the morning rounds he headed straight for the cockpit and took the controls for the fifty-minute flight to South Wales, relinquishing them only for ten minutes to confer with his aides on some points in the afternoon's speech and to snatch some lunch. When the red Andover landed at Rhoose, the small airport of Cardiff, Charles was again piloting it. "Bit heavy on the brakes," said one of his passengers, grinning broadly, of course.

When Charles got off the plane he was in foreign territory. For all the beer-fueled cheers he would hear that night at the Double Diamond, the countryside around Cardiff is a bastion of the British Labour Party's left wing, and nowhere is that radical wing stronger than in Ebbw Vale, a coal-mining, steel-making town about twenty-five miles north of Cardiff, whose fortunes have climbed and crashed with the inexorable rhythms of British industry. Ebbw Vale is the most socialist parliamentary constituency in Britain, represented at Westminster by the white-maned firebrand Michael Foot, a lifelong scourge of anything Tory or Establishment. With a certain fine historical irony, Foot became, under the Callaghan Labour Government, Lord President of the Council, a centuries-old Cabinet office once occupied by noble advisors to the Tudor and Stuart kings, and even now second in precedence in the House of Commons only to the Prime Minister himself.

It was bitterly cold when the Prince and his party arrived at Ebbw Vale; a damp, heavy mist rolled over the steelworks and on out to the Ebbw Vale Leisure Center, a lavish, government-built sports complex where Charles and his entourage halted for the day's next ceremony. The occasion was the tenth annual presentation of the Prince of Wales awards to men and women who, in the judgment of the Prince's Committee, had done the most to enhance the beauty of the Welsh landscape. The honored achievements followed no pattern: one award was given for the conversion of a derelict gazebo into a bright new roadside resting place; another went to a trailer camp club for relocating its campsites with an eye for aesthetics; still another to a man who had singlehandedly cleared litter and opened footpaths on Mynydd Machen, a Welsh mountain popular with hikers.

As Prince Charles entered the auditorium the award winners sat, spruce and eager, in the front three rows of the audience, large yellow name badges in their lapels. While the Marchioness of Anglesey opened the ceremony in the clear, cut-glass tones of the British aristocracy, the Prince sat on the dais under three flags draped on the gray brick wall above him: two of the pennants bore Welsh dragons, red on a background of green and white; a single Union Jack, symbol of the United Kingdom, hung in pride of place in the center. After several preambles, the award-giving began. Charles stood as slides of the winning projects were flashed on a screen to his right; and the winners trooped up one at a time to receive their prizes, plain metal plaques with the date and the Prince of Wales's emblem of three feathers embossed in the middle.

Charles handled the formalities with professional aplomb. While an aide handed him each plaque, the Prince shook the recipient's hand with his right, gave him the plaque with his left hand, and asked a question or two, his eyes slightly narrowed in an expression of thoughtful interest. When the ten-second exchange was complete, he indicated with a broadening smile and gentle nod of the head that it was time for the recipient to make way for the next one. From time to time Charles would use the old soldier's trick of rocking slightly from the balls of his feet to his heels and back again, or smoothing his bright brown brogues over the carpet. He has not yet learned quite what to do with his hands. When they were not busy shaking the hands of others or passing out awards he moved them almost constantly, sometimes sliding the gold signet ring on his left little finger, sometimes thrusting them deep into his jacket pockets or clasping them behind his back like his father, Prince Philip. During the speeches he made occasional notes with a gold-topped fountain pen scribbling in the margin of his own text and whispering occasional asides to Lady Anglesey on his right. A man, you would judge, who likes to be busy.

At last it was his turn to speak and he moved to the dais, spread his notes on the lectern and thrust his left hand deep into the left jacket pocket while with tight jabbing movements of his right hand he emphasized the points he was making. He was glad to see the Member of Parliament, Mr. Foot, though "as Lord President of the Council I am sure there are lots of things he ought to be doing in London." He was glad to see so many young people, alarmed to see so many people in uniform, concerned that they might have been transported to the event compulsorily by bus... but then, that would mean a few hours off school or work, and that, he supposed, would be no bad thing. He recalled the moment ten years before when the idea of a committee to work on environmental problems was first mooted. "My father," he said, "told me to go down and chair the committee and I obediently did. I was in fear and trepidation and I have been in fear and trepidation ever since." "If that's fear and trepidation..." remarked Lady Anglesey later, with sharp disbelief—leaving no one in doubt that the Prince had been an unflapped chairman from the beginning. He finished the proceedings on a note of exhortation, a blunt command redolent of the quarter deck. "So. Do your stuff. Thank you, ladies and gentlemen." Three cheers for the Prince were called for and delivered, and the company adjourned for afternoon tea upstairs. There a throng of award winners and other privileged guests sipped small cups of strong Indian tea and nibbled thin sandwiches constructed from limp, pre-sliced bread. Prince Charles moved busily among the company, shaking hands and again expressing that blend of interest, enthusiasm and genuine diffidence which has become his particular trademark.

Soon after five the Prince left the hall with Mr. Foot for possibly the strangest piece of ritual in the day. Outside the town on a windy hilltop stands a memorial to Aneurin Bevan, born in Tredegar (the town adjacent to Ebbw Vale). Possibly the greatest Welsh parliamentary orator of all time, Bevan, who died in 1960, was a virtuoso of impassioned invective, eclipsing even Lloyd George; a convinced socialist if not an active republican, he excoriated the aristocracy and condemned Conservatives as "vermin." His truculence once even got him kicked down the front steps of White's, one of London's most fashionable men's clubs.

Now, in the company of one of Bevan's disciples, the Prince of Wales himself was at Bevan's shrine: the heir to the throne of Britain was paying homage at a memorial to the greatest socialist politician his principality had yet produced. For a while Charles and Michael Foot walked in the biting wind beneath the monument, the Prince and the parliamentarian looking out over the lights of the valley towns below. Caught in the shine of the monument's floodlights, Foot, with his long white hair, looked like an Old Testament prophet. His hands moved expressively as he explained to the young visitor the geography and significance of the place, so forgetting himself in the enthusiasm of the moment that he several times clapped the Prince affectionately on the shoulder. Then the two men wandered over to a small crowd braving the early evening chill and Prince Charles asked a young boy why Wales had lost to New Zealand in the recent international rugby match. "They cheated," said the boy. The Prince seemed surprised, but the politician saved him from embarrassment. "Oh, no," Foot said, "it was because the referee was English."

This reference to the old enmity made them all laugh, and they moved away to the waiting cars, where Foot again clapped Charles on the shoulder, the privilege perhaps of one of his country's elder statesmen. "So, all the best," said Foot warmly. "And thank you for coming." Prince Charles smiled and expressed his own thanks. Then, briefly, as the heir to the throne stepped into his Rolls-Royce, Foot became Lord President of the Council again, and bowed his head in formal homage—an unexpected, slightly awkward, oddly touching movement.

With that, the Prince was away, waving again to the onlookers, en route to the plaudits of the crowd at the Double Diamond. That night, when the Welsh people sang the traditional anthem, "God Bless the Prince of Wales," they meant it. Not since the first English Prince of Wales was endowed with the title in 1301 had any of its possessors worked more diligently and attractively than Charles to know and serve his titular fief.

CHAPTER TWO

Born to Rule

ON NOVEMBER 14, 1948, a huge crowd jammed the gates of Buckingham Palace, along the road that winds around the great white memorial to Queen Victoria. Such a sizeable gathering had not been seen at Buckingham Palace, the London headquarters of the Royal Family, since the wedding of Princess Elizabeth, the heir to the British throne, to a fair, lean prince of Danish ancestry named Philip Mountbatten barely a year earlier. Now the crowd was waiting for news of an heir to their young Princess, who lay in the Palace's first-floor "Buhl Room," which had been stripped of its ornate ebony and tortoise-shell furnishings and converted into a clinically sterile maternity ward for the delivery. Sir William Gilliat, the royal gynecologist, and Sister Helen Rowe, a midwife, were in attendance on the twenty-two-year-old Princess.

Meanwhile twenty-seven-year-old Prince Philip was playing squash on the Palace court with his private secretary and old friend Michael Parker. Shortly after nine o'clock their game was interrupted by an announcement that the Princess had given birth to a seven-pound, six-ounce boy. Philip joyfully tossed down his squash racket and raced upstairs to his wife's bedside. When the Princess awoke from sedation she saw her husband hovering solicitously over her, holding a bouquet of roses and carnations.

Hundreds of years before Prince Charles's birth, fears had arisen that an alien baby had been smuggled into a royal bed and hailed as the heir to the throne of infertile parents. To prevent such rumors a leading government minister traditionally attended royal births to witness the legitimacy of the heir. This time Britain's socialist government had waived the rule, but the birth was followed by an immediate phone call to the Home Secretary, Chuter Ede. "The King has a grandson," the secretary was told. The succession was assured; the monarchy seemed secure. Within seconds of the birth a military dispatch rider roared out of the Palace courtyard on a heavy khaki-colored motorbike and rode across the city to transmit the news to the Lord Mayor of London.

Meanwhile the crowd, which had been quiet and apprehensive, sensed all was well and began to sing "Rule Britannia," the Welsh national anthem "Land of My Fathers," and even "Oklahoma." Then one of the doors of the Palace opened and the austere figure of Commander Richard Colville, Press Secretary to the King, crunched deliberatively across the gravel. The crowd, guessing the contents of the notice that Colville was affixing to the railings, broke into cheers. Intuition was confirmed in Colville's own firm handwriting, in the first official bulletin of Prince Charles's birth: "The Princess Elizabeth, Duchess of Edinburgh, was safely delivered of a Prince at 9:14 P.M. Her Royal Highness and her son are both doing well."

It was an uncommon introduction to life. The Prince's entrance into the world was hailed by the crowd gathered before the Palace gates in the cold November night. They sang "Happy Birthday," they chanted, they cheered. Eventually Michael Parker went outside to ask the people to quiet down and let the Royal Family sleep. Parker's pleas went unheeded until the secretary spotted the features of English actor David Niven pressed against the Palace railings. It was the suave Niven who finally persuaded the crowd to disperse.

The news spread fast. A mile away at the Albert Hall in Kensington six thousand ex-servicemen, gathered for a reunion, shouted out an exultant "Mazeltov" when they heard of the birth. The next morning's papers were full of the event. The London *Times* predictably (and incorrectly) said that the Prince was the first heir to the throne to have Danish blood in him since the death of King Harthacnut in the year 1042. The *Daily Express*, a rambunctious popular daily owned by the mercurial Canadian, Lord Beaverbrook, celebrated with an editorial which read "Congratulations Princess Elizabeth! The British people join in your happiness. They are delighted that it is a boy. They hope that the Prince will grow up strong and vigorous to share their struggles and achievements in the exciting years ahead." Sir William Gilliat, the King's doctor and one of three physicians who attended the delivery, announced that the infant prince "is an ideal weight," and Cecil Beaton, who took the first official pictures, declared, "The Prince is very like Queen Mary." (Prince Charles never resembled his great-grandmother in the least, but the court photographer, like everyone else, was carried away by enthusiasm.)

In the United States, where the birth was rated the tenth most important news story of the year—after the election of President Truman and the death of Babe Ruth—comment was less euphoric. The Washington *Post* thought the arrival of the Prince might prove "a happy interlude to lighten their grim living"—a pointed reminder that the British were still on wartime rations and were restricted to two pints of milk weekly and a strictly limited supply of potatoes. The New York *Times* turned the occasion into a lament for the British Empire, which was fast disappearing in a flurry of national independence celebrations. "What if they raised the last glass not to the new but for the old 'British Empire,'" suggested the *Times*, "and broke the glass." Such thoughts must have crossed the minds of many Britons in those spartan days. Englishmen were learning a bitter lesson—that the war which they believed they had won had reduced, beyond recall, their power, their prosperity and their influence.

At first, of course, the royal infant had no name. For most of us, names are relatively commonplace, uncomplicated matters, but royalty, like the rich, are different. Prince Philip, as the baby's father was generally called, had been born on the lush island of Corfu, the son of Prince Andrew of Greece. Philip was not, however, Greek, but Danish. The Danish Royal Family are a sort of General Motors of monarchy and have supplied kings and queens to countries all over Europe. Philip's family name was Schleswig-Holstein-Sonderburg-Glucksburg but understandably he preferred to be known, throughout his youth, as Prince Philip of Greece. His mother was Princess Alice of Battenburg, daughter of Prince Louis of Battenburg, who had been forced to change his name to Mountbatten in 1917. So when Prince Philip assumed British nationality in 1947, he took the name "Philip Mountbatten," even though his mother's name was Battenberg and his father's Schleswig-Holstein-Sonderburg-Glucksburg. The latter would have been an unlikely and somewhat embarrassing surname for a *British* naval officer.

When he married Princess Elizabeth Philip was given the style of "Royal Highness" and created Baron Greenwich, Earl of Merioneth and Duke of Edinburgh. If Philip's titles had been left at that, his son would have taken the title "Earl of Merioneth" (as a courtesy rather than a right), and the surname "Mountbatten." However, five days before the birth King George suddenly realized that his new grandson was going to be no more than a common or garden earl—by no means the most elevated rank in the British peerage—so he issued "letters patent under the Great Seal" by which any child of the Duke and Duchess of Edinburgh would assume the style of Royal Highness and be a Prince or Princess according to sex.

This complicated procedure ensured that the new baby was His Royal Highness Prince _____ Mountbatten, Earl of Merioneth. Or so it would seem. In fact the question of whether Prince Charles is a Mountbatten or a Windsor (after his mother), or even a Mountbatten-Windsor, has never been resolved; Hugo Vickers, a genealogical expert making a study of Prince Charles for Debrett's, the ultimate authority on the finer points of blood and birth, comments "The Mountbatten-Windsor question has always been a ticklish one, with plenty of scope for interpretation and misinterpretation. In Common Law a Queen Regnant is the last of her line, so if nothing has been done, Prince Charles would have been born the first of the House of Mountbatten. Churchill didn't like that much, so in 1952 when he was Prime Minister he persuaded the Queen to declare herself, and her House, the House of Windsor. Churchill thought the Mountbattens were a controversial lot and Earl Mountbatten had got a bad press after the partition of India where he was the last Viceroy. Besides, Churchill wanted to perpetuate the memory of George VI."

Accordingly, the Queen, using the archaic style of such pronouncements, let it be known that it was her "Will and Pleasure that I and my children shall be styled and known as the House and Family of Windsor and that my descendants, other than female descendants who marry, and their descendants who marry, and their descendants, shall bear the name of Windsor."

That seems clear enough, but in 1960 the Queen apparently changed her mind. Churchill was out of the way now, and it is said that the new edict was the result of prompting from Philip's uncle, Lord Mountbatten. The Queen apparently decided to change "Windsor" to "Mountbatten-Windsor" because, as she put it, "The Queen has always wanted, without changing the name of the royal house established by her grandfather, to associate the name of her husband with her own and his descendants."

Hugo Vickers comments: "It was an ambiguous statement because it said that all the descendants of the Queen and Prince Philip who were *not* Royal Highnesses would be called Mountbatten-Windsor, but what was never made clear was what Prince Charles's surname if Princess Anne put Mountbatten-Windsor on her marriage certificate, and it will be of interest to see if Prince Charles does the same. If so, then he will found a new dynasty—that of Mountbatten-Windsor."...

Such esoteric considerations, however, worried the royal parents very little in that November of their son's birth. They had already decided on "Charles" as the boy's first name, for the simple reasons that they liked the sound and wanted to get away from the endless succession of "Edwards" and "Georges" that had been the unexcepted rule for English kings since William IV died in 1837. They were obviously not superstitious about precedents: the first King Charles of England had his head cut off by rebellious subjects and the second, while in many ways a remarkable man and monarch, had so many extra-marital affairs that the English aristocracy was significantly enlarged by his various illegitimate offspring. No self-respecting royal personage has only one name, and so three others were added: Philip after the boy's father, Arthur for an appealing association with the legendary ruler of Camelot and George after Charles's grandfather.

On December 15, the infant was formally christened with these names at a ceremony in the Buckingham Palace Music Room. It was no ordinary baptism. The priest in charge was Doctor Fisher, Archbishop of Canterbury and senior bishop of the Church of England. The King and Queen were present, and Charles was held at the font by his aunt and youngest godparent, Princess Margaret. Among the sponsors were Lord Mountbatten's elder daughter, Lady Brabourne, the Queen's brother David Bowes-Lyon and Charles's great-grandmother, the Dowager Marchioness of Milford Haven, an old lady of eighty-five. Prince Philip's uncle, Prince George of Greece, and seventy-six-year-old King Haakon of Norway failed to make the trip and were represented by proxy. Charles was dressed in a creamy gown of Honiton lace, which had been used on similar occasions by other members of the Royal Family since the days of Queen Victoria. The holy water had been especially brought from the River Jordan.

The publicity was enormous. A special British Overseas Airways Constellation was chartered for $10,000 by Howard Hughes in an attempt to get photographs to New York in time for the next day's papers. Unfortunately, although the plane was said to be attempting a non-stop flight, it had to be diverted via Iceland and arrived late. Already a strait in the Falkland Islands, as well as a newly discovered island in the Canadian Arctic, had been named for the young prince. A pattern of massive publicity was beginning to emerge. So great was the flood of congratulatory mail into the palace that twelve temporary secretaries had to be hired to answer it.

At home the infant Charles was well-attended. His mother doted on him, breast-fed him for the first few months, and confided to a former music teacher that "he has an interesting pair of hands for a baby, rather large but fine with long fingers—quite unlike mine and certainly unlike his father's." But Charles's mother was the King's daughter, and so could not be expected to look after a baby all by herself. Two Scottish nurses, Helen Lightbody and Mabel Anderson, were hired. Nanny Lightbody had been in charge of the Duke of Gloucester's children, and her reliability was unimpeachable. Miss Anderson had got the job through a nurse's magazine. Like all the best English nannies these ladies were themselves too grand to perform routine chores and two housemaids were hired to carry out un-nannylike menial tasks. A nursery footman was added to help with heavier work; and of course there was the first of a line of personal detectives to shadow the Prince's perambulator, a high-slung Rolls-Royce-like carriage previously occupied by Charles's mother and his aunt Margaret. (The Royal Family tend to vacillate uneasily between conspicuous waste and conspicuous thrift. Despite the lavish expenditure on nursery staff, Charles slept on an old iron cot, and his hairbrush and silver rattle were the same ones that his mother had used. The mountains of baby clothes sent by well wishers were repacked and sent to needier babies.)

For the first few months of his life Charles moved between Buckingham Palace and Windlesham Moor, an opulent temporary home his parents rented from a London financier. Princess Elizabeth would nurse and play with Charles for half an hour after breakfast, take a quick lunch-time peek at the cradle and spend another hour-and-a-half with her son at bedtime. The rest of the time Charles was in the care of the royal nannies. It was a very "Upstairs, Downstairs" infancy.

The Royal Family was very close-knit. Prince Philip, five years older than his wife and the product of a broken marriage between a mildly debauched Graeco-Danish Prince and a mother who became a nun, was already a confident, rather aggressive father. His headmaster had said of Philip: "Prince Philip's leadership qualities are most noticeable, though marred at times by impatience and intolerance. He will need the exacting demands of a great service to do justice to himself. His best is outstanding—his second best is not good enough." These assessments have been borne out. When Prince Philip is good he is very, very good—energetic, resourceful, challenging; when he is bad, however, he is impatient, rude, ill-tempered. It has always been said of him that he is "a man's man," and he was determined from the first that his son should be as virile as he. Prince Philip tends to a certain contempt for intellectuals and what he considers effeminate men, and was disturbed at any signs of excessive coddling of Charles by the royal nannies and grannies.

Charles's mother was still very young—in her early twenties—and she and her only sister, Princess Margaret, had led an intensely sheltered life, privately educated by nannies and governesses. Elizabeth was small and pretty, a good horsewoman, sensitive but not sentimental, intelligent but not intellectual, and with an assiduously cultivated sense of responsibility which she was to pass on to her son.

The royal couple were, in fact, distant cousins, and both were descended from Victoria through the convoluted alliances which have tended to make European royalty a closed shop. They had lived their lives surrounded by royal or semi-royal connections, constantly moving in and out of palaces and stately homes. There was no pretending that their son could ever be "ordinary" or "conventional," no matter how like a normal growing boy he might sometimes seem.

In 1949 Charles and his parents moved into Clarence House, an impressive mansion set behind high walls between Buckingham and St. James Palaces. Prince Charles occupied the third floor of the mansion with his entourage. The pale blue nursery was light and airy and overlooked the Mall. The curtains were chintz with a pattern of 18th- and 19th-century figures on them, and there were glass cabinets filled with china figures and bibelots. Here, Nanny Lightbody presided from a wing-chair by the fireplace, just to one side of the old wireless set, and here young Charles crawled about, learning to bang a toy drum and blow a toy trumpet. Like any other British child he acquired a green ration book and an allowance of cod liver oil and vitamin-enriched orange juice, provided free by the government.

Life for the family seemed to be settling down into a predictable pattern. Clarence House made a comfortable home base. Prince Philip continued with his successful naval career and was posted to Malta in the autumn of 1949. He was given his first command—a frigate named *Magpie*. In the spring of the following year Princess Elizabeth was pregnant again. Given reasonable luck she and Philip would have plenty of time to enjoy their children without the burden of endless public engagements and attention. From time to time there were minor intrusions into their privacy, but these were usually slight enough to be endured. When Charles was inoculated against diphtheria, for instance, the news was widely broadcast in the hope that other mothers would take similar precautions. But for the most part Philip and Elizabeth were able to lead a life that was nearly normal, and it seemed that they would be able to do so for years to come. The King was, after all, only a little over fifty. There was no prospect of Elizabeth inheriting the throne for years to come, probably not until the 1970s, or the 1960s at the very earliest.

"Reasonable luck," however, eluded the royal couple. In the month Charles was born the King complained of cramps and numbness in his legs and feet. The royal doctors diagnosed early arteriosclerosis—a blocking of the arteries in the legs. The King was sent to bed and told to rest. His condition improved but he remained weak. In May, 1951, he opened the Festival of Britain, a demonstration of the best that Britain still had to offer, held on the South Bank of London's Thames River. It was obvious to all who saw him that the King was a sick man. He had never expected nor wanted to be King, and had only inherited the job after the abdication of his brother, the ill-fated Edward VIII, later Duke of Windsor. From the humiliation and disarray of the abdication King George and his Queen had regained a position of respect and affection, much enhanced during the war years when the Queen had announced: "The children won't leave without me; I won't leave without the King; and the King will never leave." Nor had he left. The family had stayed in England all through the blitz, and the Palace itself had been bombed. Now, however, the years were taking their toll. "The incessant worries and crises through which we have to live," the monarch wrote to a friend, "have got me down properly." It was worse than that. The King had cancer.

In July Prince Philip left the Navy. It was said at the time that he was on indefinite leave and technically he has been on leave ever since, but there was never much hope that he would be able to return to active duty. King George VI's illness was terminal, and it was only a question of time until his daughter took over as Queen. When that happened she would need the fulltime support of her husband. All thought of a meaningful career in the Navy for Philip had to be pushed aside. He would have loved to have emulated his uncle Dickie's success, which had been spectacular, and there was some suggestion that he could have done so. He was a good, conscientious, immensely hard-working naval officer who liked to command. Since he left the Navy he has been condemned to a permanent second place, constantly at his wife's right hand, or, rather, a little behind her elbow. He does not enjoy living in his wife's shadow, has always found his position frustrating. Despite all that Philip has accomplished, he has led, in many inevitable respects, a wasted life.

Charles remained unaware of the pervading gloom emanating from his grandfather's illness. His sister, Princess Anne, was born in August, 1950, and the two children spent that Christmas with the King and Queen at Sandringham, the Royal Family's house in Norfolk. The mere eighteen-month age gap between the siblings meant that Charles and Anne were close as children, sharing their games and many of their friends. Anne was always the more aggressive and boisterous child, and once a visitor found them playing a game called "Visitors" in which the two of them, at her direction, charged in and out of the shrubbery, "bowing to each other like state functionaries." But outside of his sister, in his earliest years Charles was surrounded almost entirely by adults—and mostly female. He seems not to have suffered or lost his taste for them.

In October, 1951, Princess Elizabeth and Prince Philip

toured North America, returning after a thirty-five-day trip on the Canadian Pacific liner *Empress of Scotland*. Prince Charles was at Euston station to greet them, wide-eyed with admiration for the detachment of Royal Canadian Mounted Police on guard duty. That Christmas was spent at Sandringham with the whole family together for the last time. The King had had a lung removed, and though he seemed cheerful and relatively fit his doctors had told him that he could expect only a few more years of even moderately active life.

On the evening of January 30, the King and his immediate family went to the Rodgers and Hammerstein musical *South Pacific*. The next day King George stood on the tarmac at London's Heathrow Airport and waved good-by to his daughter and son-in-law as they boarded their aircraft for a goodwill tour of East Africa, Australia and New Zealand. He was cadaverously thin and looked gray and melancholy.

On February 5, the King enjoyed a shoot at Sandringham during which he and a group of friends bagged 280 hare. After tea he played for a while with his grandchildren; Charles and Anne had as usual been parked with their grandparents while their parents were away. Later the Queen went upstairs to listen while Charles said his bedtime prayers. Meanwhile the King was preparing for sleep. A night watchman saw him close his window at about midnight. He was the last person to see the King alive. He had gone to bed, relaxed and happy, and had read for an hour-and-a-half over a cup of cocoa brought to him by a valet. When the valet took in the early morning tea he found that his master had suffered a massive coronary thrombosis and had died peacefully in his sleep. When his wife made her customary morning visit to her grandchildren's nursery, she was no longer Queen, but Queen Mother.

Elizabeth was now Queen of England. There is a marked lack of sentimentality in royal succession. The traditional cry on the passing of the monarch contains a bald statement of the death and an optimistic note for the new reign: "The King is Dead! Long Live the Queen!" The new Queen and Prince Philip heard the news at a game lodge in Kenya. Indeed, at the moment she became Queen, Elizabeth was almost certainly perched in the branches of a fig tree, watching African game by moonlight. Within hours she had changed into the heavy black mourning which had been packed in anticipation of such a catastrophe, and was flying home to be greeted by Prime Minister Winston Churchill and to take on the duties of royal head of State. The new Queen was only twenty-five years old.

For Prince Charles the succession meant a transfer of residence to Buckingham Palace up the road and also more of those name changes which are a necessary part of growing up in the upper echelons of Britain's class system. From being merely His Royal Highness Prince Charles, Earl of Merioneth, he became transformed overnight into Duke of Rothesay, Earl of Carrick and Baron Renfrew, Lord of the Isles and Great Steward of Scotland. Most significant of all, he bacame Duke of Cornwall. The other titles are rather grandiose relics, conferring little more than pomp and circumstance, but Duke of Cornwall has remained a position of power and wealth ever since Parliament formally bestowed the title in 1337. The Duke of Cornwall has a Duchy with land in the West Country and London. There is an estate office to run the Duchy and collect the rents, and although the new three-year-old Duke did not receive the income until he was much older, it would be the base of his fortunes until he, in turn, inherited the monarchy.

The new Queen was determined at least to try to bring her children up as normally as possible. The Clarence House nursery was recreated as nearly as could be and stuffed with handed-down royal toys—a model of Gibraltar with a working railway, cast-off royal garments to be used as dressing-up clothes, a miniature car. The Royal Family had always, like other British families, been peculiarly fond of pets, and there were two Corgi puppies, Whisky and Sherry, a rabbit called Harvey, a pair of lovebirds named Annie Oakley and Davy Crockett and a somewhat unpopular hamster called Chi-Chi. But neither such domestic touches nor Charles's early love for practical jokes (in which he was indulged by his father) could mitigate some painful artificiality in his upbringing. When the Queen returned from a six-month tour of the world Charles greeted his mother with a genteel and infinitely formal handshake. On another occasion when he came into his mother's presence, he bowed and his sister Anne curtseyed. To her credit Queen Elizabeth was so appalled that she instituted a new rule: no bows or curtseys to mummy. Helen Cathcart, an ubiquitous chronicler of British royalty, tells one story that seems typical and revealing. One day Charles found a secretary sorting through papers and asked him what he was doing.

"I'm getting these papers ready for the Queen," answered the secretary.

"The Queen? Who is that?"

"Why, it's your mother."

"The Queen is my mummy?" asked Charles, evidently incredulous.

Even now Charles never refers to his mother as "mother," or "my mother"—let alone "mummy"—even on relatively private occasions. She is always "The Queen." Anybody who refers to Elizabeth as "your mother" is met with a withering stare and at least an implied rebuke, as Charles studiedly persists in referring to her again as "The Queen."

If the Prince really didn't know that his mother was Queen his parents would have been astonished to hear it. After all, on a rainy June day in 1953 he was taken down to Westminster Abbey, where Kings and Queens of England have been crowned at least since William the Conqueror appropriated the throne in 1066. There, seated between his grandmother, now styled "The Queen Mother," and his aunt Margaret, Charles watched from the royal box the crucial forty-five minutes of his mother's coronation. It was a splendid piece of pageantry, a riot of orbs and sceptres, of velvet and ermine, of crimson and white and gold; of noble lords kneeling to pay homage, and the stately music of Handel's "Zadock the Priest," a choral rendering of biblical text which has been recited at every English coronation since that of King Edgar the Peaceful in the year 973. Charles, however, sat impassively through all this, holding his chin in his hand. Once he knelt down to fish his grandmother's handbag from the floor, where it had dropped, and on another occasion he leaned over the front of the box to get a better view. But, though he plied his grandmother with frequent questions, the small boy behaved as befitted the heir to the throne, with dignity and decorum. Later, back at the Palace, he came out on the balcony to wave at the cheering crowd and watch the flight of planes from the Royal Air Force pass by overhead. It was the nearest Charles will ever get to a full dress rehearsal of his own coronation (which will, naturally, follow an almost identical pattern), and though he has studied the books and films of the event, he remembers little at first hand. He was, after all, still less than five years old.

In many ways, however, Charles was now becoming a very mature little boy. *Tailor and Cutter,* the leading English men's fashion magazine, voted him their best-dressed young man of the year, and remarked that a certain woolly waistcoat of his had "led to a new surge of interest" in similar outfits. Bonny Prince Charlie already owned a Shetland pony and at Sandringham he went shooting with the rest of the family, dressed in rubber Wellington boots and a tweed deerstalker hat à la Sherlock Holmes and toting a toy gun. Miss Vacani, still renowned as the approved dancing instructress for practically the whole of the English upper class, was calling at the Palace to instruct Charles in her aristocratic art, and Miss Peebles, formerly governess to the household of Charles's beautiful great-aunt Marina, Duchess of Kent, was giving him regular school lessons in the Palace nursery. By Christmas the lad could read, a fact he demonstrated, somewhat falteringly, when his mother phoned from Auckland, New Zealand, at the halfway stage of her arduous post-coronation tour. That tour proved a valuable aid to Charles's geography lessons as Miss Peebles helped him pick out the various royal destinations on a large globe in the schoolroom. The governess also took her royal charge to such traditional children's attractions as the London Science Museum and Madame Tussaud's waxworks, where he laughed immoderately on seeing life-size wax effigies of his mother and father.

On April 16, 1954, Charles and Anne set out on the maiden voyage of the new royal yacht, *Britannia,* to meet their parents near the North Africa port of Tobruk. The *Britannia* is more like a liner than a yacht, and its considerable expense is justified by its dual purpose. In time of war the *Britannia* can be converted into a hospital ship accommodating 200 casualties. On the voyage to North Africa Charles was extremely seasick but he soon rallied and took some pleasure in swabbing down the decks barefoot, with miniature buckets, brushes and lengths of hose. In Malta the children stayed with the Mountbattens. When they finally joined their parents Charles and Anne watched excitedly as great-uncle Dickie led the Fleet in a dashing review, passing so fast and close to the royal bystanders that they all got wet from the spray. It was very much a family affair. Great-uncle Dickie was Commander in Chief of the Mediterranean, and his daughter, Charles's cousin Pamela, had been the Queen's chief lady-in-waiting throughout the 173-day tour. Later the *Britannia* made a triumphant return, sailing up the River Thames to the Pool of London. Charles and the rest of the family then got off the yacht and continued upstream in a royal barge to the Houses of Parliament, where they disembarked at Westminster Pier and finally returned to Buckingham Palace in an open carriage escorted by a plumed and caparisoned Sovereign Escort of the Household Cavalry.

Throughout this exposure to the public gaze five-year-old Charles carried himself with princely composure. Always a gifted mimic, he had perfected a fine salute and an accomplished smile and wave. As the royal entourage came ashore he solemnly shook hands with the waiting dignitaries and with an erect carriage and serious demeanor followed in his parents' footsteps. His only moment of anxiety seems to have been when he was alarmed by the saluting cannon, afraid that the gun blasts might sink the Royal Yacht.

Charles's ability to cope with such public occasions was a source of concern as well as pride to his parents. Years before, Queen Elizabeth had undergone the same initiation into public life. As a child she had been taken on some excursions by her grandmother, Queen Mary, widow of King George V. Mary was a splendidly regal figure with a fine understanding of what the job involved. On one outing the young Elizabeth was squirming around in her seat and Queen Mary impatiently asked if the child would like to go home. "Oh no, granny," she answered, "we can't leave before the end. Think of all the people who'll be waiting outside." Queen Mary was not amused. In fact she instructed a lady-in-waiting to take the child out by a back way and drive her home in a taxi. As the Queen's biographer, Robert Lacey, remarks, "People could get ingratiating waves in abundance from film stars but being royal was a matter of living out a role, not acting it. To cultivate an actor's concern with public relations was a step down a dangerous and slippery path, and Queen Mary made sure that her granddaughter received no encouragement to follow it."

The publicity problem had become even more acute during Charles's childhood. The presence on the throne of a young Queen, the extravagantly publicized magnificence of the coronation ceremony and a widespread feeling that monarchy represented relief from the somberness of everyday living all contributed to a near-obsession with the Royal Family. *Time* magazine had concluded that, more than any other contemporary figure—including the new U.S. president Dwight Eisenhower and the newly-arrived movie star Marilyn Monroe—the Queen represented the hopes and aspirations of the day. She managed, concluded the editors of the magazine, to "represent, express and effect the aspirations of the collective subconscious." It was difficult enough for an adult to endure this sort of assessment, but for a small child it was many times more so; and Elizabeth and Philip were acutely aware that they were faced with the responsibility not only of educating a future king but of bringing up a human being as well. Neither could very well be achieved in an existence in which, on the one hand, the young Charles was subjected to relentless pursuit by press photographers and the public at large, and on the other hand, to so many layers of figurative swaddling that he was cut off from any meaningful contact with the realities of the world beyond the Palace walls.

Accordingly, his parents focused on a number of fronts. First there was the relatively negative approach...Commander Colville, the Press Secretary, was asked to send out a request to the editors of Britain's national newspapers, asking them to keep their newshounds on a tight leash, especially when the Prince was out on his various educational visits around the nation's capital. "The Queen trusts," concluded Colville with the magisterial menace that often blighted his relations with the press, "that His Royal Highness will be able to enjoy this in the same way as other children, without the embarrassment of constant publicity." For a time this worked, but the public appetite for royal stories was such that it was difficult to keep the journalists away, and though the threat of royal disapproval might have caused some concern to British newspapers, American and Continental European publishers could not have cared less.

The time had also come now for the royal parents to make some decisions about their son's education. The more egalitarian critics were already beginning to suggest that Charles should take his chances in the State system of education, which is the lot of all but a tiny, privileged minority of Britain's children. The egalitarians argued that the Prince was growing up in a circle of friends who came exclusively from the ranks of the aristocracy. Those who attended his birthday parties or accompanied him on his excursions always came from the same tight clique. They tended to be the children of his parents' friends and relations, and while this would have been perfectly natural under most circumstances it was felt that a future king, whose task would include uniting a nation threatened by the divisions of an anachronistic class system, should have friends—or at least acquaintances—drawn from all levels of society. This was not really a very practical notion, but even the faithful Miss Peebles remarked that her charge had "only a vague relationship to the external world." For more than five years after World War II Britain had been ruled by a socialist government and there were strong signs that the socialists would again come to power. While most of those socialists were happy to support the monarchy, there have always been republicans in the British Labour Party, and their ranks were likely to grow. Besides, in the Abdication Crisis less than twenty years earlier, Charles's great-uncle had displayed such an insensitivity to public opinion that he had almost brought down the whole structure of the hereditary monarchy in the wake of his own fall and subsequent exile. It was only the exemplary sense of duty and dedication of Charles's grandparents that had restored the monarchy to popular esteem.

Perhaps if she had married a true-blue Englishman from the top drawer of English society, Elizabeth might have pursued a more cautious path, but Philip had only been naturalized as an Englishman in 1947 and had not been educated at one of the traditional English "public schools." Consequently, he shared few of the old-line prejudices. Moreover, Philip had always been heavily influenced by his uncle Dickie Mountbatten, who for all his military and naval accomplishments was widely regarded as "a bit of a red." It was not so very surprising, therefore, when Prince Philip was quoted as saying, "We want him [Charles] to go to school with other boys of his generation and to learn to live with other children and to absorb from childhood the discipline imposed by education with others."

From this distance in time that statement does not seem so very revolutionary. But at the time it was a unique break with tradition. The heir to the English throne was *always* educated at home by tutors. The idea of a prince going off at the age of seven to sit in a classroom with other boys was near-inconceivable.

Not that the school chosen for the Prince was exactly progressive. Hill House was the personal creation of Colonel Henry Townsend, an energetic figure who had once represented Oxford University at athletic events. His wife, a State registered nurse, had once worked at Guy's Hospital with Sir John Weir, the royal obstetrician who had officiated at Charles's birth, helped run the school and looked after the housekeeping and the boys' health. The Colonel was scrupulous about cleanliness (it was said only half-jestingly that the sidewalk outside the school was washed at least once a week and the railings dusted). Townsend also believed that a healthy body was as important as a healthy mind and so emphasized games and gymnastics—all of which endeared him to the Queen and Prince Philip. The school motto was a translation from the Latin of Plutarch: "A child's mind is not a vessel to be filled but a fire to be kindled." Hill House was certainly a change from being tutored at Buck-

ingham Palace, but not a *great* change. The school was in Hans
Place in the fashionable Knightsbridge district of London, just
behind Harrods, the department store with the smartest
reputation. Its 120 pupils were, of course, fee-paying. Many
were the sons of senior diplomats, for the school was in the heart
of embassy country. The remainder of the student body—
probably just over two-thirds—were scions of the aristocracy or
at least of the upper-middle classes. The boys' parents were
bankers, stockbrokers, an occasional lawyer. One parent, Lord
Longford, was an Irish peer and socialist politician who has
more recently made a name for himself as an anti-pornography
campaigner and prison visitor. But Lord Longford was not
typical of Hill House parents.

The royal efforts to evade press attention on Charles during
this period were strikingly amateur. Commander Colville had
already admonished Fleet Street (the generic name for Britain's
newspapers, most of which are in or around the street of that
name in the City of London) in his characteristically rather
heavy-handed fashion about the need for respecting Charles's
privacy. But Colville then showed distrust of the press by trying
to keep the boy's arrival at Hill House a secret. The
newspapermen, equally characteristically, responded by doing
their best to be on the scene of the story. When Charles set off on
November 7, 1956, in one of the Palace's older and less
remarkable limousines, his destination was supposed to be a
secret. He was wearing an overcoat, admired by *Tailor and
Cutter*, which described it as a "velvet collared top-coat," over
his official uniform, and *this* was intended to be a disguise.
Nothing could have been less effective. Not only was the
overcoat famous from its *Tailor and Cutter* exposure; Charles
was also the only boy wearing an overcoat of any kind. The
photographers were lined up waiting for him, and they got their
pictures. For Charles a difficult and nervewracking moment had
been made far more tense than was necessary. His first attempt
to become like other boys of his own age had served only to
emphasize his essential difference. Throughout his stay at Hill
House, Charles was dogged by both press and public.
Unfortunately, although there was a gymnasium in the

basement of the school, there were no playing fields. The boys had to walk in two-by-two "crocodile" formation down the busy Chelsea King's Road to the grounds of the Duke of York's Regimental Headquarters. In their russet shorts, open-necked shirts and cinnamon sweaters, they were a most conspicuous target. Each time a motorist stopped to allow them to cross the road, the boys raised their caps in acknowledgment. It was a simple matter to take photographs of them on the road with an ordinary camera, and with a telephoto lens, it was no problem to focus on the small Prince as he played soccer. The pictures duly appeared in the papers, and Commander Colville and the family were duly upset.

Hill House, though, was a relatively easy rite of passage for Charles. Most of the tutors were women, and their early reports were tentative to the point of being almost meaningless, full of such phrases as "keen interest" and "fair start." Charles's penmanship was evidently "good, firm, clear, well-formed," his singing competent, his wrestling (in the basement gymnasium) enthusiastic and he had a small walk-on part in the end-of-term school show. For the performance at Chelsea Town Hall, a large public auditorium, the heir to the throne wore ski-goggles in a parody of a rather tasteless nursery rhyme. It was a taste of things to come, Charles's delight in practical jokes and zany sense of humor having endured to this day. His also very real sense of dignity and of occasion has never been allowed to wholly obscure his sense of fun.

Of the summer sports, Charles enjoyed cricket less than football, though the school played an unorthodox version of the game, speeding it up so as to resemble its first cousin, baseball, rather than the drawn-out, complicated ritual to which the English enjoy devoting long summer afternoons. At the end-of-term "Field Day" Charles's parents, sister and governess came en masse to the sports ground to watch the Prince take part in some typical Hill House activities, including conventional ones like "handball rugger" and physical training. Among the less conventional games was a curiously militaristic exercise, a form of gun drill in which a wooden model of a field gun was taken to bits, pulled across an imaginary ravine and reassembled. Colonel Townsend proudly announced that the boys had managed to reduce the time of this feat from thirty to seven minutes. The exercise seems to have been modeled on a traditional annual competition between British naval units at the annual London Royal Tournament. Charles did not distinguish himself in this or any of the other events. He was in fourth position in the fifty-yard sprint when he lost concentration and finished well down the field. His arithmetic was also "below form average. Careful but slow—not very keen." But Charles showed more promise in other areas. His childhood drawings of sailboats, birds and his mother show a precocious sense of proportion and eye for detail (the Prince is today considered a gifted amateur water-colorist). Within a few years Charles was also to give evidence of a keen musical ear, and the dramatic and comedic talent that are still his forte.

While Charles was still in his first semester at Hill House his parents were devoting a good deal of thought to his educational future. They summoned to their councils one of the masters at Eton College, the most prestigious of England's private "public schools." It was this man who had suggested a day school such as Hill House for Charles's initial school experience, but Hill House was only a temporary measure. In January, 1956, the royal couple hired a young tutor, Michael Farebrother, a teacher in a south-coastal English boarding school, to improve the princely mathematics. In the summer a young Frenchwoman named Bibiane was engaged to tutor the Prince in her native language at the royal summer home, Balmoral Castle (the Prince is now, like his mother, fluent in French, once the *lingua franca* of all European courts). Miss Peebles continued in royal employment, too, but it was clear that a piecemeal approach to learning was not good enough. If Prince Charles was to take his place at the head of the nation, he would have to be educated properly.

The days of private tutors were past. Charles would go away to school to learn to be a man.

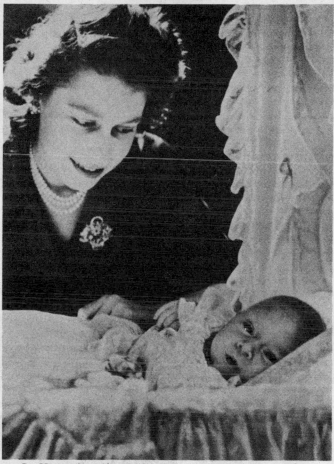

On November 14, 1948, a week short of a year after
her marriage to Philip Mountbatten, Princess
Elizabeth gives birth to a son. In this famous photo
by Cecil Beaton, the young mother looks in on
her month-old son in his cradle.

Queen Victoria's son Albert Edward,
the Prince of Wales, TOP LEFT,
lounging against a pillar at
Goodwood Races in 1873, with
a slightly seedy-looking companion.

Three Princes of Wales, past, present
and future, aboard the Royal Yacht in 1909:
King Edward VII; his son George, who became
King George V; and George's son David,
destined to be King Edward VIII.

The wistfulness of the young David gives way soon
enough to the jauntiness of a Prince-about-town.

In the music room of Buckingham
Palace, Princess Elizabeth's son
is christened Charles Philip Arthur
George. Here the Princess holds him
after the christening. Queen
Elizabeth, BELOW, sits with her
newly-baptized grandson.

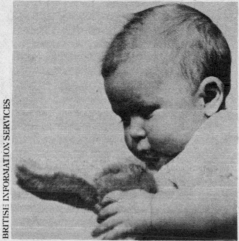

At 19 weeks, Prince Charles hugs a
toy rabbit.

In the gardens of Clarence House,
Princess Elizabeth and the Duke of Edinburgh
with Prince Charles and Princess Anne.

King George VI listens to his three-year-old grandson Charles in November 1951. Less than three months later, King George was dead, and Charles' mother was Queen Elizabeth II.

An active, five year old Charles in the gardens of the Royal Lodge at Windsor.

In a seventh birthday photo, Charles wears
the Balmoral tartan, a plaid reserved
for the Royal Family.

BRITISH INFORMATION SERVICES

Prince Philip and Prince Charles
make an entrance at the annual
Braemar Gathering in Scotland in
1955.

BRITISH INFORMATION SERVICES

Charles and Earl Mountbatten of
Burma in 1954. Mountbatten, a
brilliant World War II commander,
would become an influential voice in
shaping Charles' career.

LEFT: Charles' first school, Hill House in London's Knightsbridge district, brought the young Prince, center, into contact with the sons of foreign diplomats.

RIGHT: At Smith's Lawn, Windsor, to watch his father play polo, the Prince at eight strides along with his own polo stick.

In 1958, Cheam School becomes Charles' first venture away from home. Charles, center, after attending church services.

In his fourth year at Scotland's
Gordonstoun, 1965, Charles plays
the title role in <u>Macbeth</u>.

Two months later, Charles is off to
Timbertop, the wilderness branch of
Australia's Geelong Grammar
School.

In a 1970 Trinity College revue, Charles grapples
with a writhing bagpipe. "It is an indigenous
reptile," he explains to the howling audience.

Moving on to Trinity College at
Cambridge University in 1968,
Charles plays a chaplain in a comedy
called <u>Erpingham Camp</u>, and in the
course of the action receives
a pie in the face.

In his robes as Knight of the Order of the Garter, Prince Charles stands for a formal portrait in the Garter Throne Room at Windsor Castle.

TOP: Wearing the velvet mantle and plumed cap of the Most Noble Order of the Garter, Charles passes in procession in 1968 to St. George's Chapel in Windsor Castle.

BOTTOM: In July 1968, at a charity cricket match in Kent, Charles scores 20 runs.

KEYSTONE

At Caernarvon Castle in Wales on July 1, 1969,
Queen Elizabeth invests her son as Prince of Wales.

RIGHT: The Prince of Wales, in full regalia, walks
with his mother at Caernarvon Castle.

BRITISH INFORMATION SERVICES

Accompanied by the Duke of Norfolk, LEFT, and his
cousin the Duke of Kent, Prince Charles takes his
seat in the House of Lords in 1970.

CHAPTER THREE

Schooldays: Cheam, Gordonstoun and Timbertop

ENGLISH EDUCATION IS UNIQUE. State schools are tuition-free. They are neighborhood schools, divided into primary for children from ages five to eleven and secondary for older children. Although the majority of English children are educated at State schools, a large number of Britain's rich and powerful are products of the fee-paying schools, where by 1979 yearly tuition cost more than five thousand dollars. The fee-paying "public schools" are for boys and girls (most are single-sex) between about thirteen and eighteen. They are complemented by a similar system of "preparatory schools" whose job is to prepare their pupils for public school. The demands of the Common Entrance Exam (which has nothing common about it) are such that one really needs to go to a fee-paying preparatory school to have any chance of passing into the public school system. State schools don't teach the same subjects in the same way—the preparatory and public schools employ a classically-based educational system which uses Latin and Greek. State schools teach fewer subjects, have bigger classes and—inevitably—lower standards.

Some critics of the Royal Family argued that Charles should be sent to the nearest State primary school. Lord Altrincham, an egalitarian-minded aristocrat who renounced his title to become plain "Mister John Grigg," said that Charles should go to a State school. Some said that was all very well for Mr. Grigg; after all, he had been to Eton...

The British Foreign Office, the Armed Services and many private companies still pay all or most of the school fees for the children of their officers or executives who are obliged to serve abroad. These children, and those of others who can afford school tuition, are removed from home at the age of eight and sent to school, where they spend two-thirds of every year until they graduate at eighteen. British upper and middle-class families therefore spend less time together than any families elsewhere in the world. It is a unique phenomenon...

In view of the failure to keep the press and photographers away from Charles at Hill House, it had become clear that sending the Prince to a London school was a bad idea. There *were* London fee-paying prep schools as well as State primaries, but they were all vulnerable to inquisitive journalists. If Charles was to have any privacy he would have to be sequestered away, and since his parents had decided that he was not to be kept in the Palace, they had to find some other hideaway.

They chose Cheam. Cheam is probably the oldest preparatory school in Britain. It existed in some form during the reign of Charles I at the beginning of the seventeenth century. In 1665 the school was moved out of central London to escape the Great Plague, and settled in what was then the Surrey market town of Cheam (now a prosperous London suburb). The school remained in Cheam for more than 250 years, catering with varied success to the British upper classes. One 19th-century headmaster even had his own personalized system of aristocratic discrimination. A peer of the realm was called "my darling child," the son of a peer, "my dear boy" and a commoner, "my child." Thomas Pepys, cousin of the famous diarist, was a boy there. So was Lord Randolph Churchill, who, according to his son Winston, was "most kindly treated and quite content." The school also boasts two Viceroys of India, two speakers of the House of Commons, the commander of the disastrous Great War campaign in Gallipoli and sundry less interesting but nevertheless exotically-titled Englishmen.

From the royal point of view, however, the most significant aspect of Cheam was its connection with the Mountbatten family. When Prince Philip's grandfather, Prince Louis, was First Sea Lord he was signally impressed by two young naval officers who had been pupils at Cheam. With characteristic decisiveness Prince Louis decided that in the future all male Mountbattens should be educated at Cheam. So in the early 1930s Cheam had two Mountbattens, Prince Philip and his cousin the Marquess of Milford Haven. Philip did well at Cheam and enjoyed it. Not surprising then that when the time came to decide on a school for Charles he was as decisive about Cheam as his grandfather. As he said later: "There are a vast number whose financial limitations are such that they cannot afford to educate their children any way they like. We were certainly not limited that way, but there were many other considerations that entered into it. It would have been very difficult to select out of the blue because people would say of any selection, 'Why have they done that? There must be some reason.' They wouldn't admit that this was done for the children's benefit or because we had any particular theory of education. They would have said, 'Oh well it must be to discourage this or discourage that.' People are always looking for strange reasons. When Charles first went to school one of the problems we were confronted with was 'How do you select a prep school?' In the end he went to Cheam, where I had been. But this is something better understood in this country than almost anything else—that people very frequently do what their fathers have done. People said, 'Oh, he's gone because his father went,' and there was no further argument."

And so, in the end Charles went to Cheam because his father had gone there thirty years before. A very British reason, as Prince Philip says. Charles himself recalls: "His [Philip's] attitude was very simple: he told me what were the pros and cons of all the possibilities and attractions and told me what he thought best because I had come to see how wise he was. By the time I had to be educated, I had perfect confidence in my father's judgment."

Although he agreed to go to Cheam, Charles was not enthusiastic. Life had been a safe, contained affair until now, regulated by mother and father and nannies and governesses. Now, at the age of eight, he was to be removed from that private world where everything and everyone had a place; spirited away from the privacy of his own bedroom to a world of strangers. Cheam might be the very model of all that a prep school should be, but it was still an institution with unfamiliar rules and regulations, and, if necessary, discipline was enforced by beatings administered by one of the two headmasters, on the bottom, with a bamboo cane. Even if it wasn't quite like Dicken's Dotheboys Hall, Cheam presented a spartan contrast to life in the Palace.

The term began in September. The family came south from their Scottish castle in the overnight train, then drove to the school the following day. Since Prince Philip's schooldays Cheam had moved from Surrey and now occupied an imposing mansion on the Berkshire Downs at Headley, just south of Newbury, about sixty miles west of London. Headley is rolling, downland countryside, near some of the best horse-racing stables in England, and like so many of its rivals, the school was on beautiful and, more important, *secluded* grounds. Nevertheless, according to one observer, there were sixty-eight newspaper headlines about Charles in his first eighty-eight days at Cheam. A statistic that brought another of Commander Colville's stiff, if ineffective, rebukes along with a plea for more consideration.

The two headmasters of Cheam, Peter Beck and Mark Wheeler, had bought the school in 1947, and they were anxious that their royal pupil should be treated as nearly as possible like any other boy. Peter Beck told the parents of the ninety pupils that it was "the wish of the Queen and Prince Philip that there shall be no alteration in the way the school is run and that Prince Charles shall be treated the same as other boys." In practice this meant that the masters called him "Prince Charles," his fellow students, "Charles." Boys at British boarding schools are *always* called by their surnames. If Charles had really been like other little boys he would have been called "Mountbatten" or "Windsor" or "Mountbatten-Windsor."

Other reminders of special status kept cropping up, even though everyone tried hard to pretend that the situation was perfectly normal. Boys laughed when the vicar read out prayers for the Royal Family at Sunday Service, especially when the divine laid a lingering emphasis on the Duke of Cornwall. None of the other boys at Cheam got a special prayer. A spokesman for the Bedding Information Center announced to an astonished world that the Prince's school bed was "out of date and uncomfortable"; none of the other boys' beds were so evaluated, even though they were all springless and made from very old wood. The worst moment was on July 26, 1958, the final day of the British Empire and the Commonwealth Games. This traditional yearly athletics meet, in which all the old countries of the British Empire compete, was celebrated that year in Cardiff, capital city of Wales. To conclude the ceremonies the Queen made a special broadcast to the 30,000 spectators in the stadium (she wasn't able to be present because of sinus trouble).

"I want to take this opportunity," she said, "of speaking to all Welsh people, not only in this arena, but wherever they may be. The British Empire and Commonwealth Games in the capital, together with all the activities of the Festival of Wales, have made this a memorable year in the Principality. I have therefore decided to mark it further by an act which will, I hope, give as much pleasure to all Welshmen as it does to me. I intend to create my son, Charles, Prince of Wales today." It was, so to speak, the second creation . . .

At Cheam Peter Beck had been warned that this was going to happen, so he had invited Charles and some friends to his study to hear the speech over the radio. After the Queen's announcement the Cardiff crowd cheered, and the cheer was taken up by Charles's schoolfellows, who turned toward him, clapping and shouting. Charles was chagrined.

At Cheam, perhaps as a means of proving that for all his royal blood he was "a regular guy," the Prince was a perpetual practical jokester. In comparison with his later pranks (not to mention those of his medieval predecessor, Falstaff's *copain* Prince Hal), Charles's escapades at Cheam were pretty tame—tying together shoelaces, making "apple pies" of bedsheets and instigating pillow fights. "The Switched Hats

Affair," however, was considered quite a coup...One night Charles slipped from his bed and crept into the hall, where all the boys' caps were kept on individual pegs, each labeled with the name of the cap's owner. Charles proceeded to remove every hat from its rightful peg and transfer it to an unlikely peg, so that the smaller caps rested on the pegs of the boys with the largest heads, and vice versa. There were no names inside the hats, only on the pegs, so the next morning when the boys went to put on their caps, pandemonium, as they say, reigned. The incident resulted in a letter from the Headmaster to Prince Philip, and a royal spanking (in both senses) for Charles, but his schoolmates thought the hat-switch was a capital joke.

Nor was Charles's princely bottom exempt from the Headmaster's cricket bat when discipline was called for. Charles later recalled that the canings "all really hurt, I can tell you," but they may also have served to break the barriers between the Prince and his fellow students. Charles was indeed more popular at Cheam than some of his critics are prepared to admit. He became head of the school and captain of the football team (even though during his captaincy it did not win a single match— Charles took an expected amount of ragging about *that*, needless to say, though nobody ever directly said the dismal record was all on his shoulders. In any case, he took it in reasonably good spirits). Still, regardless of his popularity, it was evident that the Prince, like most other boys, was happier at home than at school. At home, for example, he could go fox-hunting, grouse-shooting and fishing, none of which were in the Cheam curriculum. At Birkhall, the family's Scottish house near Balmoral, he was taught how to drive a Land Rover and was a proficient driver on private estate roads by the age of twelve—five years before English law allows one to drive on the public highway. He excelled far more at such relatively solitary pastimes than he did at the regimented games and activities of Cheam. He was already, in fact, becoming something of a man apart.

Nevertheless Charles joined in at school. He won a commendation in the "Under Ten" modeling competition (with an uncharacteristically gruesome entry called "Gallows and

Stocks"); he played the malevolent Richard III in the school play, a performance about which the Cheam School *Chronicle* noted, "Prince Charles played the traditional Gloucester with competence and depth: he had a good voice and excellent elocution, and very well conveyed the ambition and bitterness of the twisted hunchback." He tried to learn the piano and failed; then attempted the trumpet but without much success, even though he enjoyed it. His mathematics remained poor, but he liked history. As his official biographer, the late Dermot Morrah, wrote, "He began to observe that history, which in the textbooks is about his ancestors, will one day be about him." Already he was conscious that the press and public took an inordinate interest in everything he did. Unflattering and distressing reports and photographs of the Prince appeared in the media. The public acquired an impression of a stout, pear-shaped little boy of ordinary intelligence. Charles, too, was acquiring impressions. Among the lessons he had learned in his first prolonged sojourn in the "real world" was that once and future kings are susceptible to the affections of ordinary mortals, or as Shakespeare's Richard II expresses it, "feel want, taste grief, need friends."

At thirteen the boys of Cheam moved on to their "public schools." Most were destined for venerable institutions in the south of England, not far from London. Some went to Eton, the smartest of them all, a centuries-old royal foundation in a small town just across the River Thames from Windsor Castle; others to Harrow, a more recently built school in the north London suburbs where Winston Churchill had gone; or Winchester, clever but rather socialist; Rugby, where the game of that name was invented; Charterhouse, like Cheam far from the madding crowd of London; Wellington with its military traditions; and so on. There was no shortage of choice.

Charles, however, went to none of these. He went, at age fourteen, to Gordonstoun, an unorthodox establishment hundreds of miles from home on the Scottish coast. Gordonstoun was the brainchild of a German-born educator Kurt Hahn, a most controversial figure. Like Cheam, however,

51

Gordonstoun was Prince Philip's old school, and like Cheam it would be accepted for that reason. As Prince Philip said later: "One of the advantages of going to Gordonstoun was that it was away from the press. It was slightly remote. It couldn't be got at, and if anything happened there it took some time to come out. If the school had been closer people would have been looking in all the time to see what was going on. The gossip would have been going to and fro, which might have been very unsettling." He was, of course, right about that.

The school was founded in 1934, after Hahn, no lover of the Nazis (nor they of him), left his native country, where he had already started a school, Salem, in Baden. As the Gordonstoun prospectus says, "It was with a few modifications, a British Public School. These modifications were of great interest to Englishmen for they represented changes to meet the new situation which developed between the world wars. The need to educate young people in independence of judgment and in strength of purpose when following an unfashionable cause, to teach the protection of the weak, the recognition of the rights of the less fortunate, and the worth of a single human life—these presented themselves as matters of urgency to Dr. Hahn as he watched the growth of the Nazi movement." Hahn identified three "decays," as he called them: "the decay of adventure and enterprise, of skill and care, and of compassion."

The site of Hahn's educational experiment was an 18th-century estate near Elgin, an isolated town in the remote county of Morayshire. The house had been built on land known—before it was drained—as "The Bog of Plewlands." For years the land had been owned by the Gordon family, of whom the most famous member was the third baronet, Sir Robert Gordon, known as "The Wizard of Gordonstoun" because of his interest in black magic. Legend has it that Sir Robert sold his soul to the Devil and then tried to escape from the deal by constructing a building of magical proportions. Which presumably accounts for the "Round Square," a courtyard surrounded by two-story stone buildings which now house the Warden's Room, the Library and Silence Room, as well as classrooms and sleeping accommodations. Round Square apparently failed to fulfill its original purpose; Sir Robert was found dead in 1704 with "the Devil's teeth marks" in his neck. His ghost is reputed to haunt the place still, and when Gordonstoun boys hear one of the old doors creaking during a fierce Scottish gale, they tend to call out, "Come in, Sir Robert."

Prince Philip, an ardent advocate of the school of which he is a model alumnus, says that Gordonstoun has never been like ordinary English schools. "The essence of the Gordonstoun system," he once said, "was that education was considered to be a much wider exercise. It wasn't simply a matter of reading up for an examination. There was a place for extra-curricular activity. This was thirty years ago and at that time extra-curricular activities were really considered rather exceptional. We played games only once or twice a week. But we did practical work about the grounds. It struck me then that education should be a very much broader concept than was general in this country."

Gordonstoun has its own fire chief (who also works for the local fire services); it runs an ocean-going yacht; on the local cliffs Gordonstoun boys man a coastguard watch that is part of the official chain of national Coastguards; and there is a Gordonstoun Mountain Rescue Service. There is also a lake for fishing, and it is possible to go skiing on the nearby Cairngorm Mountains. All of which was appealing to a boy like Charles, who was already more attracted to open-air pursuits than the more disciplined activities of football or cricket.

Hahn's view of education derived principally from Plato. "The Platonic view is that any nation is a slovenly guardian of its own interests if it does not do all it can to make the individual citizen discover his own powers; and further, that the individual becomes a cripple from his or her own point of view if he is not qualified by education to serve the community."

There could scarcely be a more appropriate educational ideal for the future leader of a people, though critics view Hahn himself as something of a crank, especially where sex was concerned. One former pupil recalls, "The first crack in my enthusiasm appeared early on when, two or three days after the term had started, he was showing me over the school. We were going through the classrooms when, in one, he suddenly stopped, gripped my arm, raised his nostrils in the air and then, in his marked German accent, he solemnly pronounced, 'Somevon has been talking dirt in this room. I can smell it!'" By the time Charles arrived at the school Hahn had long since retired as Headmaster and his place had been taken by Robert Chew, a keen sailor and outdoor man who together with Prince Philip had been one of Gordonstoun's three original pupils.

At first Charles was as lonely and isolated at Gordonstoun as he had been at Cheam. It is a special, perhaps salutary, feature of the English system that no sooner has a boy acquired responsibility and dignity as a "prefect" or "monitor" at his preparatory school than he is reduced to the ranks of a "new boy" at his new public school. Prince Charles, who had been assigned to "Windmill House," one of the school's several living units, was reminded of the school's ideal of service in a rather humiliating way—he was given the job of emptying the dustbins (garbage) every morning. An early Gordonstoun lesson in community service. Years later, during Charles's days at Cambridge, he was to bring down the house with a very funny "Dustbin Sketch" in which he described the morning machinations of the garbage collectors beneath his window at Trinity College—material doubtless worked up from his Gordonstoun apprenticeship as a "dustman."

The press continued to ferret out stories about Charles's school days, though Gordonstoun's isolation made it difficult. Almost immediately after Charles's arrival there, a journalist was found in one of the school's laundry baskets. On another occasion Charles was sent off on a punishment walk "for reading under the sheets." (Once lights had been turned out, you *had* to go to sleep.) As the Prince walked near the perimeter of the grounds, a solitary figure repenting of his awful crime, a photographer leaped out and snapped the shutter of his camera. Charles might gladly have killed him.

The Prince's worst brush with the press, however, came when he was on an excursion in the school's Bermuda-rigged yacht *Pinta*. One June day the boat put into the port of Stornaway on the Island of Lewis in the Outer Hebrides. Stornaway has a population of 5,000 and a small airport, but it is a long way from nowhere. There is some tourism, some fishing and some weaving, but the town is not exactly a hive of journalistic activity, and Charles and his genial detective Donald Green felt relaxed and happy as they strolled ashore with four other boys. The boys had been granted leave to have lunch ashore and then go on to a movie in the local cinema. Unfortunately some tourists had recognized the *Pinta* and had come to the anchorage to see if Prince Charles was on board. As he walked to the Crown Hotel Charles was identified, and a crowd began to gather. Even in the Crown Hotel people continued to stare at him, and when Inspector Green left to buy the movie tickets, Charles found the embarrassment more than he could stand, got up and hurried into the next room. A mistake. He found himself in the bar, where, under Scottish law, he wasn't allowed. Charles was only fourteen and the legal drinking age was eighteen. Charles was in a quandary. He could not go back to the crowd in the lounge; the detective was nowhere to be seen. He had to stay put, but if he stayed put he would have to buy a drink. By now thoroughly confused, he advanced on the barman, produced half a crown and asked for a glass of cherry brandy. It was the first drink that came into his head, a familiar "stirrup cup" often used in bleak British weather to warm the inner man. Charles had first been given it at Sandringham while out shooting.

Embarrassment turned to catastrophe. Just as he sipped his drink a freelance female journalist entered the bar of the Crown. Not surprisingly she recognized a scoop. PRINCE IN CHERRY BRANDY INCIDENT echoed round the world.

It was a trivial business, to be sure, but infinitely embarrassing. At first the Palace denied the story, but eventually was forced to admit the truth. The landlord of the Crown was charged by the police with serving drinks to a minor, then the charge was withdrawn. Inspector Green resigned, and when Charles got back to Gordonstoun he was summoned to Mr. Chew's study and had his "Junior Training Plan" withdrawn—which meant that he was in effect reduced to the ranks and lost some privileges. It was a windstorm in a wineglass, but the episode upset him. "At the time, when the story broke, I thought it was the end of the earth," he later told a radio-interviewer. "I was all ready to pack my bags and leave for Siberia or somewhere." He stayed to conquer.

Later, while attending the wedding of King Constantine of Greece, Charles and some fellow European princes were bathing in the Mediterranean when some photographers clambered onto their raft. Charles and the others flung them overboard. A rift seemed to be developing between the Prince and the press, and was intensified when the German magazine *Stern* carried an article called "The Confessions" of Prince Charles. Someone had got hold of one of the olive-green exercise books in which Charles wrote his weekly essays, and sold them. *Time* magazine suggested that Charles had sold them himself because he was so short of cash, a suggestion angrily repudiated by Commander Colville ("No truth whatever." "Complete invention.").

"My headmaster, poor man, was accused of selling it for some extraordinary sum in the pub in Elgin," says Charles. "I don't know. I think somebody must perhaps have come up from London or anywhere and taken it out of the classroom and then sold it." The essays were fairly innocuous—some simple condensations of a standard *History of England* by the 19th-century historian Lecky; others dealing with democracy and elections, television and the press and "how to survive on a desert island." The world learned that the Prince was "troubled by the fact that voters today tend to go for a particular party and not the individual candidate"; that he was in favor of the media's "protecting people from the government"; and would take a tent, a knife, "lots of rope and string" and a small radio set to his desert island. He added that in the event of the nuclear explosion, which was supposed to exile him to the desert island, he "would get into a frightful panic." None of this was very remarkable, but because he was Prince Charles instead of an ordinary schoolboy it was made to *seem* remarkable. As he was increasingly aware, he could hardly sneeze without making headlines. Charles did not enjoy being perpetually in the limelight, but later when he had messages he *wanted* people to get, he found that his newsworthiness could finally be turned to advantage. Today Charles has learned very well to make a virtue of necessity, and his relations with the press are generally cordial. As he told one veteran reporter, "As I shall probably have to spend a great deal of my life living with you chaps, one way or the other, I'm determined to get to know you all better." The "Cherry Brandy Affair" long behind him, the Prince now takes pains to ingratiate the press by chatting with reporters at the bar, making jokes at his own expense, which is a genuine facet of his personality.

Charles spent most of his time at Gordonstoun enduring with his classmates the rugged routine of the Hahn-inspired regime. For £519 a year the Prince was privileged to clean his own shoes, make his own bed, wake at 6:45 A.M., run round the grounds and have a cold shower before breakfast at 8:15. Another cold shower at 4 P.M. and to bed at 9:15. Conventional lessons were interspersed with regular bouts of athletics, games, and services (coastguarding, fire fighting, mountain rescue). His home in Windmill Lodge was about a quarter of a mile from the main building, where he slept in a communal dormitory. One press photograph showed this room with the windows wide open, despite the snow falling outside. It was a rugged life. The Prince felt isolated from the reassuring comforts of home. Friends were hard to make. "It's one of the things you learn through experience," he said later. "How to sense the ones who are sucking up and those who are genuine. The trouble is that very often the worst people come up first and the really nice ones hang back because they don't want to be accused of sucking up." There were, though, two boys in the school related to him and whom he could trust—Guelf, the son of Prince Philip's sister, Princess Sophie of Hanover, and Norton Knatchbull, one of great-uncle Dickie Mountbatten's grandsons. Knatchbull in particular remains one of his few close and trusted friends.

Charles's way up the school ladder was gradual. Gordonstoun has an esoteric system of promotion, but apart from the setback after l'affaire Cherry Brandy he negotiated each rung without any apparent problem. He passed through "Junior Training Plan," "Senior Training Plan," "White Stripe" and "Color Bearer Candidate" until eventualy becoming head boy, just as his father before him. Gordonstoun being Gordonstoun does not of course call a head boy a "head boy," but prefers the typically Hahnish title of "guardian." Not so inappropriate for the future "guardian" of the realm.

It was also at Gordonstoun that Charles's waggish sense of humor and skill at mimicry began to bloom, which helped contribute to his popularity with his schoolmates. He performed for his fellow students his on-target imitations of a popular British comedy group called the Goons, and brought the house down with his inflection-perfect imitations of the masters. Mr. Robert Whitby, the Prince's housemaster, acknowledges, "He could do me perfectly. So much so that he could put quite a fright up the other boys if they were doing something wrong." Whitby also remembers, "The one thing that struck me about his sense of humor was that it was always kind. It might bite a bit here and there but he never set out to hurt or upset anyone. He really enjoyed making people laugh and he was the first to laugh at himself if someone succeeded in getting his own back. He had his leg pulled often by the other boys, and it never upset him. He was the first to come back with an answering quip."

In academic work the Prince performed respectably, though not brilliantly. In 1964 he passed English Language, English Literature, History, Latin and French at the General Certificate of Education's Ordinary Level, but failed mathematics. Eventually, after intensive study, he fulfilled the math requirement. In 1967 he passed at Advanced Level in History and French, and surprised himself by gaining a distinction in the optional history paper, which placed him among the top six percent of the total entries, and was easily the best academic result of his schooldays. The secretary of the examining body (The Oxford and Cambridge Schools Examination Board) said, "I consider that his performance was extraordinary. He must have worked like a demon. I should hesitate to tackle the paper myself, it takes me back to the time when I did Greats" [the final exam in classics at Oxford University].

Athletically Charles's performance was still mixed. No good at rugby or hockey, not much at cricket. But he was learning to love the sea. At the little harbor of Hopeman, two miles from the school, he puttered about in the school boats, made a twenty-four-mile canoe trip and became a proficient sailor. He went skiing in the Cairngorms, earning a rebuke from a Free Church Minister, who attacked him for larking on the Sabbath, and he shot his first stag at Balmoral. This was a controversial thing for a Prince to do and was criticized at a public meeting of the League against Cruel Sports at the Caxton Hall in London. It also created a stir in Parliament, where one member, debating a bill for the protection of deer, complained of the Duke of Edinburgh "who goes in for this loathsome kind of sport and even brings his child up to do it." His father wanted him the macho gentleman, a representative of the people called his action "loathsome." Who could have blamed him if he wondered how you won. As an adult he would learn to handle this conundrum more effectively.

Charles continued to love music and added the cello to his repertoire of instruments, although he never played as well as he would have liked and confessed that in Beethoven's Fifth with the local Elgin Orchestra, he couldn't "play with strong enough concentration." He sang in the school choir and later said, "Singing in a big choir is marvelous." When Gordonstoun put on Britten's "Saint Nicolas," Elgar's "Dream of Gerontius" and Bach's "B Minor Mass"—three demanding vocal scores— Charles sang all three. He also sang a bit role in the Gilbert and Sullivan operetta *The Pirates of Penzance*. He continued his theatrical efforts as well, progressing from a small part as Duke of Exeter in Shakespeare's *Henry V* to the title role in *Macbeth*. The Gordonstoun *Record* was enthusiastic. The Prince was, according to its critic, "at his very best in the quiet poetic soliloquies, the poetry of which he so beautifully brought out, and in the bits which expressed Macbeth's terrible agony of remorse and fear. In the second part of the play, he equally well expressed the degenerative hardening of Macbeth's character, the assumption of cynicism in an attempt to blunt the underlying and too painful moral sensitivity." It was a satisfying achievement, viewed by an appreciative audience which even included his parents. When Gordonstoun had produced the play in the 1930s Prince Philip had been a mere spear-carrier with a paltry three-line part. The son, in some ways at least, was beginning to emerge from his father's shadow.

At seventeen Charles was leaning down, seemed tougher, more mature and self-confident, but his parents were anxious to get him away from Gordonstoun, if only temporarily. His horizons, they decided, needed extending. He needed a reminder that he was not only heir to the British throne but to Britain's overseas dominions of Australia and of Canada as well. Now seemed a good time to inspect one of these parts of the Commonwealth. In the summer of 1965 the Australian Prime Minister, that bluff old Anglophile warhorse Sir Robert Menzies, visited the Royal Family on their annual Scottish holiday at Balmoral. Asked to recommend a school for a brief stay by the heir to the throne, Menzies unhesitatingly named Australia's most famous school, Geelong Grammar, just outside Melbourne, Victoria. Geelong was modeled on the English public fee-paying school, a fine example of what some call "muscular Christianity." Two hundred miles to the north, under the slopes of Mount Buller, there was another part of Geelong, a rural colony where the regime was more Hahn-inspired, where the boys lived close to nature. The school was called Timbertop; in November it was officially announced that Charles would spend time there.

In the Australian Parliament Menzies was attacked for his suggestion. He replied that "Geelong Grammar is a school of high repute and it is not difficult for people to understand that a school that has a rural branch has attractions in this instance. I would be very sorry for the young Prince if he were at school in the middle of a crowded city in Australia with people gazing at him, with people trying to get pictures of him and with people making him a rare show. That isn't what he will be there for. He will be here to go to school and mix with ordinary Australian boys."

This was a somewhat misleading statement, since Geelong's pupils are far from ordinary. They are an elite group—privileged children from rich homes. The New South Wales Teachers Federation complained that if Charles was supposed to meet the people, then "he should meet ordinary Aussies. Geelong caters to the sons of wealthy families." Other critics were appalled by the barbarian environment in which the impressionable adolescent Prince would be living. The New York *Herald Tribune*, for instance, remarked that Timbertop appeared to be "one of those curious schools where the bleakness of life is in direct ratio to cost of tuition."

There was some truth in this, but part of Prince Philip's approach to his son's education had always been that it should be a toughening exercise. He did not want a sensitive, introverted son; he wanted a son who could, as one of Prince Charles's friends says, "do anything that a member of the Parachute Regiment can. Only better. And more." As training for this ideal, Timbertop was perfect. In the winter there was skiing down Mount Buller. In summer there were hundred-mile hikes through the bush that took all weekend to complete. Right off the bat there were three stiff inaugural hikes: up nearby Mount Timbertop, to the other side of Buttercup Creek and to the Howqua River. Other diversions included a race in which a log had to be carried across a paddock at top speed and an all-day treasure hunt which involved catching insects, fish and other wild life, as well as covering considerable areas of rough Aussie terrain.

As Charles left London's Heathrow Airport after the traditional post-Christmas break at Sandringham he viewed the exercise with some not surprising apprehension. He was still only seventeen, and this time he was really leaving the family behind. Australia was literally "down under," on the other side of the world. There was no prospect of weekends with the family, let alone long holidays at Balmoral or Windsor. His only links with home would be his detective, Derek Sharp, and Squadron Leader David Checketts, Prince Philip's Royal Air Force equerry, who would serve "in *loco parentis*." Checketts and his family were renting a farmhouse about 120 miles from Timbertop, which would be Charles's only escape from the rigors of school life; and Checketts would be his only trusted, faithful guide and friend.

As it turned out the experiment was quite a success. Charles looks back on Timbertop as a turning point in his life. "I was worried about how I would appear to them," he says, "but I had absolutely no need to worry after I'd been there an hour. Australia got me over my shyness." After his return, one of his biographers, Dermot Morrah, said, "He is now much less frightened and more confident." Nowadays Charles seems to use every excuse to go back to Australia, where he enjoys the outspoken, extroverted qualities of the people—especially when it involves, after an early morning swim, being properly embraced by a nubile western Australian model in a string bikini, as happened on his visit in March, 1979.

When questioned about the most useful thing he had learned at Timbertop, Charles replied drolly, "Kangaroo wrestling. You creep up on your opponent from behind, grab them by the tail, flip them on their backs, and then you have them at your mercy." His facetious humor was also apparent in talking about the tree-chopping contests held at Timbertop. "I think they were just getting cheap labor to clear the bush," he suggested. He might have been right.

His most public performance of the Australian trip was a visit to Papua-New Guinea, the primitive country to the north of the subcontinent, where the natives had until recently been headhunters and cannibals, and where the *lingua franca* is pidgin English. "We arrived at the entrance to the village," he recalls, "and the drums stopped and the whole village were assembled there and for some unknown reason they suddenly started to sing 'God Save the Queen,' and it was the most moving, touching thing I have ever experienced, I think, to see these people, miles from Britain, singing the National Anthem. And the tears practically rolled down my cheeks. It was the most wonderful occasion and I shall always remember that." He *is*, after all, a complete patriot.

Here Charles had seen a native civilization so primitive and unchanged that it sparked the interest in anthropology which he pursued at Cambridge University and later. He also learned more about what to expect from large crowds whose sole purpose was to see *him*. There were other Timbertopper alumni there, but the vast crowd, chanting *Egualau!* (the dialect for "welcome") was welcoming *him*, "Brother Charles." "*Nambawan pikini blong Misis Kwin.*" He found the self-confidence to respond, and when native dances were preformed in his honor he replied by leading the Timbertoppers in a spirited if imperfect version of a Scottish eightsome reel. At last he was acquiring the assurance to take charge rather than be taken charge of.

At Timbertop in winter he also taught his fellow students to ski; in summer he was the best fisherman of the lot. In his first week he had to chop logs on a baking hillside. "I could hardly see my hands for blisters after that," he said. In the Gordonstoun *Record* he wrote: "A popular cry seems to be that Timbertop is very similar to Gordonstoun. This is not strictly true. From what I make of it, Timbertop is very individual. All the boys are virtually the same age, fourteen—fifteen. [Charles had the advantage of being a year or so older.] There are no prefects and the masters do all the work that boys might otherwise do in a school. This way I think there is much more contact between masters and boys as everyone is placed in the same sort of situation. There's very little spare time and one never seems to stop running here and there for one minute of the day, from 7:30 A.M. breakfast—and no morning run, though there's worse to follow—until the lights go out at 9:15 P.M., having had tea at the unearthly hour of 5:30 P.M. If you have just done a cross-country run at 4:45 P.M. and arrived back at 5:05 P.M. it's difficult to persuade your stomach to accept food."

But there was more to this Australian diversion than pumping iron. When his much-loved grandmother came out on an official tour the Prince accompanied her on a visit to the Snowy Mountains. The Queen Mother has always been especially close to Charles, and it's said that at least twice he asked her to intercede with his parents when he was particularly unhappy at school. Certainly it was she who telephoned on his very first day at Gordonstoun to make sure that he was settled in. This time her grandson really was happy. Indeed, he had just called England to ask the Queen's permission to stay on longer. The Prince was enjoying his independence.

When this maiden visit to Australia ended he thanked his hosts in obviously heartfelt language: "It would be difficult to leave," he said, "without saying how much I have enjoyed and appreciated my stay in Australia and how touched I have been by the kindness of so many people making those six months such a worthwhile experience. The most wonderful part was the opportunity to travel and see some of the country (I hope I shall be able to come back and see the rest) and also the chance to meet so many people. I am very sad to be leaving, and yet I shall now be able to visualize Australia in the most vivid terms."

Returning to England he seemed a much more adult figure than the shy, apprehensive boy who had flown away only a few months before. At school he fitted naturally and easily into his new roles of responsibility as head of his house and later of the school. But it was in national affairs that the new maturity was most noticeable. In the autumn of 1966 he celebrated his eighteenth birthday and became First Counsellor of State, automatically deputizing for his mother on her absences abroad, and able, should she die or abdicate, to succeed in his own right without having to be a nominal ruler under the control of a Regent . . . That October there was a terrible tragedy in the south Wales coalfields when, at the village of Aberfan, a tip of coal waste slid down the hillside engulfing the school buildings and killing more than a hundred people, most of them children. As Prince of Wales Charles felt a responsibility toward the bereaved. They were his people; he was one of them, and it was his *duty* to share their suffering as well as their rejoicing. And so that bleak autumn day he made direct calls, composed and sent the first of a lifetime's messages of felt condolence: "My deepest and heartfelt sympathy to all those who are bereaved and those who are suffering. My thoughts and prayers are assuredly with you. Charles P."

He was beginning to become a Prince in more than name only.

CHAPTER FOUR

Cambridge, Trinity— The Windows Open

ON DECEMBER 22, 1965, the Queen gave a select dinner party at Buckingham Palace. Apart from her husband there were only five guests: the Archbishop of Canterbury; a Santa Claus-type prelate named Michael Ramsay who had once been a public school headmaster; the Dean of Windsor, Dr. Robert Woods, a friend of the family who had prepared Charles for confirmation and who had since become Bishop of Worcester; Harold—now *Sir* Harold—Wilson, then socialist Prime Minister of Britain and a former Oxford University academic; Sir Charles Wilson, the Principal of Glasgow University, Chairman of the Committee of University Vice Chancellors and one of the country's leading academics; and, of course, the inevitable figure of Lord Mountbatten, who had been invited not so much because he was genial uncle Dickie but because he could, as an Admiral of the Fleet and former Commander-in-Chief, speak for the armed services. It was a formidable gathering of influential and important men, and they were there to do more than drink port and munch mint chocolates. They had been summoned to advise on the future of the heir to the throne.

Charles himself was not present, though he had already expressed the hope that he might go to a university and follow a full undergraduate course like other Gordonstoun boys. There are many and differing accounts of what took place at that dinner. Someone, such as Harold Wilson, suggested that the boy should go to one of the "redbrick" universities (the mainly Victorian institutions in the English provinces). Someone else, Mountbatten, later dismissed that as a "damn fool idea." Robert Lacey, in his bestseller *Majesty*, has a memorable if improbable account of the occasion in which he has Harold Wilson utter the words, "Ma'am, Dickie has not spoken yet. Can we have his opinion?"

At which, with uncharacteristic diffidence, Earl Mountbatten "proposed the formula that came to be adopted—'Trinity College like his grandfather, Dartmouth like his father and grandfather, and then to sea in the Royal Navy ending up with a command of his own.'"

In fact it did not take this august gathering long to agree that Cambridge University was a sound choice; but the question of a college was more difficult. Charles had already suggested Cambridge, and as Prince Philip said a year later, "There are three kinds of university: there are the old universities... the 'redbrick' universities and the new universities. We discussed this at great length, and in the end we came to the conclusion that it is so difficult to choose between any of the new universities, and that particular associations which existed between one or another were so marginal that the consensus of opinion was that it should be one of the older ones. And Cambridge, I think, suggested itself for a number of reasons. His cousins had been there, his grandfather too... and East Anglia is relatively close to Sandringham, and in a sense all reasonable arguments seemed to point to Cambridge."

There was no need for Philip to sound so apologetic about the choice. Cambridge is the second oldest university in England and shares with its arch-rival, Oxford, the reputation of being the best institution of higher learning in every conceivable respect. Its alumni have become prime ministers and Nobel Prize winners, poets and actors, writers and scientists. The campus is extraordinarily beautiful, the light blue colors of its athletic teams compete with distinction in almost every competitive sport and its Footlights acting revue achieves professional standards year after year. Like Oxford, Cambridge is a collegiate university and since much of life is lived within the colleges, the choice of a college is important. Each college has a subtly distinctive image and reputation. Magdalene, for instance, is sometimes thought snobbish; King's rather effete; Christ's somewhat too keen on sport. Robin Woods, the Dean of Windsor, was dispatched to the city of Cambridge to do some canvasing of the colleges and fact-finding. When he returned he recommended Trinity College, where he himself had been an undergraduate.

Trinity is the biggest of the Cambridge colleges and can lay some claim to being the best. It was founded in 1546 and has produced a succession of famous men, including more than a quarter of all British Nobel Prize winners, at least six prime ministers, the scientists Newton and Rutherford, the poets John Dryden, Lord Byron and Alfred Lord Tennyson, philosopher Bertrand Russell, composer Ralph Vaughan Williams and hundreds of other men distinguished in their various fields, including such unexpected figures as A.A. Milne, the man who wrote *Winnie the Pooh*.

The deciding factor in choosing Trinity was its Master, Lord Butler, known to generations of English politicians as "Rab," widely acknowledged as "the best Prime Minister the country had *never* had," a notably liberal Conservative with an impressive record as a Minister especially when running the Education and the Home Office. Lord Butler had recently been appointed head of Trinity College. He was wise, not only in an academic sense but also in the ways of the world, and the Queen knew and trusted him. He would be an admirable overseer of the Prince's university career.

Later Charles and his parents were to be less than pleased when Lord Butler granted a very frank interview to the searchingly inquisitive Ann Leslie of the London *Daily Mail*. Miss Leslie, an Oxford scholar with a plausible manner, asked Butler what his original plans for the Prince had been. Butler immediately recalled the precedents: Charles's grandfather and other members of the family had been to Trinity but theirs had been fleeting, almost peripheral visits.

"They'd lived out of town in mansions with their own staffs, and the college tutors came to them," said Butler. "Well, we were absolutely determined that Prince Charles was going to live in college and share as far as possible in the everyday life of the ordinary undergraduate."

This earnest echo of the hopes expressed by the authorities at Hill House, Cheam, Gordonstoun and Timbertop was, surprisingly, more difficult to realize at Cambridge than anywhere else. To begin with, there was some rather unwarranted carping by everyone from Teachers' Associations to schoolchildren about the apparent injustice of the Prince's admission; his two A-levels were undistinguished but did meet the minimum entrance requirement.

"Quite unjustified," Butler said of the criticism. "The boy has great gifts, great gifts. I think he's really very clever, even more so than his parents."

The remark about Charles's parents was somewhat tactless, and the Queen and Prince Philip were not amused by the old politician's further comments: "Quite frankly, you know, the Queen and the Duke are not university people—they're horsey people, commonsense people. The Queen is one of the most intelligent women in England and brilliant in summing up people. But I don't think she's awfully interested in books. You never see any lying about her room when you go there, just newspapers and things like that. Whereas Prince Charles has a tremendous affinity for books—they really mean something to him."

As far as the academic side of the Prince's time at Cambridge was concerned, there was little or no bending of the rules. For the first year of his studies he read archaeology, physical anthropology and social anthropology—which are concerned with "those characteristics of mankind which spring from the fact that man is a social animal." This seemed a useful grounding for a young man whose future was to involve so much dealing with man as a social animal, and in some respects the course was tailor-made for Charles—social anthropology includes the study of kinship, inheritance and succession, military organizations and religious institutions. Charles, who would one day inherit the crown, the command of Britain's armed forces and the supreme authority over the Church of England, was a walking, talking case-history for his fellow students. He enjoyed his studies and sat for an end-of-year exam like everyone else, passing with honors and obtaining a 2.1, which put him in the top half of the class. Only very clever and hardworking students get "firsts," which are generally regarded as the virtual passports to fame and prosperity. Charles's 2.1 was a vindication for Butler, the A-level examiners and others who had always regarded him as university material. In the next two years Charles specialized in history. This time he did less well in the final exams, slipping a class to a 2.2. Butler irritated the family by asking them to let Charles concentrate on his studies and not force him to take on public duties, which would include a lengthy stay in Wales. "I really wanted them to leave him alone, you know. That's why I was so against him being sent off to Aberystwyth, where I knew he'd have to waste time being fêted by lord-lieutenants and suchlike. But I'm afraid my arguments didn't prevail. His family were set on it." Butler did, however, compensate by giving Charles some informal instruction on his future constitutional role. "He'd often come up to my study in the evening and we'd sit here and discuss politics very frankly and I'd tell him who was a bloody fool and who wasn't, and I'd explain things about the Constitution to him and tell him all about the part he'd have to play. Oh yes, we enjoyed ourselves enormously and got on very well. He's a tremendously cheerful chap, you know."

A cheerful chap but not, of course, an ordinary one. Most Cambridge undergraduates are provided with a room, or possibly two rooms, but they share bathrooms and their cooking facilities are rudimentary. Charles, however, had his own private bathroom and kitchen. Butler recalls dining *chez* Charles. "He did most of the cooking and I must say it was very good. Poor chap, though, the college servants were dying for the honor of helping him so they sent along a waiter, which I think rather annoyed him as he'd wanted to do it all himself." Squads of plumbers and painters had been sent up from Sandringham to make sure everything was spick and span, and on the day the Prince arrived at Trinity in a jaunty little Austin-Morris Mini he was greeted by a crowd of squealing groupies in mini-skirts. The girls threatened to pounce, but before they could perpetrate any frightful indignity "several burly bowler-hatted gentlemen proceeded to drag shut those magnificent wooden gates to prevent the crowd following in." Charles described the episode as "rather like a scene from the French Revolution." Few undergraduates owned their own cars and cars were expressly forbidden to freshmen. Nevertheless, Charles kept a blue MGB sportscar the entire time he was at the university, but he was extremely discreet about using it in his first year. His detective (who stayed in Cambridge all the time and was christened "Oddjob" after the character in the James Bond film) used to pick him up outside Trinity and drive him off to the MGB's garage in his Land Rover. Butler, like all university provosts, had a good intelligence system and was keen to let everyone know that he was more or less omniscient. He used to watch prince and detective sauntering casually across the courtyard on their way to the illegal car, and finally he could bear it no longer. "I knew they were going off to pick up his car, and when I told him one day that he couldn't fool me, his face fell a mile. Poor chap thought he'd got away with it."

The English university is traditionally a place not only for book-learning but for growing up, for making friends and most of all for talking. Charles got on well with other people at Trinity and he never seemed to "pull rank." The previous Prince of Wales had been forced to wear a velvet cap with gold tassels during his student days, and when he attended debates at the university Union everyone was expected to stand in his honor. Prince Charles eschewed such formalities, but his efforts to mix with his contemporaries were not wholly successful. At first he took meals in the communal dining hall along with everyone else. "Didn't keep it up though," says Butler. "He told me he felt a bit lonely in a college as large as this. He'd go into Hall, make friends with the chaps sitting on either side of him and then, after the meal was over, probably never come across them again. After a while he had his meals sent up to his room, which you can do here if you've got the money. And money was hardly one of his problems."

Most of Charles's friends, perhaps inevitably, came from the middle and upper classes, what Butler called "conventional huntin' and shootin' Army types from public schools." Charles may wince at this terminology but he concedes that "a person's closest circle of friends, whatever his position, is determined by his interests and way of life. For instance, I enjoy shooting; therefore I see a lot of people who shoot. A number of them are 'members of the aristocracy.' Not all. But it isn't that they are landed gentry which is the cause of my seeing them. It's shooting."

Students of humble birth may have been timid about making overtures of friendship to the Prince of Wales; this problem persists today. "Unfortunately," he says, "the nicest people are those who won't come up and make themselves known. I think, good God, what's wrong? Do I smell? Have I changed my shoes? Yes, it's usually the nicest people who want to be friendly. But they're terrified of being seen to be friendly in case I won't talk to them or something. So you can imagine I then have to make the running, which becomes a bit of an effort sometimes. I have to show that I'm a reasonable human being."

At Cambridge the Prince and seven friends formed an exclusive all-male dining club which they named the Wapiti Club. Its dinners involved tuxedoes and formal invitations which Charles issued, using one of his more romantic sounding titles: "The Lord of the Isles." On one occasion when the friends went to the Marx Brothers' movie *A Night at the Opera*, Charles adopted another pseudonym, "Charlie Chester," which is the name of a well-known old-world English comedian. The alias was both a tribute to British comedians (many of whom are frequently invited to the Palace by Charles, especially The Goons, at whose celebrations the Prince has often been guest of honor) and a sly allusion to one of Charles's legitimate titles, Earl of Chester.

The members of the Wapiti Club, so named because it was a "stag" organization, were all affluent and privately educated. Although three-quarters of Trinity's 650 members were from State schools, the majority did not play polo, enjoy (even if they could afford it) dressing up for smart dinners or share the essentially conservative views of the Prince of Wales. Even one of his fellow Wapiti members remarked, "I don't think anyone gets to know him really well." The fault, if fault it was, lay on both sides. People were as bashful about approaching the Prince as he was about approaching them.

An exception to this rule was Hywel Jones, the Welsh son of a non-conformist minister, most of whose friends and relations had been, according to him, "either railwaymen or miners." He was the president of the Trinity Students Union and had rooms leading off the same staircase as Charles. Ordinarily Charles and Hywel, who appear to have had nothing whatever in common, might never even have met, much less become friendly; but when Charles quizzed Butler about politics, the Master suggested that he look up Jones and see how it worked at the college level. The discussion would give Charles some grass-roots instruction. Later, after Jones had become an academic at another university, Charles cited their friendship to demonstrate that he had got to know students outside the round of "Hurrah Henries" that Butler suggested were his exclusive companions. "We write to each other, but we don't meet as much as we did because he's in the North of England and I'm down here. The fact that I don't 'mix' with him as much as I did isn't because he's a different kind of person—or because he comes from a different 'class'—it's a matter of circumstance."

At Cambridge Jones and Charles used to sit in their dressing gowns arguing over their coffee into the early hours of the morning. Charles listened more than he talked, although, Jones says, "those views he did express were surprisingly open-minded and flexible, given the sort of background he comes from. In fact, his thinking is far less hide-bound and stereotyped than I think most people would suspect."

It was also at Cambridge that Charles met Lucia Santa Cruz, the attractive daughter of Chile's Ambassador to the Court of Saint James. She had taken an undergraduate degree at London University and then did postgraduate work at Oxford before moving on to Trinity, where she was helping Lord Butler on his memoirs. A bright, vivacious and highly intelligent girl, she became one of the first to be linked with Charles in the popular press as a regular and intriguing girlfriend. But, as important if not as titillating, she was a provocative conversationalist and gave him some useful, informal advice on further reading. It was largely at Lucia's instigation that Charles embarked on a long and exhaustive study of the English novel in his leisure hours.

The Prince's intellectual growth was also fostered by conversations—both formal and informal—with his senior tutor at Trinity, now a fellow of the college, Dr. Denis Marrian. Dr. Marrian recalls a humorous exchange which occurred between himself and his royal pupil one night when the Prince caught him emerging from the wine cellar of his house by a coal hole in the ground that served as the entrance to the cellar.

"I've always wondered where the senior tutors have their quarters," said Charles. "From now on I shall have to call you Dr. Mole."

When the embarrassed tutor explained that he had been in his wine cellar, the Prince replied, "What an excellent idea, it *does* make it rather difficult to go back for a second bottle when you want it but don't really need it."

Anxious to reestablish decorum, "Dr. Mole" assured the Prince, "As you can see, sir, when I've been down there once, I rarely need to visit it a second time on the same night."

The Prince answered, "Well, sir, you must ask me to dinner one night, and we'll see what we can do about that."

"Throughout my relationship with him," Dr. Marrian later recalled, "I always found him to be very quick at this kind of off-the-cuff remark. We had almost Boswellian conversations. The only time when Prince Charles was not being funny was when he was learning. When he came to see me he was thoughtful and serious and never mucked about. But when the day's work was done he was a hoot."

He had always had a sense of humor—ever since the childhood practical jokes that he shared with Prince Philip—and Cambridge was an ideal outlet for the Prince's talents as a comic. The University's Footlights is a revue group dedicated solely to humorous productions, and over the last few years the group has spawned any number of successful shows and performers, including, most notably, *Beyond the Fringe, Monty*

Python, David Frost and John Cleese. The Footlights performers were drawn from all over Cambridge, but each college also had its own theatrical group specializing in a peculiarly British variant of the sort of student humor that the National Lampoon made famous. In the case of Trinity the revue group, named the Dryden Society after the poet, put on a show called *Revu-Lution* which Charles later described as "an awful sort of *Beyond the Fringe*-type show full of the most awful sort of groan jokes." Like his father, Charles is notoriously prone to "awful groan jokes," so after a quick consultation with Butler, who told him he might as well join in because "it's essential for you to learn how to deliver throwaway lines," he auditioned and was accepted. In the course of a two-hour show Charles portrayed a cello-playing pop star (lightly mocking his own more serious musical leanings), the Duke of Wellington deriding Napoleon's army for having made a mess of the Eton playing fields and a Victorian lecher, Sir Cummberbund Overspill, whose parting line as he exited left wing with a pretty nymphette in tow was, "I like giving myself heirs." It was archetypal undergraduate humor, and his own imitations and funny voices owed more than a little to his early addiction to the radio "Goon Shows" of Peter Sellers, Spike Milligan and Harry Secombe. The publicity Charles as comic received from the national press was uniformly favorable; an heir to the throne who was prepared to laugh at himself in public made a refreshing change. Next year he was at it again, appearing in twenty-five of the thirty sketches which made up the Trinity Revue, *Quiet Flows the Don*. This time Charles had a meaty role as a weather forecaster on the BBC. Coming on stage in a gas mask and flippers, the Prince announced: "It is 0600 hours. Virility will at first be poor. Promiscuity will be widespread. The Naval review at Portsmouth will be warm and sunny—so there will be no cold navels. Listeners are advised to avoid falling barometers and on funday and boozeday there will be bold and rowdy conditions."

Having delivered this mildly risqué bit of humor the Prince began to blow bubbles from a toy pipe and continued: "There is a manic depression over Ireland. But there is a warm front over

Sweden which will be followed by a cold back."

The audience was appreciative. Charles seemed to have them eating out of his hand, and then, as happens occasionally even to professional actors, he "dried up." The house was so silent you could hear a pin drop, but Charles could not remember his lines. They never did come back to him—instead, he saved the day by turning to the wings and asking, with a loud laugh and an exaggerated stage whisper, "What the hell comes next?" When the laughter died down, Charles was ready with a saving, "It doesn't happen like this on the BBC." He also appeared in several other sketches in the revue, including as an expert in Bong Dynasty bidets, a quiz-show contestant who is unable to identify a set of Scottish bagpipes which he mistakenly describes as "an indigenous northern reptile with stuffed tentacles." As if to prove his point, the "reptile" attacked him.

But it was not all fun and games. On June 17, 1969, the Prince was installed as a Knight of the Garter at Windsor, joining other members of his family in the oldest surviving order of European chivalry. He was resplendent in flowing robes, an ornate feather hat, and a badge inscribed with the motto *Honi soit qui mal y pense* ("Evil to him who evil thinks"), which was what King Edward III said to his courtiers when Joan, Countess of Salisbury, dropped her garter and he picked it up. The courtiers were giggling and nudging each other knowingly, and the King was concerned to demonstrate that he and Joan were "just good friends." As it happens, the courtiers were almost certainly justified in their suspicions, but that didn't stop the King from founding the order which is now nearly six-hundred-and-fifty years old.

By now Charles was attending many of the great State occasions at which the Royal Family's presence is *de rigueur*. He was at the funeral for Britian's great wartime leader, Sir Winston Churchill, and he was at the State opening of Parliament in 1967, looking slightly ill at ease in a formal black tailcoat with a hint of white handkerchief protruding from the breast pocket. (He had to miss a meeting of the University Madrigal Society to get to Parliament that day.) The educational visits which his old governess, Miss Peebles, had instituted had now been translated into adult form, and Charles was making his first fact-finding tours, listening intently as he was taken round a new elevated highway in West London, the construction site of a section of the London underground railway system, an evening paper in Scotland, and one of Britain's leading motor-racing tracks. He was beginning to become a genuinely public figure.

Perhaps more surprising to those who recalled the child who had seemed timorous and sedentary, the young man was beginning to come out of his shell, conquer his inhibitions and play the daredevil. His MGB was a spiffy sportscar and he drove it fast. Now he was also learning to fly, relishing the danger and challenge. "I always thought I was going to be terrified," he said. "I was dreading the moment when I was going to have to go up, but because the weather had been so bad for so long I put in quite a lot more hours than is really vital and so I had quite a lot of experience. But the day I went on my solo the instructor taxied to the end of the runway, having landed, and he suddenly climbed out and said, 'You're on your own, mate'... So there I was. And I only had time to have a few butterflies in my tummy, and then I taxied off, and took off, wondering whether I could do it, and the moment I was in the air it was absolutely marvelous. There was no instructor to breathe fire down the back of your neck, and the airplane flew much better, because he'd gone and the weight was out of the airplane and I had a wonderful time."

This account of flying came during his first radio interview. A short time later he gave his first television interview. It was all a prelude to the real baptism of fire, the culmination of the promise his mother made to the people of Wales at the Empire Games in Cardiff. When he heard it over the radio in Peter Beck's study at Cheam he had been a nervous, embarrassed little boy. Now the Student Prince was poised for an initiation rite as symbolic and ancient as those he had studied in his Cambridge textbooks. He was about to become the Prince of Wales.

CHAPTER FIVE

The Mantle of the Black Prince

"I SEEM TO HAVE quite a lot of Welsh blood in me," remarked Prince Charles shortly before his investiture as Prince of Wales in 1969. Indeed, he is, by some obscure genealogical process, descended three times over from the original Welsh princes who once held sway over the 8,000 square miles of Britian which comprise the ancient principality. Yet Prince Charles, owing to a misunderstanding of his father's family background, has been denigrated as "Charlie the Greek." On any count, he looks English with possibly a trace of Scots blood—a casual observer would never guess Charles to be Welsh. Indeed the Royal Family has seemed to pay scant attention to Wales until the heir to the throne became its prince. There are, for example, no royal palaces in Wales, though there are several in England and two in Scotland; and while the royals pass quite easily from the role of English lord to that of Scots laird they have seldom seemed so assured in Wales. It is perhaps significant that the most Welsh member of the family was Anthony Armstrong-Jones, who took the title Snowdon from Wales's highest mountain and has now divorced Princess Margaret (though he remains an obvious favorite with the Queen and Charles and is still regularly asked to take official royal photographs). In 1969 Charles was so far removed from firsthand experience of Wales that he confessed, "I've hardly been to Wales." He added, "You can't really expect people to be over-zealous about the fact of having a so-called English Prince to come amongst them and be frightfully excited."

At no stage in its long history has Wales exactly welcomed outsiders. In 61 A.D., for example, the Romans invaded and were met by an army described by the historian Tacitus: "The enemy lined the shore, a dense host of armed men, interspersed with women clad in black like the Furies, with their hair hanging down and holding torches in their hands. Round this were Druids uttering dire curses and stretching their hands toward heaven. These strange sights terrified the soldiers." Some two thousand years later the natives, or many of them, were still just as violently opposed to outside influences, and for a time their hostility focused on the young, otherwise inoffensive figure of Charles.

The principal cause of the Welsh fury was the issue of language. Theirs seemed, over the centuries, to have fallen into disuse. Welsh patriots insisted, however, that it had not so much fallen as been pushed—by the English.

Not all Welsh people agreed. There were plenty of Anglophiles in the country and many more moderates. One hundred seventy-five students at the University College in Aberystwyth had even signed a petition asking that Prince Charles be sent there to acquire a knowledge of Welsh language and culture. The main nationalist party, "Plaid Cymru," had recently won a parliamentary election at Carmarthen and sent its leader to Westminster and the London Parliament. The Plaid wanted a measure of self-government for Wales, and was prepared to work for it democratically. Not so the Welsh Language Society and the Free Wales Army, which were said to be training in the mountains. When an RAF warrant officer was injured in an explosion the Language Society was blamed (wrongly as it turned out) and thereby earned the hatred of the moderates. "I had some in my taxi the other day," said a Welsh cab driver. "I turned them out. Them in their bloody green jackets. They spoke to me in Welsh. I'm Welsh but I don't speak

Welsh. They said I was ignorant. So I turned them out. They're like the Hitler youth."

The Language Society specialized in blotting out the English names on road signs and scrawling up Welsh equivalents. They were making inroads. Phone boxes had already become monolingual. There was no sign in them saying, "To contact the operator—dial 100." Instead the legend ran: *Os cawch anhawster—deialwch 100*. At the Sip-y-Pethe in Aberystwyth, which is literally Welsh for "shop with everything," there was a gramophone record called "Carlo," sung by the Welsh Language Society's leader, Dafydd Iwan. The song which made the top of the Welsh hit parade mocked the Prince, describing his mother telling a Welsh "friend" that "Carlo, Carlo, Carlo is playing polo today...with his Daddy." The song went on sarcastically to exhort the Welsh "serfs" to join in the chorus of their liege's praise.

On November 17, 1967, when hundreds of Welshmen gathered in the capital city of Cardiff to discuss plans for Charles's investiture, a bomb went off—the first of thirteen to explode during the build-up for the investiture.

It was into this simmering cauldron that the Royal Family loosed its son and heir. Eleven years before, when he was still a boy at Cheam, Charles had heard his mother's fateful announcement that he would one day be invested at Caernarvon Castle. To that baptism of fire there was now added the further ordeal of a term at the University in Aberystwyth. In the final stretch of his Cambridge education, just when his academic studies were at their most crucial and just when he had come to feel at home at Trinity, he was sent off to a strange college in a totally strange town in what was in essence a totally strange country. He admitted to being apprehensive: "Having read in the papers an awful lot about the sort of things that might happen and the anti-feeling there was in Aberystwyth and in Wales, naturally misgivings built up." Even the principal of the college, Dr. Thomas Parry, a founding member of Plaid Cymru, seemed to regard the exercise as a form of intellectual warfare. He described it as "mutual indoctrination" and went on, "He will learn something of the problems, idiosyncrasies and prejudices of the Welsh—right or wrong . . . it will be a very fine opportunity for extremist friends to put the Welsh nationalists' view to him in its most rabid form."

Nor was it simply the Welshness of the place that was intimidating. Cheam was an upper-middle-class establishment with paying pupils from "the right sort of home." So was Gordonstoun. Timbertop, however spartan, was a branch of another exclusive private school and, finally, Trinity, although it admitted bright working-class boys funded by the State, had the sophistication and tradition to assimilate a royal student without batting an eyelid. Not so the University of Wales. Not so Aberystwyth. The University of Wales belongs firmly in the "redbrick" class. Almost all its students come from relatively poor homes and only a very few have been at schools like Gordonstoun. If his fellow pupils at other establishments had felt nervous and cut off from the Prince, how much more so would the people at Aberystwyth. And then there was the place itself. Aberystwyth is pretty much a one-horse town at the end of a single-track railway line. It has a population of about ten thousand, excluding students and tourists, who are the main sources of income. It has a rather decrepit pier and the air of having seen very much better days. (Since cheap package holidays have become all the rage, British seaside resorts have obviously suffered, and few would visit Aberystwyth with its rocky beach and icy Cardigan Bay water when they could have the Mediterranean for the same price. The impression is correct. Aberystwyth *has* seen better days.) Most important, it was the sort of town which would not, like Cambridge, take a royal prince easily in its stride. The sophisticated natives of Cambridge react to celebrities by pretending not to notice them. The natives of Aberystwyth, on the other hand, tend to rubber-neck. Every morning a little knot of matrons were gathered outside Charles's hall of residence to speed him on his way to the language laboratory where he was learning Welsh. These women were almost more embarrassing that the people who demonstrated against him. Once the Prince turned the tables on them by greeting the most vociferous one in Welsh. "*Bore da, sut 'rydych chi,*" he said, to which the woman, rather discomfited, said, "I'm very sorry but I don't speak Welsh." With demonstrators who opposed him the Prince was just as forthright, and would march up and try to engage them in some form of dialogue. It didn't always work. "They were standing there," he said of one such occasion, "and they were, I thought, perfectly ordinary people and I thought one could talk to them as perfectly ordinary people. One somehow feels that because they're demonstrating and they've got placards that they're a group apart. Instead, I thought, 'Might as well go up and see.' So I asked one chap who was holding a placard what it meant, because it was in Welsh and I'm afraid to admit I haven't learnt it properly yet. So I asked him and he just in fact hurled abuse at me and said it was 'Go Home Charlie' or something like that. After I'd asked him more questions I gave up. There was no point."

At the neo-Georgian hall of residence, halfway up the hill on the outskirts of town, he was registered simply as "Windsor, C. Room 95." On his first night his next-door neighbor, a Welsh nationalist, invited him down for dinner in the communal dining hall, but he probably made fewer friends during this period than at any other time in his life. There was nice Mrs. Morbyth-Branan, who cleaned his room and exchanged a bright "*bore da*" (good morning) with him every day. And more significantly there was Edward Millward, his tutor. Millward was a vice-president of the Plaid and their parliamentary candidate in nearby Montgomeryshire (he lost easily—Montgomeryshire is Liberal country). Millward, a fervent Welsh nationalist, was also a civilized, intelligent man as well as a fine teacher. Not only did he get Charles's Welsh up to a standard which sounded brilliant, he also argued with him articulately and forcefully, never giving ground. "I've had some very interesting talks with Mr. Millward," said Charles, "and he had enlightened me a great deal about Nationalist aims, ideas and policies."

As far as Charles was concerned, Millward was possibly the best thing about Aberystwyth, and he certainly managed to make the prediction of the college president, Sir Ben Bowen Thomas, come true: "He might leave with a very strong Welsh accent," said Sir Ben. In fact, by the time he left Wales Charles was at least able to deliver a speech in a faultless Welsh style. "I haven't found it too bad," he said, "because I think I can imitate accents reasonably well, and it helped to actually speak Welsh." It was surely an improvement on his previous learning of languages. "I learned French for about ten years and hardly ever spoke it; and whenever you spoke it they all laughed at you and you felt you were rather silly." When he first spoke Welsh at a Welsh League of Youth Eisteddfod no one laughed and he didn't feel remotely silly.

But excellent tutor though Millward was, he could never become a friend. It was rumored that the Prince was lonely. Charles denied this, but he did admit, "I haven't made a lot of friends, if that's what you mean, and I haven't been to a lot of parties or anything. There haven't been very many, and I've had a lot of other things to do. I've been round Wales a lot, looked at things and visited people." In the final analysis, he conceded, "It is, I suppose, compared with other people's lives, more lonely."

In his spare time he used to drive about the countryside in his blue sports car with its silver plume of feathers on the front. (He drove an MG in those days—a less expensive and less powerful car than the Aston-Martin of his later years.) On these royal drives his only companion was the detective who had a room down the corridor at the Pant-y-celyn hall of residence; there were no journalists or photographers in tow. He therefore felt quite free to stop and pass the time of day with anyone who happened to cross his path. There were some happy encounters with Welsh farmers, including one discussion on the merits of artificial insemination of cattle. Sometimes he would spend a weekend with a local dignitary or even go north to Caernarvon to inspect the castle where he was later to be invested and to meet the Lord Lieutenant, Sir Michael Duff. More often he would nip into Mrs. Griffith's Bay Hotel on the front at Aberystwyth and spend the evening watching television. Or, if he was feeling like a decent dinner, he might drive a few miles east to Ponterwyd, where Miss Withers, the elderly proprietor of the George Borrow Inn, served the best food for miles. "Roasts are properly cooked and so are the fresh vegetables," remarked the Good Food Guide. "Non-residents must book and meals are served on the gong." Charles went out there to dine on the gong at eight, and developed an affection for Miss Wither's homemade trifle. (He has always had a sweet tooth. His favorite meal is smoked salmon and scrambled eggs followed by peach melba with lashings of whipped Devon cream.)

In the course of his term in Aberystwyth Charles certainly learned something about Wales and the Welsh, but he was conscious, too, of being a long way from home. Aberystwyth was very unlike Trinity with its nearby polo, or Sandringham and Windsor, which were within easy driving distance. It was, in a strange way, an even tougher, more demanding experience than Timbertop. As a prelude to the investiture it was, however, useful if not wholly enjoyable. When his predecessor was invested in 1911, the Prime Minister of the day, David Lloyd George, "the Welsh Wizard" who was Member of Parliament for Caernarvon, coached the young Prince, rather unsatisfactorily, in such apposite Welsh phrases as "*Mor o gan yw Cymru i gyd*"—"All Wales is a sea of song." In Charles's case no such coaching was necessary. Nor did he face the prospect of the ceremony with quite the misgivings expressed by the hapless twentieth Prince in 1911. "The ceremony I had to go through," recalled the Duke of Windsor, "with the speech I had to make, and the Welsh I had to speak were, I thought, a sufficient ordeal for anyone. But when a tailor appeared to measure me for a fantastic costume designed for the occasion, consisting of white satin breeches and mantle and surcoat of purple velvet edged with ermine, I decided things had gone too far." Poor Prince. He had been used by Lloyd George and Alfred Edwards, Bishop of St. Asaph, as a political pawn. The two men had wanted a sumptuous piece of pagentry to emphasize the unity of England and Wales, and the Prince had been the obvious person to star in the pageant. The ceremony was virtually their own unprecedented invention.

The earliest Princes of Wales had been entirely Welsh and for many centuries had led their countrymen in battle with conspicuous success. As late as 1256 the great Llewellyn took on the English and drove them out, and it was not until the end of the thirteenth century that Wales was finally abolished as an independent state. King Edward I proclaimed five Welsh counties, announced that they would all come under the King's Dominion and borrowed £19,000 (more than five million dollars at today's rates) to build a magnificent castle at Caernarvon at the foot of the Menai Strait, which divides the North Welsh mainland from the island of Anglesey. Here the King presented the vanquished Welsh with their first conqueror Prince. "You asked for a prince who spoke not a word of English," he said, and according to legend, displayed his infant son, Edward, at his fortress in Caernarvon. This might have been a good medieval joke but it has, not surprisingly, rankled with the Welsh ever since. It brought little joy to Edward either. He grew up an effete and lost one of the most disastrous battles of English history when he was defeated by the Scots at Bannockburn. He was finally forced to abdicate by his wife Isabella and was murdered at Berkeley Castle in 1327, in the most frightful manner possible, by men with a red-hot poker.

Since then the Princes of Wales have been a motley collection. Only twelve of them actually went on to be King. Some, like Henry VIII's elder brother Arthur, died young (he was not yet sixteen). James II's son went into exile and became known as the "Old Pretender." He ended his days in Rome where he "created" his son, later known as Bonny Prince Charlie, Prince of Wales, a title which was as meaningless as that of King, to which he also laid claim. Two Princes were actually born in Wales, but none was invested there until 1911. Indeed, the investitures were usually conducted with scant ceremony at one or other of the royal palaces in London or in the House of Lords. There was certainly no thought of turning the investiture into the great gala which confronted Charles until the bishop and Lloyd George hatched their plot in the early years of this century.

"I think it will probably mean quite a lot," said Charles, when asked about the day. "I think on the whole I will be glad when it's over—put it that way. But that doesn't mean to say that I shan't get any meaning out of it. One could be so cynical about this sort of thing and think, well, it's only a ceremony, and some people are against it, and perhaps it's for television, you know, it's just a show. But I like to think it's a little more than just that. Perhaps it's symbolizing *Ich Dien*, if you like, in some way. It will be an exhausting day and an enjoyable one, because I do enjoy ceremonies, and I think the British people do them so very well, particularly the Duke of Norfolk. He's a wonderful man. With all the people who've taken part and helped, and who hope it's all going to go well, it will probably be a marvelous day, as long as the weather stays fine."

The Duke of Norfolk, Earl Marshal of England, was the country's most aristocratic Roman Catholic, which made him a strange choice for England's official impresario. As the nation's Cecil B. de Mille he was responsible for such Anglican pageants as coronations and State funerals such as Sir Winston Churchill's (regarded by many as Norfolk's finest hour). He was everyone's idea of an English lord, passionately fond of cricket (he managed an English cricket tour of Australia and owned England's most attractive cricket field at Arundel, next door to his castle). He was also rather prickly and not too clever in an academic sense.

The man who played Barnum to Norfolk's Bailey was George Thomas, a thin-faced Welsh socialist MP for West Cardiff who went on to become Speaker of the House of Commons. At the time of the investiture he was Secretary of State for Wales and greatly endeared himself to the public by prefacing many of his remarks with "Me and me mam," a reference to the venerable mother with whom he still lived. A devout Methodist, he was in almost every respect a perfect foil for the Duke. They were an archetypal odd couple, but it seemed appropriate that such an unlikely pair of promoters should take charge of this unlikely event.

The day was set for July 1. The preceding months were full of meticulous preparation. In the enormous gardens behind Buckingham Palace the Duke of Norfolk marked out an imitation Caernarvon Castle and moved members of the Royal Family about as if they were pieces in an Alice-in-Wonderland chess game. To his chagrin he was allowed only £200,000 to stage the show, and he grumbled that he would have preferred half a million to do the thing properly. It soon became clear that this was, as Charles had suggested, a television spectacular. The castle itself could only accommodate four thousand guests, but thanks to the marvels of modern telecommunications an estimated five hundred million people would be able to watch it in their homes. The BBC would be devoting six hours to the investiture and, all in all, the castle would contain more than fifty cameras, much to the irritation of the chairman of Independent Television's special events section, who complained: "More than fifty cameras were doing the work of twenty-five. Attempts to bring reason to bear upon this absurd situation failed."

Shortly before the great day Charles gave two interviews, the first on radio to Jack de Manio (who coincidentally was a director of the same public relations company as Charles's secretary, David Checketts), the second on television to Cliff Michelmore of the BBC and Brian Connell of ITV. The Prince was becoming public property with a vengeance, though he managed both interviews with an easy, modest charm which won him a good deal of support. "I wasn't really nervous for some extraordinary reason," he said later. "I like acting and I enjoy imitating which helps enormously when appearing in public." He added that he thought he should only appear on the box when it was absolutely necessary and when he had something specific to talk about. He looked forward to appearing again—but sparingly.

Meanwhile the castle was being prepared. Special souvenir chairs with vermillion cushions of pure Welsh wool were commissioned by the Ministry of Works, which promised to sell them off afterward as souvenirs at £12 apiece. That meant an extra £48,000, which cheered up the Duke of Norfolk. Twenty-six banners, twenty-three feet, six-inches long, were hung on the castle walls, and a special plastic canopy for the royal dais was tested in the British Aircraft Corporation's wind tunnel, in case the castle was subjected to one of the sixty-mile-an-hour gusts which attack it every ten years on the average.

The genealogists of the College of Arms were poring over their records and found the form of investiture used for King

James I's son, Henry, in 1610 and repeated for his brother
Charles after the former's untimely death. The Mayor of
Caernarvon, initially unhappy about the occasion, now
succumbed to an extravagant fit of Welsh euphoria: "You could
put a suit of armor on that boy," he said, "and send him to
Agincourt. I reckon he's the ace in the royalist pack. Wales has
reached a point where we need friends—from Buckingham
Palace upwards or downwards. The investiture is the spur that
has got us to do things we wouldn't ordinarily have done. We've
put a shilling on the rates and begun a crash program for the
streets. It's a bit like asking a village to run a cup final, but life
would be very dull if we didn't have any pageantry. The castle, of
course, is not a symbol of oppression but of our toughness
... There's no oppressor any more. It's a privilege for the Prince,
as well as the Principality..."

The mayor may have been exaggerating when he made his
references to Agincourt, a famous English battle of the fifteenth
century, but he was right about the reference to a "village
running a cup final." Before the great day Caernarvon was
already full to bursting. There were journalists everywhere and
part of the castle had been turned into a sort of military
compound for television crews only. Tempers frayed. The entire
Daily Express team of about twenty was thrown out of its hotel
for allegedly drunken and rowdy behavior, and there were ugly
scenes when press men learned that the Caernarvon Sunday is
officially dry. Accommodation was in such short supply that the
heralds from the Royal College of Arms had to be quartered in a
hotel at Beaumaris, half an hour's drive away on the other side of
the Menai Strait.

And there was still the threat of an attack on the Prince.
Charles was irritated by rumors that he would wear a
bullet-proof vest, but £23,000 *was* spent on security, and
although most of the 2,500 troops under canvas in the grounds
of Sir Michael Duff's house at Vaynol were there for show, there
were some who were not. On Investiture Eve a homemade bomb
built with two sticks of gelignite and a wristwatch exploded at
the Cardiff post office. And the royal train bringing Charles and
his family north from London was delayed at Crewe for an hour

when another bomb was found hidden under a bridge near Chester. This one was a hoax: an alarm clock and two sticks of plasticine.

As the train traveled toward Wales a great crowd gathered spontaneously in the square outside Queen Eleanor's Gate of the Castle. Inside, a full rehearsal of the investiture was held; the parts of the Royal Family were taken by substitutes but everyone else was present, although in plain clothes. It was the Duke's last chance, and he, like George Thomas, was well satisfied. In the square, around the statue of Lloyd George, the crowd sang as only the Welsh can, quite without direction yet in perfect harmony, ranging through the whole canon of Welsh music from dirge to battle hymn, though noticeably less enthusiastic over "God Bless the Prince of Wales," the words of which are, of course, in English. It was a fine and moving occasion, a demonstration of patriotism and loyalty and a little of that uniquely Welsh quality they call *hwyl*, a Welsh Welshness, which knows no translation. The Oxford dictionary inadequately describes *hwyl* as "emotional quality, inspiring impassioned eloquence." In any event, the scene was set for the next day.

The waiting became tiresome. At 10:45 A.M. the royal party disembarked from their train and went to Michael Duff's for a champagne breakfast. Charles wandered off to look at one of Duff's horses; then, when a nearby television set was turned on, complained at seeing himself yet again. "I'm so bored with my face," he said, "can't we have someone else?" After breakfast the royals piled back into their train and traveled the few hundred yards to the special railway station erected for the event. Royal ceremony is sometimes a curious business. Waiting to greet them, in the uniform of Her Majesty's Lord Lieutenant, was the beaky figure of Sir Michael Duff, with whom they had just had breakfast. "I'd no idea I should see you again so soon," said the Queen rather flippantly.

Charles arrived in the castle at 2:40 P.M., driving to the Eagle Tower with George Thomas in an open carriage. In the castle the 4,000 guests (mostly Welsh, but including a smattering of foreign notables such as Tricia Nixon and President Tubman of

Liberia) heard the cheers of the huge crowd outside, sweated slightly over a sharp explosion that could have been a small bomb and then sighed with collective relief as Prince Charles's own personal standard, including the arms of the last native Prince of Wales, Llewellyn ap Gruffyd, was broken from the pole of the tower. Moments later a tiny figure in the dark blue uniform of Colonel-in-Chief of the Royal Regiment of Wales with the lighter blue sash of the Order of the Garter across his chest stood on the green, green grass, and everyone rose for a thunderous rendering of "God Bless the Prince of Wales." Charles was then marched off to a dark octagonal dungeon to wait for a half-hour until his mother summoned him for the investiture proper. It was, in all honesty, a bit of a pantomime: the Lord's Prayer recited in Welsh or English according to choice; Lord Snowdon, constable of the castle, in a green uniform he had designed himself and which made him look not unlike a bellhop at the Waldorf-Astoria; a piece of charade involving the key to the castle specially invented for the 1911 investiture by Lloyd George; an odd mixture of English Gentlemen-at-Arms in high boots and hats with plumes of swan feathers; and berobed figures from the National Eisteddfod Court including Gwnn o'r Llan, Rhys ap Gruffyd and Elisabeth of Wendraeth. Finally the Queen gave Charles the silver gilt sword, a golden rod, a golden ring, a mantle of purple and ermine and a new electro-formed coronet donated by the Goldsmith's Company, while James Callaghan, the Home Secretary and Member of Parliament for one of the Cardiff constituencies, intoned the Letters Patent, which described how "Elizabeth the Second by the Grace of God of the United Kingdom of Great Britain and Northern Ireland and of Our other Realms and Territories Queen Head of the Commonwealth Defender of the Faith" was "granting, confirming, ennobling and investing Our Most Dear Son Charles Philip Arthur George." This done, Charles, kneeling in front of his mother, his hands in hers, declared: "I, Charles, Prince of Wales, do become your liege man of life and limb and of earthly worship, and faith and truth I will bear unto you to live and die against all manner of folks."

89

That was the climactic moment. Afterward Charles listened, sitting on his mother's right, to a loyal address, then made his own speech in resonant Welsh and English, including an oblique reference to comedian and singer Harry Secombe (of The Goons) whom he described as "a very notable goon." It was perhaps not one of the Prince's best jokes, but it got a titter of recognition and was a useful ice-breaker. From that moment the spontaneity grew as Charles went from one side of the castle to the other to show himself to the crowds gathered outside in a strange echo of that legendary, Edwardian gesture of almost seven hundred years before. The crowd cheered his appearance. The investiture had been a great success. The television audience had topped the six-hundred-million mark.

"I frankly believe it could not have gone better," said the old Duke of Norfolk, giving himself a well-deserved pat on the back. "There is still a great sense of pride in this country, thank God."

And the Duke's partner, George Thomas, more lyrical and more Welsh, enthused: "The support of the populace exceeded my wildest dreams. I don't want to be guilty of the Welsh sin of exaggeration, but it was a far greater triumph than we had a right to expect. He really was the Prince Charming."

What followed was, perhaps inevitably, a marginal anticlimax. For three days Charles made a royal progress through the Principality, meeting his people. The crowds were enthusiastic, especially the women who stood with flags, tears in their eyes, sometimes bursting into verses of his increasingly familiar anthem, "God Bless the Prince of Wales." In the coal fields of the south it was especially moving to see the miners coming up from the pit-face to watch the Prince pass, their faces black with coal dust except for the white patches around the eyes where their goggles had been. It recalled the frustrated despair of his great-uncle David, who had made a similar tour in the Depression and had so won the hearts and minds of the Welsh with his heartfelt cry that "something must be done."

Two incidents stood out. Once, Charles stopped to talk to a small girl with her grandmother. "Is this your nan?" he asked her, correctly using the Welsh term for grandmother. The remark was overheard by the press, which has used it against him to this day, assuming that by "nan" he meant "nanny" and was shocked that he should be so out of touch as to believe that an ordinary Welsh child would have a paid nanny. Charles was right and the press critics were wrong, but the gibe stuck. The second notable incident, at Carmarthen, was the meeting with Gwynfor Evans, leader of the Plaid Cymru. The meeting was relaxed and cordial, though Evans said, "If the investiture was intended as a political exercise it has entirely misfired. In fact it has strengthened both the Welsh language and our national confidence."

Prince Charles would not have disagreed. The ceremony had, indeed, made an honorary Welshman of him. "I am the Prince of Wales," he said later. "I have an association, a relationship, a title. I want to make it real, productive and as effective as possible."

Now he had to return to Cambridge and finish his studies; then enter the services and take on his brief naval career. But, like General MacArthur, he would return.

Princess Anne and brother Charles at
Sandringham, one of the Royal Family's favorite
places of retreat.

Silver Wedding Anniversary of the Queen and
Prince Philip in October 1972. Between the Queen

and Princess Anne are Prince Andrew,
standing, and Prince Edward.

Charles after advanced flying training at the Royal
Air Force Academy at Cranwell in 1971.

Wearing his Balmoral tartan, Charles at 24 dances
on the heath with his 8-year-old cousin,
Lady Sarah Armstrong-Jones.

On active duty with the Royal Navy in
1973, Charles walks down the
gangway of the frigate
H.M.S. <u>Minerva</u>.

At Caterham Barracks in Surrey, Captain Idris
James of the Welsh Guards fixes a leek to the hat
of his colonel, Prince Charles. The presentation of
leeks is a traditional gesture on the feast of
St. David, patron saint of Wales.

Charles cuts a rakish figure at
Princess Anne's wedding in the fall
of 1973.

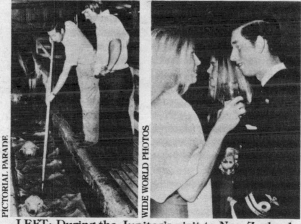

LEFT: During the <u>Jupiter's</u> visit to New Zealand,
Charles lent a hand in sheep-dipping.

RIGHT: A California blonde came into Charles' life
during the <u>Jupiter's</u> stop in San Diego—Laura Jo
Watkins, the daughter of a U.S. Navy rear admiral.

As communications officer aboard the frigate
H.M.S. Jupiter in 1974, Charles headed a division
of radiomen and "tactical operators," the men who
handle the signal flags and lights.

Charles got a taste of helicopter flying in a training session at the Royal Naval Air Station at Yeovilton.

Charles strides across the field with his helicopter instructor, who called the Prince "a natural pilot."

BRITISH INFORMATION SERVICES

Charles makes pre-flight checks on his Royal Navy Wessex Mark V helicopter.

WIDE WORLD PHOTOS

At Resolute Bay in Canada's Northwest Territories in 1975, Charles takes an arctic dive.

ECHAVE & ASSOCIATES

On the bridge, the bearded Charles
looks strikingly like his sailor-king
great-grandfather, George V.

KEYSTONE

In February 1976, Lieutenant
His Royal Highness the Prince
of Wales got his own command, a
wooden-hulled mine hunter, H.M.S.
<u>Bronington</u>.

Sporting an Edwardian beard after one of his cruises on the <u>Bronington</u>, Charles turns up at the Badminton Horse Trials.

PICTORIAL PARADE

Between the weeks at sea, there is just enough shore leave to keep the press guessing about Charles' romantic attachments. One favorite is Davina Sheffield, seen here strolling with Charles at the polo field at Windsor.

With Davina Sheffield, the Prince drives out in a coach-and-pair at Windsor.

Lady Sarah Spencer, daughter of Northamptonshire landowner Earl Spencer, has been a friend of Charles since childhood. Here she joins Charles for a summertime polo match.

At the races in 1977 with Lady Camilla Fane, daughter of the Earl of Westmoreland, Charles is elegantly turned out in morning suit and top hat.

The London newspapers make her a mystery lady
when this photo first appears in 1970, but
Charles-watchers soon learn that the stunning
young woman is Lucia Santa Cruz, daughter of the
Chilean ambassador to Britain.

When Prince Charles visits the White House in the
summer of 1970, Tricia Nixon in still single,
and the President, it is rumored, would
welcome a match.

Princess Marie-Astrid, daughter of
the Grand Duke Jean of
Luxembourg, still rumored as a
possible bride for the Prince.

One of the most durable of Charles'
companions is the striking Lady Jane
Wellesley, the daughter of the eighth
Duke of Wellington. Here, in the
spring of 1978, Lady Jane and
Charles walk across the course at the
Quorn Hunt in Leicestershire.

CHAPTER SIX

Golden Eagle, Red Dragon, Blue Sea: "From Boy to Man"

THE EARLY 1970s were awkward years for the future King of England to enter the military. He had, of course, served almost two years as Colonel-in-Chief of the Royal Regiment of Wales and Honorary Colonel of several other Army commands, but those were largely ceremonial duties. Now he was set to enter active service, first in the Royal Air Force, next, for a much longer period, in the Royal Navy. But the U.S. misadventure in Viet Nam had aroused pacifist sentiment the world over, and Britain was not exempted. The voices of criticism were not many, but they were a strident minority. Charles found himself on the defensive, having to explain a choice that his forebears had made with almost universal approval.

He selected his platform adroitly. In March, 1971, the City of London offered him the Freedom of the City, an ancient medieval honor that even royalty can only earn, not expect. (Indeed, in 1978, the city fathers of Edinburgh voted narrowly *not* to give Charles the freedom of the Scottish capital, on the grounds, said one opponent, that he had done "nothing to deserve it.") To receive his accolade from the London establishment Charles rode in an open coach from Buckingham Palace to the old city Guildhall where he was given a rousing ovation. Elegant in his dress uniform as Colonel-in-Chief of the Royal Regiment of Wales, wearing the riband and star of the Order of the Garter, the twenty-two-year-old Prince listened as a herald certified his legitimacy as the son of "Prince Philip, Duke of Edinburgh, citizen and fishmonger of London, and that he was born in lawful wedlock . . . so they all say."

After the City Chamberlain, a certain Richard Whittington, presented Charles with a scroll attesting to his Freedom of the City, the Prince rose to reply. There were the usual generous acknowledgments, and then the message, forthright and unmistakeable. "It is pointless and ill-informed to say that I am entering a profession trained in killing," said the Prince. "The Services in the first place are there for fast, efficient and well-trained action in defense. Surely the Services must attract a large number of duty-conscious people? Otherwise, who else would subject themselves to being square-bashed, shouted at by petty officers, and made to do ghastly things in force ten gales? I am entering the RAF and then the Navy because I believe I can contribute something to this country by so doing. To me it is a worthwhile occupation and one which I am convinced will stand me in good stead for the rest of my life."

It was, in a sense, a farewell speech to civilian life for nearly six years to come. The very next week Charles was off to the RAF College at Cranwell in Lincolnshire to earn his Royal Air Force wings.

Though the Navy was his ultimate goal, the RAF seemed a logical first choice. He had been flying since his Cambridge days, soloing at twenty. Since then he had qualified in the twin-engined Basset, giving him enough flying hours, even as he entered the RAF, to be awarded the rank of flight lieutenant. He slid easily into place among a new class of university graduates ("Graduate Entry One") who had just completed their Basset training and were moving on to jets. Apart from a flamboyant operational code name—"Golden Eagle"—which he found a touch embarrassing (he was called "Wales" by his superior officers), the Prince was treated like any other cadet officer, put up in a bachelor apartment with three others in the graduate program, sharing an enlisted aide (a "batman" in British military parlance). There was only one other royal touch: a detective also shared the duplex apartment.

Like other cadets, Charles pedaled around the base on a government-issue bicycle, but on his time off he accelerated the pace, climbing into the new dark-blue Aston-Martin Volante he had bought to celebrate his twenty-second birthday the previous autumn. Then he was off to country-house parties—at Belvoir Castle, for one, where he starred at a charity ball given by the Duke and Duchess of Rutland and set tongues wagging by dancing more than courtesy required with his hosts' daughter Charlotte. Back at the base Charles indulged his comedic streak on April Fools' Day, arranging a phony announcement over the public address system. A certain London shoemaker, the announcement declared, had discovered a fault in the design of some shoes that many cadets had bought. Those who had purchased such shoes, it went on, should turn them over to the school porter (who was in on the joke) for return to the firm. Dozens of pairs were turned in before the cadets realized that their legs had been literally pulled by a royal practical joker.

About this time Charles made his famous appearance at the Master Tailors' Benevolent Association charity dinner at a West End hotel. He described the incident three years later at a Variety Club in Manchester: "About three years ago I was elected as one of the world's best dressed men. The following year I was elected as one of the world's worst dressed men. At a tailor's dinner just after, I decided to have my own back. I arrived wearing my white tie and an old tweed jacket over the top. The British are such a splendid race. They pretended that I was perfectly normally dressed. They are far too polite to comment."

By now Charles had earned the nickname "The Clown Cadet," but his pluck was acknowledged in another nickname, "The Chinfull Wonder" (aristocrats are supposed to be chin*less*, the mark of a weak will and timidity). Actually Charles had little time for either dormitory pranks or derring-do. He and his classmates had barely five months to rush through the intensive course of jet training. By the end of three months he had logged more than eighty hours in the subsonic Provost trainer, twenty-four of those hours solo. Soon he was in RAF front-line aircraft, making sorties over the North Sea in the Nimrod maritime reconnaissance jet at speeds over 1000 mph. Which earned him membership in the RAF's Ten Ton Club (a "ton" in pilot's lingo being 100 mph). On one training mission in a Vulcan jet bomber, Charles joined in a simulated attack on the city of Doncaster, showering railway yards and locomotive works with "direct hits."

Despite all the action, he still chafed at the bit. He had not been allowed to try parachuting as the other cadets had, and he very much wanted a chance at it. It was not something he relished trying, more a fear he felt he had to conquer, as he explained to Douglas Keay of *Woman's Own* magazine in 1975. "Of course there is danger," he said of his various daredevil exploits, "but I am trying to be as responsible as I can because I'm totally aware that there are people who will have to take the can if something goes wrong. But I do feel that in my position I must set an example. I must show people that I am prepared to do things that they are expected to do. Perhaps it's because I am constantly feeling that I have to justify myself, my existence. I want to prove to myself that I can accept challenges, and mentally accept things which are perhaps dangerous or slightly frightening. I want to overcome that fear, if I have any." He most certainly had a fear, the Prince admitted candidly, of "jumping out of an airplane on a parachute." But "I'd always wanted to do it because I wanted to see how I'd react. I managed to do it in the end."

The Queen ultimately gave permission ("I cannot stand in your way," she is reported to have said, with perhaps a conscious touch of Windsor humor), but the exercise was more like an expedition. Charles jumped into the sea, a mile offshore, on a perfect summer day, diving out of a twin-prop Andover at 1200 feet, after experienced officers had jumped to test the wind drift. "Out I went," Charles recalled later. "The slipstream is terrific. You appear to be flipped on your back and the next thing I knew my feet were above my head, caught in the rigging lines, very odd. I thought, 'They didn't tell me anything about this.' Fortunately my feet weren't twisted round the lines and came out very quickly. The Royal Marines were roaring around in little rubber boats underneath and I was out of the water in ten seconds."

Golden Eagle, to the command's great relief, graduated in one piece and with official applause. As a late entry into the class he was ineligible for prizes (a young Scot from Charles's quarters, Flying Officer Gavin Mackay, won most of the flying trophies), but his final report showed more than mere deference to royalty. The Prince, it declared, would "make an excellent fighter pilot at supersonic speeds." He displayed "a natural aptitude for flying," an "all-around ability," and "excelled at aerobatics in jets."

At the graduation ceremony, which Prince Philip attended in his gold-encrusted uniform as Marshal of the RAF, there was just a mild touch of rue in the words of Air Chief Marshal Sir Denis Spotswood. "We have the honor and distinction of witnessing the graduation of the first heir to the throne to have completed a flying course at the college. It will not have escaped anyone's notice that the Prince of Wales has had to so compress his experience of Royal Air Force life that he graduates and leaves the active list at the same time." The next stop would be a humbling experience for the newly graduated flight lieutenant. Within a month he would be at the Royal Naval College at Dartmouth, an acting sub-lieutenant once again starting up the ladder of rank in what is known in Britain as "the Senior Service." It was a self-imposed discipline. Had he wanted to, he could have transferred into the Navy as a lieutenant.

The Royal Navy has changed dramatically since the third son of King George III, young Prince William, went to sea in 1779 at the tender age of fourteen. So brutal was the life at sea then that enlisted ranks often had to be kidnapped into the service by "press gangs" and thereafter lived under the life-and-death rule of martinet captains who could order a hundred lashes or a keelhauling for a trivial offense. Even for a midshipman of royal blood the training was strenuous and the life hard: Prince William, later Lord High Admiral and eventually King William IV, did not earn his name, the "Sailor King" with ease. In the two centuries since, the cruelties have been abolished and the hardships ameliorated by technology, but one tradition has remained. Since the time of William's niece, Queen Victoria, one of the royal princes, usually a younger one, has been sent to sea to make his career.

It was accident, however, that made the Royal Navy a training school for kings. William himself was two brothers away from the succession. Queen Victoria's second son Alfred was allowed to enter the Navy as a youth while his elder brother, the Prince of Wales, had to fret for years before being allowed even to serve in the Army. Only reluctantly did Victoria let the Prince of Wales send his own two eldest boys into the Navy, and when the older one, Prince Eddy, died, Prince George had to leave the service to train for his own eventual succession to the throne. With thirteen ships and the hard-earned rank of commander behind him, the man who became King George V would look back on his naval career as the *sine qua non* of manly training.

Curiously, George V's enthusiasm for naval training seems to be borne out by the separate royal paths followed by his two eldest sons. When King George came to the throne in 1910, the naval career of his first-born son, David, was cut short before the new Prince of Wales was out of Dartmouth; wider duties for the new Heir Apparent were deemed more appropriate. It was the younger of the two, Prince Albert, who stayed in long enough to see service at the famous Battle of Jutland, the greatest naval engagement of the First World War. And it was Albert who succeeded to the throne as George VI when his brother, Edward VIII, abdicated in 1936. That the Royal Navy should turn out two Kings as dutiful and selfless as George V and George VI was not lost on those who helped to chart Charles's future. Charles's great-uncle, Lord Louis, Earl Mountbatten and longtime First Sea Lord, one of those who joined in shaping Prince Charles's career, often recalled an incident in December, 1936, when he stood beside the new King George VI. "I'm only a naval officer," protested the bewildered, inexperienced monarch. "It's the only thing I know about."

"That is a curious coincidence," Mountbatten remembered himself saying. "My father once told me that when [Prince

Eddy] died, your father came to him and said almost the same things that you have said to me now. And my father answered: 'George, you're wrong. There is no more fitting preparation for a King than to have been trained in the Navy.'"

The family vote in favor of the Navy was doubtless influenced not a little by Prince Philip, who had already persuaded Charles to trace his former footsteps through Cheam and Gordonstoun. Philip himself had been an eighteen-year-old cadet at Dartmouth in 1939 when he first caught the eye of the thirteen-year-old Princess Elizabeth, who was visiting the school with the King and Queen. Young Philip won the King's Dirk (a ceremonial dagger) for his excellence at Dartmouth, and went on to serve with distinction in Royal Navy warships during World War II—and then won the King's daughter as well.

Charles acknowledges that he discussed the Navy with "my father and Lord Mountbatten," but insists the choice was ultimately his. "I wanted to go into the Navy anyway, partly for historical reasons, partly because it was a form of tradition in my family, but basically because I felt I had been brought up in the Navy in some ways, heard so much about it. It was the Service I had always known about, having been on the *Britannia* every year as a child."

The Britannia Royal Naval College at Dartmouth has no connection except coincidence with the name of the Queen's luxurious seagoing royal yacht: the college was the successor to the old wooden-hulled training vessel on on which George V, for one, had served as a cadet. By the time Charles reported to the green military campus on the Dart River in Devon in 1971, Dartmouth was a far different place from what it had been when Prince Philip was there thirty-two years before. For the long-term cadets, it still provided a blend of college-level academic studies, naval sciences and military discipline, together with a touch of the traditional hazing bestowed on newcomers by their seniors. Some Dartmouth staff officers insisted, too, that the College still lived up to its reputation to "treat 'em mean and keep 'em mean." But to other staffers it seemed to have become a place both civilized and rigorous, a serene setting that produced toughened young men. "Anyone who has not been to Dartmouth has no idea what it's like," Chief Petty Officer Henry Phillips told newsmen shortly before Charles's arrival. "It's right out of this world; it's the only place I know with flower beds around the parade ground." The results remained remarkable. "They come here with long shaggy hair and white faces. After a fortnight they are totally different. You virtually see them change from boy to man."

Charles, in any case, would not have to endure the rigor of the full program that once put George V and Edward VIII at the mercy of their classmates' hazing. The Royal Navy, like the R.A.F., had begun to recruit university graduates to supplement its ranks of cadets, and generously commissioned them as acting sub-lieutenants when they entered Dartmouth—the equivalent of the U.S. Navy's rank of ensign. For the usual graduate cadet, the stay at Dartmouth was short, a mere three months, and not unpleasant. Charles, for example, was assigned Cabin A-30, an airy room on the second floor of one of the college buildings, with broad windows overlooking the Dart River. He shared the services of a steward with several other officers; the food was good and plentiful, and though the workday was full (barely more than two hours of "free time") there was no compulsory reveille so long as one turned up at morning formation promptly at 7:50 A.M. Most of the day was a pell-mell crash course in naval subjects: navigation, seamanship, marine and electrical engineering and basic shipboard administration. Then it was off to the real school—the sea—for the balance of a year.

Charles's term at Dartmouth was shorter by half than most cadets', a hectic six weeks. It was so brief, in fact, that his family hardly took notice of the graduation parade. Prince Philip was in Berlin, Princess Anne in Hong Kong. But Lord Mountbatten flew down to Devon for the occasion, pleased, as he put it, that "my great-nephew was top in navigation and seamanship, and that is all we seamen care about." Then Charles boarded Lord Louis's chopper to be flown back to Windsor for lunch with the Queen. In early November, after attending the opening of Parliament, he flew to Gibraltar to complete his training aboard the 6400-ton guided-missile destroyer H.M.S. *Norfolk*.

Charles's dual role as fledgling naval officer and Heir Apparent was swiftly driven home in Gibraltar, where he arrived unheralded in an ordinary troop transport plane and was unceremoniously hauled off in a Land Rover to meet the docked *Norfolk*. Local citizens, involved in a struggle to preserve their sovereignty from Spain, were unhappy that the Prince did not lend his royal presence to a parade; the Spanish Foreign Ministry was distressed enough to send off a message to the British Embassy in Madrid protesting Charles's mere presence on the Rock. The Embassy tried to put the proper face on the matter. "His Royal Highness' movements as a serving officer are subject to normal operational requirements and are purely a matter for Her Majesty's government." All the same, for the next five years Her Majesty's government would have to watch nervously as Charles sailed the seas.

The *Norfolk* was sleek, fast, new: a guided-missile destroyer designed to add a special punch to the NATO Fleet with a long-range surface-to-air missile called the Sea Slug, a weapon so expensive (more than $100,000 a shot) that it was rarely fired more than once a voyage. One of Charles's principal duties was to serve in the ship's elaborate electronics operations room as part of a gun director team, but the sophisticated Sea Slug was not his responsibility. Instead, his equipment controlled the shorter range anti-aircraft Seacat missiles and the ship's two conventional 4.5-inch gun turrets. "When we have to use those," said one *Norfolk* officer of the close-combat guns, "we are in trouble."

Gunnery was just one of many jobs for the royal sublieutenant as he labored among the 35 officers and 450 crew of the *Norfolk* to learn its workings from stem to stern. Captain J.W.D. Cook, a forty-nine-year-old commanding officer of the destroyer, described what might be a typical day at sea for Charles.

"His steward might call him at 3:30 A.M. for the 8 A.M. watch, as second officer of the [bridge] watch. Then he would have breakfast and spend the rest of the forenoon in the operations room. In the afternoon he probably would be attached to a department, perhaps the engineroom, for general experience.

After tea there would probably be another watch, and in the evening he would have to get on with his studies. Of course he would have to go to bed early, because he might be required for the middle watch, midnight to 4 A.M." The *Norfolk*, fortunately, offered its new sailor a bit more than just a bruising schedule. Chief Petty Officer Edward Moriarty, the wardroom cook, was renowned fleetwide for his curries, and daily laid a table with a choice of several hot and cold main dishes. And for the first time in years there was no detective tagging along. When Prince Charles went to sea, the Navy took responsibility for his security. His cabin measured only seven by seven feet—but he was at last *alone*.

The pace scarcely let up after the *Norfolk* returned home for Christmas. Through the first months of 1972, while the *Norfolk* crew spent most of their time doing the drudgery of upkeep and maintenance in Portsmouth, Charles's naval godfathers saw to it that he got maximum exposure to other kinds of duty. In January, 1972, he literally plunged into the submarine familiarization course at Gosport, and—after gaining the express permission of the Queen and the Prime Minister—made his required three ascents from a submarine escape tank. The next month he was off for a twenty-four-hour patrol off the Scottish coast in the nuclear submarine *Churchill*, and then bounced over to the Fleet Air Arm frigate *Hermione* for yet further temporary duty—all the while remaining officially assigned to the *Norfolk*. Conceding a bit wearily that he was getting "a shortened course of introduction to the Navy," the Prince gamely declared, "I have to try that little bit harder to be as professional as possible . . . to assimilate all the vast problems rather more quickly."

The drop-in duties were rarely dull, though. One day in March, 1972, Charles found himself aboard the *Scimitar*, the Royal Navy's fastest torpedo boat, a streamlined craft with the rakish hull of a racer and an engineroom half the size of the boat, housing twin gas turbines that could turn up 7,000 horsepower. Charles was aboard for the Thursday War, a weekly naval exercise staged off the Dorset coast near Portland. The *Scimitar*'s mission was to intercept and destroy a formation of frigates and other warships trying to break through a ring of submarines and torpedo boats. As the *Scimitar*'s skipper plotted the torpedo problem, Charles took the wheel, piloting the torpedo boat at close to 50 mph straight for the frigate *Andromeda* and her companion ships. "Fire," shouted Lt. Paul Haddacks, the *Scimitar*'s twenty-five-year-old skipper. Crewmen discharged flares, signaling torpedoes running toward their targets, and the royal helmsman swerved the torpedo boat toward safety, leaving a dense smokescreen behind. After the mock battle Charles returned to the *Norfolk*. Over a bunk in the *Scimitar*'s wardroom Haddacks and his crew posted a discreet card noting simply: "Prince Charles slept here, 8/9 March."

Soon the *Norfolk* sailed for the Mediterranean again, with Charles again aboard. He honed his seaman's talents further, but was obliged to join the Queen in Avignon and then Paris during a State visit to France. In June, while the *Norfolk* was in Malta and the Prince visiting Premier Dom Mintoff, sad news came from home: the Duke of Windsor was dead. The man who had been King Edward VIII and was transformed into a royal exile came home to Windsor in death. Prince Charles, who had visited the Duke twice in Paris, flew home for the funeral. On June 3, he led the Duchess of Windsor gently into St. George's Chapel, where the former Prince of Wales lay in State. Thirty-five years before, the King had renounced his throne to marry the woman he loved.

Charles left the *Norfolk* in the summer of 1972. For the next two years he would shuttle between advanced naval studies ashore and sea duty on a pair of *Leander*-class frigates, among the trustiest workhorses in the fleet. The schools, in a pleasant affectation of the Royal Navy, would sound as if they were ships. The H.M.S. *Mercury*, in the hills above Petersfield, was a Signals School (teaching communications), where Charles would learn the vagaries of longwave and shortwave radio, the finger-numbing exercises of assembling cryptographic rotors, the art of writing and answering naval messages. Nearby, at H.M.S. *Driad*, he would take other advanced courses, ranging from watchkeeping on the bridge (American nomenclature: Officer of the Deck Underway) to nuclear defense, an exercise that tries to imagine how a flimsy naval vessel can survive a nuclear attack.

The schools were welcome respites: they kept regular hours and working days, providing Charles with opportunity to go up to Windsor in his Aston-Martin for a rugged weekend of polo. The summer, however, found its tragedy when Charles's thirty-one-year-old cousin, Prince William, Duke of Gloucester, died in a crash during an air race, but Charles nonetheless returned to Cranwell for refresher training in Provost jets. In the best tradition of the stage—and the Royal Family always seems to be marvelously close to National Theater—the show had to go on.

From the *Driad* it was a brief skip to H.M.S. *Heron*, which is not a ship but an airfield, the Naval Air Station at Yeovilton in Somerset where the Prince was due for an "Air Acquaintance" course. No one knew then how close and how fond the acquaintanceship would become: Charles posed cheerfully in the cockpits of Mark V Wessex helicopters and fell in love with the machines almost at first sight.

Says one of the Prince's former helicopter instructors, "We seriously recommended that he should continue the course because he would have quite definitely become one of the finest helicopter pilots in the history of that aircraft. He expressed a wish to stay with us because he enjoyed it so much. But his parents did not want the Prince to specialize. They wanted to give him an all-round experience of military life and so he had to move on."

So Charles moved on, spending two weeks aboard a minesweeper, H.M.S. *Glasserton*, before reporting for duty to the frigate H.M.S. *Minerva*.

There are Navy men in any service who contend that there is no school like a frigate. The names and often the sizes vary: the ship can be called a destroyer escort (or an escort destroyer), a destroyer (the U.S. Navy preference), or a frigate (the British and Commonwealth parlance). The bigger, modern vessels of their kind may earn another name by dint of guided missiles or nuclear propulsion, but the function remains essentially the same. They are hunters—hunters of enemy aircraft and enemy submarines, equipped to blow a submarine out of the water or an aircraft out of the sky. If they belong to fleets that still treasure capital ships, they form protective screens around the heavy-gunned cruisers and the vulnerable aircraft carriers. (The battleships, everywhere, are gone.) If they don't, they patrol vulnerable waters like greyhounds on the scent of prey. They are small, fast and tough: men aboard them learn to work together to survive. Charles could find no better school.

H.M.S. *Minerva* was his first frigate, his home for most of ten months. With it he embarked, in early 1973, for the West Indies, on a voyage more eventful than might have been imagined. The Queen had deputized her son to perform diplomatic functions as well as naval chores, and at his very first stop the Prince found himself walking through the gardens of Bermuda's Government House with Sir Richard Sharples, Governor of Bermuda. The conversation waxed late: it would be one of Sharples's last. A week later, walking with a young aide through the same garden, Sharples and his colleague were shot dead by an assassin.

Charles did not return to Bermuda with his ship. Instead he was transferred for the interim to H.M.S. *Fox*, a hydrographic vessel then involved in an attempt to refloat the grounded Swedish bulk carrier *Ariadne* from a coral reef. But the rest of the Caribbean cruise was less ominous. On St. Kitts, Charles officially reopened an antique fort known as the Prince of Wales Bastion. In July he presided over Bahamas independence celebrations and witnessed an inadvertent comedy: a great awning collapsed on the assembled dignataries, completely enveloping fine-gowned ladies, bewigged justices and morning-coated officials. No harm was suffered, except to dignity, and the Independence Day celebrants were again in good spirits by the time of the State Ball, where they stood around the dance floor to watch Charles perform a spirited version of the local dance known as the *merengué*. Said Charles later: "I love tunes and I love rhythm. Rhythm is deep in me. If I hear rhythmic music I just want to get up and dance. That's one of the reasons I had such a marvelous time in the West Indies."

A curious man, this royal sailor, an acting lieutenant now. In one role he was the Queen's own ambassador; in another he was still something of the collegiate cut-up. When visitors to his cabin looked for photos of girls, Charles would say, "Climb up on my bunk. They're behind the bulkhead shaft." There, just as he said, were a half-dozen beauties in various states of dress or undress; he never volunteered to identify them, and, as one visitor put it, "something in his eye forbade one to ask." The photos may, of course, have been nothing more than princely window-dressing, winsome passports to the aggressively masculine life aboard ship.

The *Minerva* returned home in early September, with Prince Charles poised to embark on a doubletime schedule of royal engagements. It was not exactly a four-month shore leave: in between official engagements he wrestled with a three-week navigating course for frigates at H.M.S. *Driad*, a short course in personnel management at H.M.S. *Victory*, near Nelson's old flagship at Portsmouth, and a Flight Deck Officers Course at H.M.S. *Osprey* in Weymouth, Dorset, where he learned to bring in and send off the helicopters that land on the deck of this particular brand of frigate.

There were duties and pleasures. Among the duties, the Queen had left him as Counsellor of State while she journeyed to Australia, enabling Prince Charles to welcome and accredit new ambassadors. More privately, Charles huddled regularly over dinner with Princess Anne and Mark Phillips about their impending marriage. Like any brother of the bride Charles worried about what to get his sister and her fiancé as wedding gifts. He rose to the occasion, presenting Mark with handsome leather cases for his hunting guns and Anne with a diamond brooch. When the Queen returned, Anne and Charles rode with their mother to the State opening of Parliament, the last time they would do so as unmarried sister and brother.

Soon Charles himself became the focus of popular wishful thinking, when 10,000 Britons descended on Sandringham at New Year's to see his girlfriend of the moment, Lady Jane Wellesley, daughter of the eighth Duke of Wellington. The tide of speculation retreated some only as Charles headed east for

Singapore on the second day of the New Year, there to join the frigate H.M.S. *Jupiter*.

Prince Charles joined the *Jupiter*, a sister ship of the *Minerva*, on January 4, 1974. The *Jupiter* had been at sea since the previous July when she sailed from Plymouth, the great British naval base from which Sir Francis Drake had sailed four hundred years ago to defeat the Spanish Armada (after first finishing his game of bowls on Plymouth Hoe). The *Jupiter*'s voyage is a fascinating passage in recent history. Off the East African coast she had taken part in the "Beira Patrol," designed to prevent oil supplies reaching the rebel colony of Rhodesia—a blockage now seen to have been essentially a paper one. From there she went on to a ten-day exercise in the Indian Ocean with warships from Iran, Pakistan, the U.K. and the U.S. (these were the days before Pakistan became an Islamic Republic under General Zia and Iran was still under the rule of the Shah). In Singapore, once the jewel in Britain's imperial crown, the *Jupiter* was undergoing an assisted maintenance period at what once had been the Royal Naval Dockyard but had been turned over to the Singapore Government with a proviso that a "maintenance capability" would be kept up for those few British ships that found themselves east of Suez.

By the time Prince Charles arrived in Singapore to be greeted by his new commander, John Gunning, the ship was ready to go to sea again. The men, who had been temporarily quartered at Woodlands barracks, were now back on board, as was the Wasp helicopter the *Jupiter* carried with her. Charles was assistant flight deck officer, which meant that he was second-in-command of the helicopter, and he soon became a familiar sight on the flight deck, controlling the chopper in the approved manner with devices that looked suspiciously like ping-pong bats strapped to his hands.

His most important job however was that of communications officer, with responsibility for all communications on board, as well as the twenty-three men who made up his section. On a more lighthearted note Charles was also entertainments officer, responsible for setting up concerts, quizzes relayed over the loudspeaker system and parties for local people at ports of call. He was conspicuously successful.

There were frequent crew changes on the long voyage. Even the commanding officer was replaced at Mombasa, Kenya, in October, and at Singapore Charles was one of three new officers joining ship. His full and formal designation was, as before, His Royal Highness, Lieutenant the Prince of Wales. If he was being formally addressed over the loudspeaker the form would be: "Would His Royal Highness, Lieutenant the Prince of Wales report to the bridge?" In the wardroom, where officers shared their meals and recreations, he was known semi-formally as "Prince Charles." He would, as is the custom in the Royal Navy, always address the commanding officer and first lieutenant as "Sir" because in naval terms they were senior to him. Members of the ship's company addressed him, in turn, as "Sir" because, again in naval terms, they were junior to him. As one senior officer remarked, "He was not there as the Prince of Wales, but as *Lieutenant* the Prince of Wales." That may sound like hair-splitting, but the distinction was vital to his naval career. Without it life would have become intolerable; and to those involved there was absolutely nothing peculiar about it. When, on occasion, Charles went ashore and reverted to his role as Prince of Wales, his commanding officers would call him "Sir" without a moment's hesitation.

Four days after Charles joined the H.M.S. *Jupiter* in Singapore, the ship slipped anchor and headed out into the ocean en route for Australia. There were a few days of exercises to give the crew a chance to shake off the last vestiges of their Christmas and New Year hangovers and then it was full speed ahead for Brisbane, Western Australia, on the sort of "flag-showing exercises" that rarely occur nowadays, government economies having brought most of the British fleet back to home waters.

On January 11 there was a moving moment when the *Jupiter* passed almost directly over the watery grave of her predecessor, the fifth H.M.S. *Jupiter*, which had sunk in 1942 after striking a mine in the Battle of the Java Sea. The Allies had been heavily outnumbered by a Japanese force and every ship, including the *Jupiter*, was sunk. Miraculously, many of the crew escaped and made their way in open boats to the safety of the north Australian coast. As the present H.M.S. *Jupiter* passed by at sunset, the ship's company gathered on the flight deck. As the last post sounded, a bareheaded Prince of Wales cast a memorial wreath on the ocean. Once (for a brief period when his famous ship the *Kelly* was in dock), the wreck that lay at the bottom of the sea had been commanded by Charles's great-uncle, Lord Mountbatten. Charles thought of all the past *Jupiter*s and the men who had sailed in them, ever since the first fifty-gun, fourth-rate frigate was launched on the River Thames in 1778. Naval history means a great deal to Charles ... "I think it's very important that I should understand something about the defense of one's own country," he says. "I think the Navy ought to mean a great deal to this country—this island."

Early the next morning Charles was brought back to the present with a jolt. He was officer of the watch when an S.O.S. came through from the Tembaga reefs 120 miles away. An ocean-going tug and two barges had gone aground and needed assistance. Charles decided immediate action was necessary. The captain was awakened and the *Jupiter* made her best speed toward the reef which, it turned out, was surrounded by an uncleared minefield. A classic naval rescue took place. The Wasp helicopter landed a boarding party; the master of the tug, the *Mediator*, signed Lloyds' "open form" after some argument; and rescue began. It was dull and wet, the tide was falling and so was night, but somehow the *Jupiter* inched her way through the minefield and got close enough for the boarding party to get a 200-foot towline across. At the third attempt they pulled tug and barges free and reversed out through the minefield and on to safety and an anchorage at Baai Van Suuenep. The whole operation took thirteen hours and did not end until one o'clock in the morning. (The only marginal mistake was when the *Jupiter* sent food over to the *Mediator*'s crew. Unfortunately they sent pork to the all-Moslem crew.) Like his fellow officers, Charles received a reward for his work in the form of salvage dues. Unlike them, he gave away the money (between thirty and forty pounds) to charity. Charles never touched a penny of his naval salary—it all went to charity.

Finally, after journeying halfway around the world, the *Jupiter* docked at Brisbane—and the crew learned the unwelcome news that they would have only two days in port. There were receptions, a dance, a cricket match and "open ship" for a day. Although the pretense that Prince Charles was "just a member of the ship's company" was scrupulously maintained by the men and officers of the *Jupiter*, it was impossible to persuade the Australians to do the same. Press coverage—not to mention the number of invitations to festivities—was unprecedented. But normal etiquette was followed. If someone wanted to invite Prince Charles they had to invite the captain and other officers and hope that the Prince was included. There was no way they could ask Prince Charles on his own. The Mayor called on the captain. The captain called on the Mayor. If the captain chose to take the Prince along for the ride, then that was the captain's business. If the Prince had more pressing duties on board ship, then he attended to them. It was an interesting contrast to his predecessor's world cruise; great-uncle David had been promoted to full captain, given his own aide-de-camp (Lord Mountbatten) and generally maintained a languid and lordly presence, much to the irritation of the Navy's professional officers. Prince Charles's evident determination to be as professional as possible was much appreciated by his colleagues. "He was absolutely typical," was the way one of his brother officers put it.

The Brisbane visit was marred by the death of one of the men in Charles's own communications section who was knocked over and killed by a car while hitch-hiking during the last night of the visit. The Prince had to deal with all the gruesome details of identification, informing the next of kin and supervising the auction of the dead man's kit (an old naval custom that is a practical way of providing for the deceased man's family). In this case the auction raised more than £1,500.

On January 23, the *Jupiter* was back at sea running before heavy winds, forerunners of Cyclone Pam. They had hoped to get the ship spruced up and painted before reaching New Zealand but it was too rough, so they anchored in Queen Charlotte Sound, a quiet secluded spot off the northeast of New Zealand's South Island. There they painted and polished in preparation for ceremonial duties as escort to the royal yacht *Britannia*, which was the temporary home for the Royal Family during the Commonwealth Games at Christchurch. Briefly, Charles ceased being *Lieutenant* the Prince of Wales and reverted to Prince of Wales only, with his parents and sister and brother-in-law attending the games and flying to the State opening of the New Zealand Parliament in Wellington. Later, at the Bay of Islands, sometimes described as the most beautiful place on earth, there was a pageant evoking the history of New Zealand and a memorable extra escort of an ancient Maori outrigger paddled by sixty warriors. The next day the *Jupiter* awoke to find herself abandoned. The warships of the New Zealand Navy, the royal yacht and the outrigger canoe had vanished, and the frigate, its crew and the Prince were back to conventional status.

Almost. The next stop was Suva, capital city of Fiji. At the Independence Day ceremonies of this idyllic island state in 1970, the Queen had been represented by the Prince of Wales; and even if Charles was now a mere naval lieutenant there was no way the Fijians were about to let him pass without festivities. They fêted Charles with a ceremonial fish drive, a display of firewalking and a feast at which everyone ate tropical fish, turtle meat and taro, the Pacific potato. Afterward there was dancing to a local band, the local ladies eagerly leading the way. During this visit Charles assumed equal status with his commander, John Gunning, the two men strolling side by side in their long white shorts, bareheaded and garlanded with flowers. As entertainments officer Charles put on cricket, soccer and volleyball matches. The Fijians won them all!

At times this trip seems to have been all wine, women and song. At Tonga there was more dancing and some of the crew were entertained with late-night cheese and champagne aboard the French minesweeper *Le Dunkerquoise*. In Western Samoa, where they suffered a delay due to contaminated water in the boilers, there were barbecues and rugby matches. And as they crossed the equator all those making their first crossing were subjected to the lighthearted ritual associated with "Crossing the Line." Members of the crew dressed up as "Queen Aphrodite" and "Neptune," and Charles, along with sixty others, was force-fed on spaghetti and a stomach-turning "magic elixir" before being daubed with cream and ducked in a makeshift swimming pool. In Hawaii, where the *Jupiter* went into dry dock because of a leaking stern gland on the port shaft, they were practically given the freedom of Pearl Harbor.

Still, apart from the parties and the sight-seeing, the ship had always to maintain an efficient front-line fighting capability. The two 4.5-inch guns, the two 20-mm cannon and the *Seacat* anti-aircraft missile system were not just for show. As the ship neared San Diego there were a series of exercises with U.S.S. *Hollister* and U.S.S. *Southerland*. As Charles himself says of life on shipboard: "I had a very glamorous, romantic idea about it which isn't always borne out because there are an awful lot of mundane tasks." In the words of one officer, "It was Fortress Jupiter once the gangplank was up."

San Diego, however, was parties. On March 14, the *Jupiter* crawled into port through a thick pea-soup fog to find the jetty lined with newspapermen and photographers jamming the dock. Invitations outnumbered sailors and for once Commander Gunning lost his *sang froid* as female guests clustered around Prince Charles in the hope of having their picture taken. "I can't stand those ladies posturing round him like that," Gunning snapped as he put a stop to the picture session. Here the pretense that Charles was just another seaman was even more difficult to maintain than usual. At first he scarcely ventured off the ship—and when he did it was to visit the exclusive Palm Springs estate of millionaire Walter Annenberg, former ambassador to Britain. Charles breakfasted with Annenberg and his house guests, Governor Ronald and Nancy Reagan, and lunched with a group of celebrities including Bob Hope and Frank Sinatra. Despite the 94-degree heat and his known aversion to the game, Charles played a shirtsleeved round of golf with Annenberg, turning down the tempting offer of a game of polo nearby. After dinner, which included caviar (a present from the Shah of Iran) and Château Lafite Rothschild '59, Charles and his hosts watched a special showing of *Anne of a Thousand Days* in the private Annenberg movie theater. Charles also toured Hollywood and shared a cup of tea with Barbra Streisand. "I've never played *that* Palace," remarked Barbra when Charles suggested she might like to call in next time she was in London.

There were one or two unexpected extra diversions. A stunning long-haired blonde named Laura Jo Watkins monopolized Charles for fifteen minutes at a party, and immediately found herself the center of press attention. Laura Jo's father was an American admiral, and she combined the sex appeal of Jean Harlow with the Doris Day air of the girl next door, though some of Charles's *Jupiter* colleagues found her a bit pushy. Charles's flirtation with Laura Jo was the only public suggestion of sex on the whole trip. More seriously, he learned in San Diego that a man had attacked his sister's limousine as it traveled up the Mall a few hundred yards from Buckingham Palace. Using his privileges as the ship's communications officer he called London and established that Anne was quite safe, but a jittery San Diego police authority immediately ordered highway patrol cars to escort *Jupiter* sailors on their way back to the ship after a visit to Disneyland; and in the huge naval base where forty major fighting ships were berthed every incoming vehicle was subjected to a detailed search.

Some of the publicity was deflected from Prince Charles when a former Royal Navy sailor, claiming to be Ordinary Seaman John Talbot arrived at the ship and tried to give himself up to the Captain. Talbot had been on board H.M.S. *Calcutta* when she docked in Montreal in 1920. In 1942 he had joined the U.S. Navy. Now, at this late date, he had decided to surrender. Commander Gunning was somewhat nonplussed, but subsequently Talbot was given a free pardon by the Lords of the Admiralty.

And so the *Jupiter* began her homeward trek, making brief stops in Acapulco (which was far less hectic and more relaxed than other ports of call), Puerto Rico, Bermuda and the Azores before the ship finally dropped anchor in Plymouth Sound exactly nine months after leaving. She had sailed 50,609 miles.

During the trip her crew had been paid £410,000 in wages, eaten 114,108 pounds of potatoes and 4,669 pounds of sausages (which would stretch out for two-and-a-half miles if placed end to end) as well as 6,439 eggs and 7,290 oranges. Charles had enjoyed himself, proved himself, become an integral and well-liked member of the ship and learned some important things about leadership ... "I often think there are two types of leadership," he said later. "One for the more aggressive, dominant person who imposes his will forcibly on people and gains their respect through his sheer determination and ability. The other for someone who tends to charm people and is more friendly. People feel it's worth doing something for him because they like the person." There was little doubt which category Charles would put himself into—as the ship reached its journey's end a truck was waiting on the dockside to greet her. Charles had arranged for the truck and along its side was the slogan: "*Jupiter* Officers for the Tower!"

As flying had always been one of Charles's great loves, he was delighted to be posted next to the Royal Naval Air Station at Yeovilton, Somerset, for a conversion course to helicopters. He says he enjoyed this more than any other period with the Navy: "I adore flying and I personally can't think of a better combination than naval flying—being at sea and being able to fly. I find it very exciting, very rewarding and stimulating. Also bloody terrifying sometimes."

It was a difficult course made all the more difficult because it was crammed into far less time than normal. "People expect one to be a genius," he said, "and to achieve the impossible rather sooner than in the immediate." Not for the first time, though, official royal duties interfered with military ones. Charles was a week late in starting his training because he had to attend the funeral of the Prime Minister of New Zealand and in the middle of the course took a month off for official duties in Fiji and Australia. His colleagues took nineteen weeks to complete their training. He had to do the same in just over seven weeks and rack up 105 flying hours in forty-five days. His helicopters were Wessex 5s, the frontline commando helicopter of the Royal Navy that he learned to fly in North Wales, where he winched up an old cannon in a maneuver designed to help his conservation interests in the Principality, and in Devon where he flew at heights of only a hundred feet above Dartmoor, navigating with a one-inch ordnance survey map. In Weymouth Bay he practiced deck landings in a force-ten gale and at nearby Portland he fired the SS 11 wire-guided missile and did better than his instructor. When he finally passed he was awarded the Double Diamond trophy for the man who had made the most progress on the course.

From the training squadron, dubbed the Red Dragons, Charles joined an operational squadron, which was based at Yeovilton but serviced the Navy's Marine Commando Carrier H.M.S. *Hermes*. He was learning more than flying. "It's considered a good idea for the pilots to find out what the Marines have to put up with from firsthand knowledge," he said. "So I went down to do the Marines' assault course at Lympstone in Devon and also to do what the Marines charmingly call a 'Tarzan' course—a most horrifying expedition where one has to swing over small chasms on ropes, slide down ropes at death-defying speeds and then walk across wires and up rope ladders strung between a pole and a tree." After that there was a survival course involving tunnels half-full of water and a brisk run across the moor. It was on exercises such as this that he earned a momentary notoriety after being spotted at a sex-comedy film called *Percy's Progress* in Okehampton and again in a local pub where he bought half a pint of rough cider, locally known as "scrumpy." It produced echoes of the long-ago Cherry Brandy Incident at Gordonstoun, but Charles was an infinitely more mature person now, and instead of being upset he was merely irritated by the quality of the press reporting. In the pubs, for instance, "Marvelous old boys in caps came up and said 'Like ter shake yer 'and.' They were charming. One old boy produced his Home Guard certificate signed by my grandfather. But that sort of thing never gets reported. It's all this business about looking for scrumpy. Everyone must think I'm an alcoholic."

In September, 1975, after accompanying the *Hermes* on tours of the western Atlantic and the Caribbean, and after a freezing spell under canvas in New Brunswick (at a Canadian Air Force base inappropriately named "Blissville"), Charles enrolled in a lieutenant's course at the Royal Naval College at Greenwich, outside London. He then got what he had always dreamed of, and what, in the minds of his father and Lord Mountbatten, had always seemed the culmination of Charles's naval career: a command of his own.

Charles's ship, H.M.S. *Bronington*, was a 150-foot, 360-ton minehunter with a bad habit of rolling from side to side in the most placid sea. The Navy says that she would "roll in wet grass." In bad weather lunch consisted of a meat stew in a pot lashed to a stove. Most people were too sick to bother. As captain, Charles had his own cabin, nine-by-eight feet, and also his own washbasin.

The bathroom was communal. The other four officers shared their accommodations, as did the thirty men on board. "It's a bit like living on a yacht," says another minehunter commander. "Everybody knows everybody else. The captain has decided views on all the crew members and they on him. They let you know what those views are by talking in very loud voices as they go past your door."

The Royal Navy maintains a fleet of some thirty to thirty-five anti-mine vessels, all of which used to be mine*sweepers* and all of which are, like the *Bronington*, at least twenty years old. Ten years ago sonar devices became so sophisticated that the Navy converted half their sweepers to hunters. The *Bronington*'s job was to detect mines or "mine-like objects." The minehunter either blows them up with a charge or sends a diver down to bring it up. Sometimes the "mine-like object" turns out to be a bicycle. Because the vessels are tiny and have a draught of only eight feet they are also extremely useful for goodwill visits to places inaccessible to the fleet's aircraft carriers and cruisers. While Charles was in command in 1975 he took the *Bronington* to Lubeck, on the Baltic coast of Germany, and Port Talbot, South Wales. But most of the time was spent looking for mines.

He was based on Rosyth in the Firth of Forth, just north of the Scottish capital of Edinburgh, and for the first few weeks he went about the Forth getting accustomed to ship and crew. "I

116

don't think I'm breaking any confidences when I say that he was a very good ship handler," comments a fellow officer who knew Charles at the time. "Those ships have a tremendous power/weight ratio. They're really little tugs, designed to haul all the minesweeping junk through water. But when stripped of that as the hunters are they become very good on the accelerator and pretty good on the brakes. Quite fun to drive." Charles consequently enjoyed driving the *Bronington* almost as much as he enjoyed driving his Aston-Martin, even though the *Bronington* made him feel more seasick than his automobile. As the same officer remarked, "They enjoyed themselves on the *Bronington*. That was obvious. He's tremendously whole-hearted in everything he does."

After his early workout Charles was sent off on his own to work on the Clyde, the great river on Scotland's other coast, which serves Glasgow and is home for Britain's ten nuclear submarines. The clearance of mines from a waterway is obviously vital. At the end of the day one needs to be able to swear he can sail an aircraft carrier through it, and if he can't it's the clearing officer's fault. "They're very busy little ships," said a fellow officer. "There's always more to do than they have time for, and he really stood or fell on his own. It's a tremendously exciting and stimulating experience but the buck does stop with you." Throughout 1976, when Charles was in command of the *Bronington*, his naval superiors were acutely conscious of the fact that the buck did indeed stop with Charles and that if anything went wrong there could be a terrible furor. Fortunately there were no accidents.

The little ship was known to the rest of the Navy as "old quarter-past eleven" because her pennant number was 1115. Throughout that year she worked like a Trojan. When really stretched she was on a twelve-hours-on, twelve-hours-off routine, but she seldom went more than three days without returning to port for supplies. The longest passage she could make would be about a week, which was the length of the Lubeck visit.

The routine of the *Bronington* was varied. She visited the NATO mine school at Ostend (when Charles is supposed to have

117

made a brief excursion to Brussels for a lunch to discuss his marriage to Princess Marie-Astrid—a lunch never admitted by the Palace.) In May the *Bronington* shadowed a Russian Whiskey Class submarine down the English Channel, and in February Prince Philip called in for tea and cucumber sandwiches. To every expedition Charles brought a brand of easy formality and *joie de vivre*. And then, too, there were the special perks of royalty—once the *Bronington* sailed up the Thames to the Tower of London so that Charles could attend Remembrance Day services at Whitehall. He always flew his own personal standard and displayed his coat of arms on the bridge, even though both are in defiance of strict naval regulations. He also grew a full set of beard and whiskers, then shaved off the beard leaving only the mustache. That, too, is contrary to naval law, but no one seemed to mind. Charles endeared himself to an admiring crew by taking every chance to slip into a wet suit, climb overboard and take his mini-sail off on a quick skim across the waves. It was exhilarating and unusual, but in December affairs of State loomed once more and Charles announced, "It has been great fun, but there are other things to do."

On December 15, Charles said a final farewell to the *Bronington*. He was wheeled ashore in a wheelchair by enthusiastic shipmates. Around his neck hung a souvenir toilet seat engraved in gold with the words "H.M.S. *Bronington*." Above him hung a placard saying, "Command has aged me," an allusion to Charles's joking remark, made earlier in the year, that he was surprised his beard was not yet gray. A considerable change from the days of Nelson's Navy when retiring commanders were rowed ashore by their officers in a longboat! The ships and jetties of the Rosyth dockyard were lined with cheering sailors as Prince Charles was finally wheeled to his car. He bid his men good-by, with a cheery, "See you behave yourselves, boys." The days of Lieutenant the Prince of Wales were over. Those of His Royal Highness the Prince of Wales were just beginning.

CHAPTER SEVEN

H.R.H.: The Woman Who Will Be Queen

LADY GEORGINA PETTY-FITZMAURICE, daughter of the Marquess of Lansdowne, Lady Henrietta Fitzroy, daughter of the Countess of Euston (as she then was), and Margot Cholmondeley, daughter of the Earl of Rocksavage, all have something in common. So have Princess Clarissa of Hesse, Princess Maria Claudia of Saxe-Coburg-Gotha and Princess Margarita of Rumania. Not to mention Sandra Butter, Marilyn Butter, Rohays Butter and Rosaleen Bagge. All these, and many more, have solemnly, seriously and repeatedly been touted as appropriate and imminent brides for the Prince of Wales. The list goes on and on—and so does the speculation. No matrimonial intentions have been more anxiously and intrusively considered by the British since the abortive relationship between the London Zoo's pandas An-An and Chi-Chi. Mixed in with the rumors is an occasional grain of truth, not the least of which is that Prince Charles is extremely fond of female company, and not the least disturbing of which is that he is under considerable pressure to get married and settle down to producing a respectable family full of heirs of his own.

Some of the rumors take on a life of their own, like this one about alleged contender in the Royal Marriage Stakes Princess

Marie-Astrid of Luxembourg. Like many a wild surmise about the future Queen of England, it began amid the clacking typewriters of London's Fleet Street, where the national press is quartered. It was, in fact, a marvelous story, suggesting a Ruritanian romance straight out of Hollywood: over an elegant luncheon table in a sumptuous palace, royalty were earnestly settling the fates of dynasties; high and politically shrewd churchmen were solemnly weighing the spiritual impact of their decision. At the edge of the gathering, their conversation politely animated but noncommittal, their eyes perhaps trying to sense each other's mood, sat the prospective bride and groom.

That, at least, was the sort of image a reader of the London *Daily Mail* might conjure up from an EXCLUSIVE REPORT FROM LUXEMBOURG at the end of March in 1977. SECRET TALKS, ROYAL APPROVAL for Prince Charles's marriage to Princess Marie-Astrid of Luxembourg, revealed the irrepressible columnist Nigel Dempster. According to Dempster, who is surprisingly accurate for a so-called gossip columnist, the secret meeting had occurred the previous December, when Charles was still skipper of the *Bronington,* and had put into port at Ostend, Belgium. There a British Embassy car picked him up and sped him to the lunch at Laeken Palace, just outside of Brussels, the royal home of Belgium's King Baudoin and Queen Fabiola, who were hosting the luncheon. Prince Philip, ostensibly in Brussels for a meeting of the International Equestrian Foundation, was present, along with an unnamed representative of the Church of England and Leo-Josef Cardinal Suenens, the Roman Catholic Primate of Belgium. Near Prince Charles was the twenty-three-year-old Princess Marie-Astrid—"Asty," as Charles is said to have called her.

The purpose of the lunch, according to Dempster, was to discuss the Princess's marriage to Charles and the serious issue it raised. How could Charles, who as King would become head of the Church of England, marry a Roman Catholic princess from a devoutly Roman Catholic country like Luxembourg? Under the British Constitution, either Charles would have to renounce the throne to marry the Princess, or she would have to become a member of the Church of England to marry him. The lunch was supposed to resolve this knotty problem. But did it ever take place? Dempster, widely resented for his scandal-mongering but *still* extremely well-informed, stuck to his guns.

Buckingham Palace swiftly denied that the meeting had ever taken place. The Palace could hardly do otherwise, however, and conjecture continued to boil. By June the *Daily Express* categorically insisted that the royal engagement would be announced on the following Monday, a prediction that drew withering scorn from the Palace. "I am authorized by the Prince of Wales to make the following statement," declared TV journalist Ron Allison, then the Queen's Press Secretary. "There is no truth at all in the report that there is to be an announcement of an engagement of the Prince of Wales to Princess Marie-Astrid of Luxembourg." The next day, to reinforce his point, Allison went further: "They are not getting engaged this Monday, the Monday after, or any other Monday, Tuesday, Wednesday or Thursday. They do not know each other and people who do not know each other do not get engaged. The Royal Family do not go in for arranged marriages. If the Prince and Princess Marie-Astrid have met at all then it has been briefly at official functions."

That brusque denial was not treated with the respect it demanded. Journalists remembered that the Palace had been wrong before. Buckingham Palace had barely finished denying the engagement of Princess Anne to Mark Phillips when the two announced they would wed. On March 3, 1973, Princess Anne was reported as saying: "There is no romance and there are no grounds for these rumors of a romance between us." Two weeks later the man she was rumored to be romancing with added, "Princess Anne and I are just good friends with a common interest." (This last was taken to be a reference to horses, a common passion of both Princess and Captain Phillpps.) Five weeks after that an announcement appeared in the *Court Circular:* "It is with the greatest pleasure that the Queen and the Duke of Edinburgh announce the betrothal of their beloved daughter The Princess Anne to Lieutenant Mark Phillips, the Queen's Dragoon Guards, son of Mr. and Mrs. Peter Phillips."

"I know it sounds off," said a spokesman, "but at the time they really had no thought of getting married. It was only decided over the weekend after the Badminton Horse Trials."

This, needless to say, was greeted with some skepticism—a skepticism that increased when Robin Ludlow, then the Queen's Press Secretary, left his post shortly after, having held the post for an unprecedentedly short time. The incident rebounded on Charles. Denials about his amorous adventures and marriage plans are often given short shrift. As he says himself, "The great problem as a result of my sister announcing her engagement, having said only a few months previously that there was no truth in the rumors, is that the press, I know, will never again believe it if you say there is no truth and we're just good friends."

The feeling persisted, and persists still, that the Queen herself was enchanted with Marie-Astrid. After a visit to Luxembourg in late 1976 she had apparently come back charmed by the pretty, talented Princess, who, among other accomplishments, is a trained nurse.

The rumor came back to haunt—if that is the appropriate word—Prince Charles once again at the beginning of November in 1978 when Parliament assembled at Westminster to hear the Queen's speech. As the gathered MPs marked time in the corridors, a Labor MP wondered why the Mayor of Luxembourg City, a certain Madame Colette Flesch, was receiving red-carpet treatment in London, and even lunching with the Foreign Secretary. It seemed an undue fuss to make over a minor mayor. Another MP observed that Luxembourg's Grant Duke Jean, Marie-Astrid's father, had just become the first person to be granted a private audience with the new Pope John Paul II. And why was the Archbishop of Canterbury, asked another, the first Anglican primate since the Reformation to attend an installation of a Pope? A listener added still further evidence: Luxembourg had doubled its budget for official uniforms. As the MPs edged in to hear the Queen's speech, fresh news was filtering out from West Germany: Charles himself, hunting in Austria, had met the Grant Duke and Duchess of Luxembourg just the previous weekend. Didn't it all add up? asked the London *Times* with tongue poking slightly in cheek.

The Pope had been consulted on the difference in religion; Mayor Flesch was in town arranging wedding plans; the new uniforms were for the ceremony; and Charles was meeting his future in-laws. West Germany's biggest newspaper, *Bild Zeitung,* was certain: CHARLES: MARRIAGE, ran the headline. WILL QUEEN ABDICATE? The match would be announced, predicted *Bild Zeitung,* on November 14.

From Buckingham Palace came a categorical denial so sweeping that it even surpassed the furious riposte of the previous year. Charles had indeed met Marie-Astrid's parents, a spokesman conceded, but "there was *no* question of marriage being discussed at all and certainly *absolutely* no question of an engagement either on November 14 or at any other time to Princess Marie-Astrid or anyone else." At least some of the clues the curious MPs had discussed were, it seemed, more red-herrings than real. Luxembourg's Mayor Flesch had lunched with a junior minister, *not* with the Foreign Secretary. The new uniforms in Luxembourg were for the Army, not for the Court staff. The Archbishop of Canterbury's presence for John Paul II's elevation to the papacy was a generous ecumenical gesture.

It really, though, depended on one's perspective. Charles himself raised further skepticism by protesting too much. He denied that he had even met the Princess, then said that if he had met her he didn't remember it. At the time of this writing the engagement has yet to take place—which is not to say it won't.

Prince Charles has been called the world's most eligible bachelor. At times, especially on trips abroad, the crush of female admirers around him resembles a horde of groupies in pursuit of a rock star. When he toured the United States in the autumn of 1977, young women and their mothers vitually threw themselves in his path, harassing local British representatives with requests for dates with the Prince. The British Consulate in San Francisco finally issued an appeal to the mothers to stop calling. Governor George Busbee of Georgia even appointed his daughter Jan, a public relations woman, as a sort of official chaperone to keep the more aggressive southern belles away from Charles. Jan Busbee did her job efficiently; at the principal dinner at the Governor's Mansion in Atlanta, the youngest woman at Charles's table was fifty-two.

In Hollywood, at a charity dinner attended by such veteran matinee idols as Cary Grant, Gregory Peck and Charlton Heston, it was the Prince of Wales who starred. On his left sat Angie Dickenson of the television series *Policewoman,* on his right Farrah Fawcett-Majors of *Charlie's Angels.* Angie Dickenson pronounced herself "the luckiest girl in the world." Charles, she said, was "a beauty. We had a charming conversation. Anything I could say about him would be an understatement." Farrah Fawcett-Majors, only slightly less impressed, declared the evening to be "one of the best times of my life." Even her husband, TV star Lee Majors *(The Bionic Man),* had "enjoyed himself—and he usually hates parties." Sophia Loren, meeting Prince Charles for the first time, was charmed by his "great sense of humor." And Lauren Bacall, who got to sit next to Charles at a luncheon at 20th Century Fox the next day, was "enchanted." Beyond that, she would not reveal any details of the "wonderful conversation" they had. "The next time I see him I want him to smile at me," Ms. Bacall said. "If I tell everybody what he told me today, he might not smile at me the next time."

Some of the response was presumably the special wonderment that one kind of celebrity feels toward another, but Charles does seem to possess—especially as he has grown older and his face has mellowed into maturity—a genuine allure for many women. It may have much to do with the aura of royalty, as if the monarch's touch carried some kind of miraculous power, as it was once supposed to. Or, as the New York *Times* suggested just before his 1977 trip to the United States, Charles's mystique may have a good deal to do with more earthly powers. "He has a 'lover's voice,' as one English woman puts it," reported the paper, "and deep blue eyes that fix a woman steadily as he talks and listens." Not every woman has succumbed to the royal charisma, though. Out on the town in Montreal in 1975 with shipmates from the carrier H.M.S. *Hermes,* Charles approached a girl he had met earlier and asked for a dance. The girl, identified only as Phyllis, turned him down. "No, thanks, I'm really tired and I want to go home."

Such a brush-off is rare. After his visit to Chicago during his U.S. tour the Prince announced roguishly: "I received numerous delicious Chicago kisses." In Fiji for an anniversary of that island's independence, he was whisked into an enthusiastic dance that later was revealed to be a fertility rite. In South America in 1978 he sambaed into the night with a stunning Brazilian beauty, to the delight of following photographers.

Amid such adulation Charles has perhaps more chances for casual sexual encounters than almost any other young man in the world, only show business idols excepted. When he so much as joins Lady Jane Wellesley for a week of hunting in Spain, or Lady Sarah Spencer for a skiing holiday at an Alpine chalet (with plenty of rooms, friends and a bodyguard), the suggestion in some of the more raffish papers is that an affair has commenced.

In other eras Princes of Wales did pretty much as they pleased about their sex life—at least once they attained their majority, and often before. Queen Victoria's son, Prince Albert Edward (later Edward VII), was not yet twenty when fellow officers of the Grenadier Guards stationed with him at Curragh Camp in Ireland smuggled a young actress named Nellie Clifden into his quarters. Although the gossip reached aristocratic circles all across the Continent (and deeply wounded Edward's family), it escaped the newspapers. Earlier this century a reticent British press kept quiet for years about Edward VIII's romance with Wallis Warfield Simpson until the American press had made it a cause célèbre that could not be ignored.

The British press has consistently publicized Charles's relations with eligible girls, but it has been much more careful in its approach to the subject of Charles's sex life. Only the satirical *Private Eye* magazine (which refers to Prince Charles by the obscurely humorous code name "Brian") gets near to suggesting that the Prince shares his great-uncle's fondness for married ladies. Nigel Dempster, who does turn-and-turn about as *Private Eye's* "Grovel" columnist and is the writer of a gossip page in the tabloid *Daily Mail*, has mentioned the names of several married women, whose husbands are also close to Charles, as princely paramours.

The Palace tends to take the position that Charles's sex life is nonexistent. Biographer Robert Lacey found this out when he submitted his manuscript for *Majesty* to Buckingham Palace for official clearance. The book was, after all, a semi-authorized biography of Queen Elizabeth and her family, and the Palace had reserved the right to check it. Among the lines that were excised was a simple statement about Charles that was discreet but tantalizing: "Prince Charles enjoys a normal, healthy sex life." Earlier, before Charles had begun to display his obvious enthusiasm for female companionship, the Queen confided that he "was neither totally interested nor totally uninterested in girls. In point of fact he'd scarcely met any." If Charles does enjoy a "normal healthy sex life" in this age of mass communication, it can only exist in circumstances in which he is protected by a tight circle of impeccably discreet friends. "I've discovered it's not really a good thing to go by yourself with a girl somewhere public," he says. "It's much better to go in a party and then nobody knows in whom you are particularly interested." Nevertheless, according to one of the Prince's biographers, Simon Regan, Charles indulges in late-night rendezvous with women who are checked out by his best friend, Nicholas Soames.

Charles still, however, seems to enjoy a quiet dinner with a few close friends as much as anything. On his twenty-first birthday, for example, he gave a dinner and concert, with music by Yehudi Menuhin and friends, also choosing the music, which included two pieces by the 18th-century Frederic, Prince of Wales, a Haydn cello concerto, Mozart's A Major violin concerto and Beethoven's Romance in F Major. Later there was a disco at which women guests were allowed to wear pants-suits (some traditionalists winced). The previous year Charles had celebrated his birthday with a gala showing of the film *Romeo and Juliet* followed by a dance, and danced with Olivia Hussey, who had played Juliet in the film. "He's a good dancer, we did have a terrific Charleston," was her verdict. Charles's thirtieth birthday was celebrated by a gala party at Buckingham Palace with numerous beautiful ladies and music by the Three Degrees, but he left at midnight—for this moment a Cinderella Prince—to prepare for the busy day ahead.

Charles goes to parties as well as gives them. Sometimes these are in the line of duty—there was one at the end of a recent tour in Ottawa—but occasionally they are private. However, the grand private dance that was a dominant feature of British social life is not quite what it was. Two years ago Queen Charlotte's Ball, the highlight of the London season, was abandoned altogether, and today if people do throw extravagant parties they are not likely to advertise them the way they once did . . . "They don't like bloody-minded journalists ringing up and asking how much it costs," remarked one man-about-town, "and fewer people have that sort of money anyway."

Last September, just before the annual balls on the island of Skye, Charles arrived at a dance in Oban, Scotland, an Argyllshire resort famous for its tweeds and its whisky. Oddly enough the Scots tend to be more conservative than the English about dress balls. At the annual Caledonian Ball in London, for instance, gentlemen are required to wear either full highland evening dress, or white tie and tails and not just tails but tails with facings—colored silk on the lapels of their jackets—and gentlemen not entitled to regimental or club facings are recommended to go to the Scotch House, London's leading Scottish shop, where they may have bright scarlet facings sewn on. At the Oban Ball national dress was the rule, and like the other men Charles wore a kilt (of Balmoral tartan) with a black velvet jacket, black bow tie, frilly shirt, diced stockings with a dirk (a small Scottish dagger) stuffed down the side and a cummerbund at his waist. "He didn't dance a lot," said one girl, "he spent most of his time talking to people. But when he did dance he was all right. Not first division, but perfectly respectable."

Scottish dancing is complicated, and unlike the tango it takes more than two. It is, indeed, a form of team game and if one man gets any steps wrong, the team suffers. Older folk consider it great sport to sit about on the outskirts of the dancing, watching for the young dancers' mistakes. "To make a mistake on the third step of a reel is a most appalling gaffe," said a former officer in the most famous Highland Regiment, "The Black Watch." "It's a bit like your kilt suddenly falling down in the middle of dinner."

Charles, originally coached by Madam Vacani in the privacy of Buckingham Palace, coped adequately with eightsomes, foursomes and a popular favorite called "The Duke and Duchess of Edinburgh." In between the Scottish dancing there were waltzes to such tunes as "Maire's Wedding." Charles danced some of these but sat out more.

It was altogether a very Scottish occasion. The main decoration was heather, which was everywhere, and the women wore long white dresses with plaid sashes—married women with their sashes over the left breast, unmarried over the right (a telltale distinction originally to avoid ardent males directing their attention to unavailable females—in Hawaii they position a flower behind the appropriate ear for the same reason). As for the refreshments, "Men drink whisky," said one guest, "women drink orange juice. It is very hard form to get drunk." Charles sipped decorously and stayed sober.

Inevitably, any public encounter with a young woman— especially one who has been touted as a possible Princess of Wales—brings reporters and photographers (especially photographers) out in battalion strength. Yet Prince Charles did manage to keep the world from learning about his brief romance in Fiji with Jeanette Stitson, the stunning blonde daughter of Colonel Charles Stitson, Minister of Finance to Fiji. Jeanette managed to elude the three official photographers who accompanied the royal expedition, slipping off with Charles for intimate evenings together aboard a small ship at sea. A story is told by one member of the royal entourage, who claims he had it from Charles, that the morning after being introduced to Jeanette for the first time the Prince went for an early dip in the Stitson's swimming pool and, thinking he was alone, decided to skinny-dip. The Prince was no sooner in the pool than Jeanette appeared at the pool's edge. While Charles was pondering how to retrieve his robe on the other side of the pool Jeanette slipped out of her own robe, and joined the Prince in a nude swim. During the celebrated Fiji fertility dance, which Jeanette viewed with the Prince (although she kept herself in the background to avoid publicity), Charles remarked to her, "Well, it beats the changing of the guard, doesn't it?"

A more publicized encounter was the first meeting between Prince Charles and Princess Caroline of Monaco, the daughter of Princess Grace and Prince Rainier, in May, 1977. No matter that this was precisely the time that some British papers were betting firmly on a royal marriage between Prince Charles and Princess Marie-Astrid of Luxembourg. For years gossip columnists had been trying to pair Charles and Caroline as Europe's perfect royal match, despite the fact that Caroline, like Marie-Astrid, was Roman Catholic. Now the two were finally to meet in Monte Carlo at the star-studded annual awards of Variety Club International.

Caroline and Charles arrived separately at Monte Carlo's Hotel de Paris, slipping up in the elevator to its rooftop restaurant, Le Grill. There, at a $3,000-a-plate benefit dinner hosted by London nightclub owner John Mills, Charles and Caroline finally met over a table shared with her brother Prince Albert, the Mills family and Roger Moore of the James Bond movies. Charles did not mince words. He said teasingly, "I'm supposed to be marrying Caroline, aren't I?" Later, when Charles and Caroline descended together in the elevator, waiting photographers besieged them and wound up in a near-riot. While Charles and Caroline escaped in different directions, a number of photographers were carted off to jail, while other papparazzi mourned damaged equipment.

The long-touted romance between Caroline and Charles did not come off. The night after the scuffle with the press, at the gala closing dinner of the awards ritual, Caroline was again seated between Charles and her brother Albert, but this time she appeared bored. When Charles cheerfully sampled a package of Givenchy fragrances on the table, it was another nearby woman—not Caroline—who offered a wrist to be sniffed. Thirteen months later Caroline married Philippe Junot.

The speculation about foreign princesses is not altogether

idle. In the nineteenth century Queen Victoria and Prince Albert scoured the Continent for a suitable princess for their own Prince of Wales, settling finally on the beautiful Princess Alexandra of Denmark as the only princess attractive enough to turn their stubborn son's head. The necessity of marrying a princess, or even the daughter of nobility, has faded since then, but Charles himself conceded its advantage in his first serious public comment on a future wife. In a television interview just days before his investiture as Prince of Wales in 1969 he observed that "when you marry in my position you are going to marry someone who perhaps one day is going to be Queen. You have to choose somebody very carefully, I think, who could fill this particular role.... The one advantage about marrying a princess, for instance, or somebody from a royal family, is that they do know what happens."

He has not changed his opinion appreciably since then. In 1974 he suggested looking at the question "from the woman's point of view. A woman not only marries a man, she marries into a way of life, into a job, into a life in which she's got some contribution to make. She's got to have some knowledge of it, some sense of it, or she wouldn't have a clue about whether she's going to like it, and if she didn't have a clue, it would be risky for her, wouldn't it?" Two years later on Canadian television in 1976 Charles virtually repeated his 1969 remarks about marrying someone who knows "what happens."

Yet he has set himself a difficult goal. Despite his reiterated praise of princesses he added a qualifying aside even in his 1969 remarks: "The only trouble," he said, "is that I often feel I would like to marry somebody English. Or perhaps Welsh. Well, British, anyway." Over the years Charles has followed that inclination more earnestly than his pursuit of princesses. Most of the girls at his side at Smith's Lawn and Ascot and Covent Garden have been Britons. It is difficult, of course, to be certain which of these attachments are serious and which casual. Charles has learned over the years to be carefully discreet.

Charles seems to have something of a split personality on romance and marriage, as if he had been brought up in another age. In 1975, in an interview with Douglas Keay of *Woman's*

Own magazine, he acknowledged forthrightly that "I've fallen in love with all sorts of girls and I fully intend to go on doing so, but I've made sure I haven't married the first person I've fallen in love with. I think one's got to be aware of the fact that falling madly in love with someone is not necessarily the starting point to getting married." One of the advantages of marrying at about thirty, suggested Charles at the time, was the long apprenticeship. "By this time you've seen a great deal of life, met a large number of girls, been able to see what types of girls there are, fallen in love every now and then, and you know what it's all about. I would never recommend getting married too young. You miss so much. You get tied down...."

Charles nourishes a curious image of roguishness mixed with naïveté. Meeting actress Susan Hampshire at a royal gala a few years ago he noted her decolleté gown and told her, "Father told me if I ever met a lady in a dress like yours, I must look her straight in the eyes"—lest, of course, a photographer catch him casting a too appreciative glance. Yet on that occasion and others Charles has been caught in precisely that attitude. Margaret Trudeau, the estranged wife of Canada's Prime Minister, also noticed the Prince's roving eye, claiming that on one occasion, out on the dance-floor with Charles, she noted him peering down the front of her dress. When she scolded him, she says, the Prince blushed.

If the anecdote is true, it would seem more typical of an inexperienced fledgling than a seasoned man of the world. For all of the Fleet Street stories about his romantic life, that image of Charles blushing suggests something more along the lines of the adolescent hero of Eugene O'Neill's *Ah, Wilderness* than an apprentice Edward VII. At the same time, innocence—feigned or real—can be a potent allure for women who perhaps would ignore more forward approaches. Charles's very boyishness may be the deadly bait—so long as it can last.

"Innocence" is not a word used much lately in connection with Margaret Trudeau, and it is not surprising that she found Charles sexy. She apparently found his little brother Andrew (sometimes known as "Randy Andy") sexier still, and when questioned by us on the subject of the princely sex appeal lowered her eyelids and murmured, "Of course I found them attractive. Wouldn't you?"

Apparently Mrs. Trudeau tried to do something about that attraction. On March 30, 1979, the New York *Post* reported that three months after separating from her husband she was in Paris, from where she called Charles on his private number at Buckingham Palace. According to her account he agreed to a secret rendezvous in Paris and said he would call back in forty-eight hours to fix the details. In the meantime, Mrs. Trudeau, pursued by the press, moved from the Grand Hotel to the Manchester, where she booked in under her maiden name of Sinclair. When, she said, Charles finally phoned back his call was not put through because the staff at the Manchester did not make the connection between "Trudeau" and "Sinclair." Mrs. Trudeau finally found out the mistake but when she phoned Buckingham Palace she discovered that Prince Charles had disappeared. Hoping that he was on the way to their allegedly planned love-nest in France she waited eagerly, only to discover that he had actually gone to Scotland for a family holiday. Mrs. Trudeau then flew off to the Bahamas, to the welcome of Perrier-water president Bruce Nivens.

"When he first saw me in Ottawa," says Margaret, "I knew I'd get him interested in me." Which may well be true, but it is also true that Charles is considered too canny to become entangled with anyone as outspoken (some might say indiscreet) as the peripatetic ex-first lady of Canada. No matter how much he fancies her....

To hear Charles discourse on the subject of marriage is to hear a man who sounds older by decades. Indeed, some of his considerations would have sounded quite seemly coming from the lips of his great-great-great grandfather, the solemn Prince Albert, the husband of Queen Victoria. "Marriage is a much more important business than falling in love, as I think a lot of couples probably find out," he declared in 1975. It is "not just for the sake of living with a girl." Rather, he suggested, it is "essentially a question of mutual love and respect for each other. Creating a secure family unit in which to bring up children, to give them a happy, secure upbringing—*that* is what marriage is all about, creating a home." As for a suitable mate, he observed, "Essentially you must be good friends, and love, I am sure, will grow out of that friendship."

Douglas Keay, interviewing Charles in *Woman's Own*, suggested that the Prince's attitude sounded "as if you believed you fell in love several times before you got married and then married a friend." Replied Charles: "On the whole, yes." His position was different from that of other people, he said. "I have to consider the whole business of marriage a bit more carefully, particularly because, whomever I marry, I hope it will last the rest of my life." Mismatches among his own family and acquaintances do seem to haunt him. "It's very important to find the right partner with whom one can be as happy as possible. In my position, obviously, the last thing I could possibly entertain is getting divorced."

Those poignantly serious reflections do contrast rather markedly with the Prince's public romances—or at least with what the press has tried to make of them. From the time he was a teen-ager at Gordonstoun Charles could hardly talk with a pretty girl without some journal somewhere making at least a petit—if not a grand—passion out of it. When some of the girls at Elgin Academy near Gordonstoun took part in a production of Gilbert and Sullivan's *Iolanthe* with the Gordonstoun boys, one young woman, the daughter of a local lawyer, threw a cast party. Charles attended—and made the mistake of spending some ten minutes in conversation with an attractive blonde girl. In Paris *France Dimanche* breathlessly published the tale of "Charles's love affair," a ludicrous sample of things to come. The surprised girl tried to explain: "I asked him what he was going to do after school and he said he really didn't know yet. And I said, 'Well, I suppose I'll have to curtsey to you,' and he said, no, he'd let me off that for the rest of my life. He was a super dancer, once he got going. I hope he marries someone as nice as himself."

Though the *Iolanthe* party produced nothing but bogus headlines, Charles did not spend the entire year cooped up at Gordonstoun. He was, after all, home for four months of the year, and he used some of that time to make friends with a girl named Rosaleen Bagge, the daughter of a Major John Bagge, who lived near the Royal Family's home at Sandringham. A pretty brunette girl, she soon took herself out of the royal sweepstakes by marrying a captain in a smart cavalry regiment. But while she was at hand, she was devoted: she and Charles corresponded while he was both at Gordonstoun and Timbertop. She also set something of the tone of many of the girls that Charles would later find attractive: refined, vivacious English roses of the upper-middle to aristocratic classes.

At Cambridge Charles tended to loosen up—but never settled down, as many of his classmates did, into the pattern of easy sexual relationships that became more and more tolerated in the late 1960s and early 1970s. "When he first came up he was touchingly naïve and old-fashioned about girls," one of the Prince's Cambridge friends told British writer Ann Leslie. "He certainly wasn't one of the permissive generation. He really thought that girls who slept with their boyfriends weren't quite 'nice.' I think he got rather confused when he started to meet girls at Cambridge who were clearly *very* 'nice' and equally clearly no longer celibate." Also to the point, indiscriminate sex for the Prince was clearly hazardous.

He was by no means shy, though. Lord Butler, the Master of Trinity during Charles's years there, observed that "he's very good value at parties, you know, and he's got a very easy social manner with girls." Cambridge classmate John Molony put it even more strongly: "He's not a man's man at all," said Molony of the Prince, who would later become such a successful "man's man" in the Royal Navy. "He's much more of a ladies' man. I'm not saying that he's a Casanova, simply that he gets on very well with women and seems to prefer their company." Charles certainly enjoyed the company of a pert, eighteen-year-old blonde woman named Cindy Buxton, who was one of his earliest girlfriends at Cambridge. At one Cambridge ball, as the newspapers eagerly noted, Charles kept trying to kiss Cindy instead of dancing. A Cantabrigian herself, Cindy was also the daughter of Prince Philip's old friend from East Anglia, television executive Aubrey Buxton. (While Charles was at

Cambridge the Queen provided him a ten-room cottage on her Sandringham estate to serve as a weekend hideaway for him and his friends. In his book *The Clown Prince,* Simon Regan reports that Charles used the cottage often.)

Almost invariably during his undergraduate years Charles dated the daughters of families who were close to his own. Sibella Dorman, one of his more frequent companions at Cambridge, was, like Cindy Buxton, a fellow student. Perhaps just as important, Sibella's father, Sir Maurice Dorman, was Governor-General of Màlta, a career diplomat knighted by the Queen and a country gentleman in possession of an impressive manor house some seventy miles west of London. Both Charles and his sister Anne visited Malta as the Dormans' guests, but Sibella, like so many others, faded from the running and eventually married someone else.

There were the usual false alarms in the Cambridge years. After a gala party to celebrate his twenty-first birthday—a soirée that saw the Prince dancing into the early morning hours—Charles left Buckingham Palace at 7 A.M. with dark-haired, twenty-year-old Lady Leonora, daughter of the extraordinarily rich Duke and Duchess of Westminster. In a private plane Charles flew with Lady Leonora to her family's vast country estate near Chester in the west of England. Charles had enjoyed earlier weekends there, and had also been at Ascot and Windsor with Lady Leonora, but a Palace spokesman defused the rumors. The Prince would spend the weekend shooting on the estate (so huge that it includes two hamlets, a golf course, two rivers and a church) and would attend a ball to meet some of the local young people. "Oh dear, oh dear," the Palace spokesman said. "If they are going to read romance into it every time Prince Charles goes out with a friend that is what we must expect." In private at least one of Prince Charles's girlfriends complains bitterly that press and public are too prurient to accept that friendship can be platonic.

Rumors again circulated when Charles and Princess Anne visited the U.S. in the summer of 1970 and stayed at the White House. Tricia Nixon was not yet married, and Washington *Post* columnist Maxine Cheshire unsubtly hinted that "If Tricia's

Prince Charming turns out to be someone other than law student Ed Cox, her parents certainly will not be displeased." Tricia herself threw ice on the speculations of romance by noting that Charles was only her sister Julie's age (twenty-one), while she was twenty-three. And though Charles paid dutiful attention to Tricia during his stay, he seems to have allowed his true feelings to slip out during a visit to Florida a few years later. At a benefit party in Miami Beach Charles was asked about his White House stay. "I didn't like it much when they started matching me up with the older daughter," he was reported (by *Women's Wear Daily* in May, 1975) to have said. "Which one was she—Tricia, isn't that right? I found her to be artificial, plastic. I did like the dark-haired one, Julie. She's bright—warm personality."

Charles's most lasting attachment at Cambridge was with Lucia Santa Cruz who, as noted earlier, was the daughter of the man who was then Chile's Ambassador to Britain, Don Victor Santa Cruz. Lucia was four years older than Charles, a strikingly attractive and certifiably brainy person then working on her second postgraduate degree. When she met Charles she was helping Lord Butler with the historical research for his memoirs. Charles and Lucia seemed to share, as much as anything else, an intellectual camaraderie, including a droll pleasure in testing each other on historical minutiae. According to Helen Cathcart, one of the Prince's biographers, Lucia, seated opposite Charles at dinner one night, told him of plans to write a book on King Charles IV. "Really?" replied the Prince, pretending ignorance. "Who on earth was he?" Lucia drily countered that he was the second son of Charles III. "That's right," Charles came back. "Weren't both kings of Spain when we had George the Third?" (George III is one of the Prince's favorite historical figures: "I see him as a person whom I'd love to have talked with. He was a marvelous eccentric.")

Lucia left Britain with her father when the newly elected Marxist regime of Salvador Allende recalled him from London, but when she returned in 1972 she was immediately invited to Balmoral Castle for the weekend. When the couple returned from Scotland to London by overnight train, Lucia told reporters, "There's no romantic attachment between us." Even

H.R.H.: The Woman Who Will Be Queen

Fleet Street was more circumspect than usual in predicting a marriage: Lucia was, after all, a foreigner, a commoner and a Roman Catholic, no use at all as a potential Queen of England. But she had touched Charles's life permanently. He has spoken of a close personal friend who gave him a long list of important books he should read, a project he has worked on over the years. Lucia has probably been Charles's secret tutor. Commoner or no, she had dignity and intelligence, and was undoubtedly a benevolent influence. Now she, too, is married.

Charles has shown a continuing and endearing weakness for women who are intelligent as well as attractive. In 1970, for instance, there was Bettina Lindsay, blonde, twenty-year-old daughter of Lord Balniel and a thirteenth-generation descendant of King Charles II through a son by the King's famous mistress Nell Gwyn. Bettina had begun to study acting at a famous Parisian mime school but gave it up to become a teacher. Her family coolly down-played the relationship. "Prince Charles is a good friend of Bettina—just one of many friends," Lady Balniel explained to the press. Just as well. Within months Bettina was among the also-rans.

Another of Prince Charles's girlfriends was Georgiana Russell, daughter of Sir John Russell, former British Ambassador to Brazil. Georgiana was a young woman who had so charmed Brazil that one newspaper there called her "the living expression of all that is young and free in Britain today." A slim, small blonde woman with an arrestingly lovely face and elegant taste in clothes, Georgiana was also a startlingly gifted linguist who could speak French, German, Greek, Italian, Portuguese and Russian. Like nearly all of Charles's women friends, she worked, serving as a Girl Friday for the British *Vogue* magazine. Charles first met her at Arundel, the historic home of the Dukes of Norfolk, in 1970, but they didn't see much of each other until 1972, when stories of a serious romance began to circulate. It lasted about a year, culminating in a report that Sir John and Lady Russell would soon announce an engagement. The announcement never came, and no one, it seems, can or will explain what happened. Whatever the reason, the romance was over: Georgiana is now married to Welsh landowner Brooke Boothby.

Despite Charles's heavy schedule in the Royal Navy, romances were now beginning to overlap. He was still squiring Georgiana Russell about London when he began to appear, now and again, with petite, dark-haired Lady Jane Wellesley, daughter of the man who has since succeeded to the title of eighth Duke of Wellington. The encounters were expectable: Charles and Lady Jane had known each other since childhood and their parents were close friends. With the press and the public, the occasional dates did not begin to add up to something serious until the fall of 1973, especially when Charles went off to join a hunting party at the Wellington estate in Spain.

The estate, Molino del Rey ("Windmill of the King") was Spain's gift to the first Duke of Wellington, the victor of Waterloo for driving Napoleon's armies out of Spain in the Peninsular War. Some 2,300 rolling acres of olive groves, wheat and potato fields and grazing land for sheep and cattle, the estate lies in the dramatic southern coastal region of Spain near Granada. It is also good hunting land. On his first day in the field Charles bagged twenty-four partridge—and, according to villagers employed to assist the party, managed to hug and kiss Lady Jane several times. That was enough for the press, which descended on Molino del Rey en masse only to be turned away by Spain's tough Guardia Civil. Charles's personal detective, Inspector Paul Officer, denied there was any romance. "The whole affair has been built up from a molehill to a mountain," he declared. "It is just not on. The two are just very good chums. The Prince will not be a party to deception. That is why he has declined to be photographed with Lady Jane. They are just two young people relaxing with friends for a few days."

Yet, again, denial convinced very few. For the New Year's holiday at the beginning of 1974 Lady Jane was a guest of the Royal Family at Sandringham, and Britons were convinced that the next Queen was being fêted. Despite the serious fuel shortage that had followed in the wake of the 1973 Yom Kippur War and the subsequent Arab oil embargo, more than 10,000 people journeyed to Sandringham to catch a glimpse of Lady Jane.

One member of the Royal Family contends that any serious relationship between Jane and Charles was spoiled permanently by the relentless pursuit of the press, that the hounding by journalists must surely have given Lady Jane pause during those hectic months at the end of 1973. The day after her New Year's holiday at Sandringham, Lady Jane was telling reporters once again that "there is nothing for anyone to get excited about...this is all so ridiculous." But in fact the fleet, not Fleet Street, had parted the couple: Charles was already off to Singapore to report for duty on the *Jupiter*. He would not be back for months.

In the years since, Lady Jane has proved a durable friend. She has not married, as have so many of Charles's other women friends. An "ideal pupil" during her student days at St. Mary's Church of England Convent School in Berkshire, she has moved steadily ahead in her career. During the pressured weeks of 1973 she worked in an art gallery; soon after she moved to the British Broadcasting Corporation, where she rose to deputy head of research for its weekly *Radio Times* and became "Father of the Chapel"—trade union secretary. (She would, if chosen, be the first trade unionist Queen in British history.) Mostly recently she moved into the public relations department at the BBC-TV Center. She has not abandoned Charles. In 1977 she visited Balmoral again, and in the fall of 1978 Charles was once again at Molino del Rey. If it is only a friendship it is an enduring one. And Charles has talked seriously of marrying a friend.

There have also been many other friendships with women, at least one or two of them intense, since the to-do over Lady Jane, and even during it. Just after the *News of the World* first bruited the romance of Lady Jane and Charles in September, 1973, the rival *Daily Mirror* was on the trail of a girl called Rosie Clifton, daughter of an Army lieutenant-colonel and prosperous landowner. Rosie Clifton was all but engaged to a wealthy, polo-playing young man-about-town named Mark Vestey when she began seeing Charles, dining with the Prince occasionally at Buckingham Palace and visiting him at Balmoral. "I know Charles has to be in the public eye, but I don't think I have to be—or Mark, either," she complained. "It is really a personal matter. It's just between the three of us." As it turned out, it was just between the two of them. Rosie, in the end, married Mark Vestey....

As mentioned earlier, it was in March, 1974, that Charles met California blonde Laura Jo Watkins, the daughter of an American admiral, when the frigate *Jupiter* made a port call in San Diego. Charles made Laura Jo "feel at ease," she said. At the barbecue where they met, Laura Jo recalled, "He loaded up a double hamburger with every kind of sauce on the table and ate it without spilling a drop. There's one thing you can't be delicate with—and that's an American hamburger. Only a man with the most delicate manners could have got away with it."

Charles did not forget the meeting. When he got back to London, he suggested that Laura Jo be invited to the farewell party for the U.S. Ambassador Walter Annenberg. Laura Jo flew to London, where she listened to Charles's maiden speech in the House of Lords—a thoughtful sixteen-minute discourse on the recreational needs of the young. The Prince could not attend the Annenberg party because of the death of his great-uncle, the Duke of Gloucester, but he did take Laura Jo on a private visit to Kensington Palace. Laura Jo's mother was amazed at it all. "Surely," she said, "he must have lots of English girlfriends." As for Laura Jo, it was a bit overwhelming. Life in Royal Britain was "fascinating," she told friends on returning to the United States, but it was "unlivable" for an American girl.

Another blonde woman was soon to play a visible part in Charles's life. According to the New York *Times* of September 11, 1976, the Prince had once described his ideal woman as "tall, slim and long-legged," and though he had often chosen girlfriends who did not answer that physical description, Davina Sheffield did. She was just a half-inch short of six feet tall—half an inch taller than Charles, considerably taller in heels. She was leggy, with golden hair that hung just to her shoulders and a mischievous, openly seductive face. She became Fleet Street's darling—the *Daily Mirror* dubbing her the "perfect girl" for Charles.

She had been more adventurous than almost any other of

Charles's women friends. She had opened an Irish crafts shop in London, watched it fail and sold it. When an earlier romance broke up she went off to Saigon to care for orphans just as the Communists were making their final push to capture the city. "I feel a real sense of purpose here," she told a Saigon friend. But as the besieged city was falling, Davina finally had to flee for safety to Bangkok. Back home there was sudden tragedy: her mother was brutally murdered by thieves. Her father, an Army major, was dead. However, her debutante credentials were still adequate—a grandfather had been a Lord.

Davina's name was first linked with Charles's in 1974 when she was invited to Balmoral to spend the August Bank Holiday. At the time her romance with James Beard, a professional boat designer, was simmering, and she did not catch the public eye again until June, 1976. Her return was rather spectacular: she joined Charles for a coach-driving competition at Windsor, and to the delight of thousands of spectators Charles later drove out with her, at the reins of a coach-and-pair. The splash of publicity was a bit of an embarrassment to Charles, who had begged off attending a royal wedding in Sweden because of the "pressures of work."

A bombardment of headlines lasted into the fall. At one point pursuing newsmen drove Davina home from a holiday trip with friends at the island of South Uist in the Hebrides. There were spurious hints of a "love nest": Charles had sometimes stayed at nearby North Uist, but he was at sea on the *Bronington*. Davina had returned to London, she explained amid tears, because she could not subject her friends to the hounding of the press.

The press *was* relentless. The Sunday *Express* told of a "hidden cove" near an unnamed "seaside hamlet" in the West Country where Charles took Davina to a "secret beach." It was not so private, though. Village fishermen took the couple to the beach—inaccessible by land—and the Prince's detective stood guard at one end of the beach. "We all keep fairly quiet about it," said one villager, "so that the Prince isn't bothered."

There was less discreet news to come. James Beard rather ungallantly let it be known to a Sunday paper that Davina would make a fine wife. She had lived with him for a while in a thatched cottage near Winchester, he said, and "is very domesticated and a marvelous cook." The revelation seemed to doom Davina. One Royal Family spokesman said (in the *Daily Express* of October, 1976) of her chances of becoming Queen: "Not in a month of Sundays." Yet Davina, like Lady Jane Wellesley, has proved resilient. When Charles arrived in Western Australia in March, 1979, to celebrate the state's centennial, a report came from London that Davina Sheffield was soon to join him there.

The long interlude between Davina and the return of Davina was not exactly a solitary time for Charles. Lady Jane was back and in early 1977 there was a brief encounter with a young woman named Fiona Watson, the twenty-three-year-old daughter of soap millionaire Lord Manton, but Fiona, it turned out, was living with a young man named Patrick Anderson, and, for good measure, had permitted her unveiled figure to be spread across eleven pages of *Penthouse* magazine three years earlier. "Prince Charles was meant to be taking her out tonight," Anderson told an inquiring newspaper, but he "rang to apologize because he couldn't make it." Exit Fiona Watson.

A considerably more acceptable, young woman soon filled the void: Lady Sarah Spencer, willowy, red-haired and twenty-two, renewed a childhood friendship with the Prince at the Royal Ascot race meeting in 1977. Lady Sarah herself was clearly a "thoroughbred." Her father, Earl Spencer, is former equerry to Queen Elizabeth and the Queen was one of the guests at his Westminster Abbey marriage to Sarah's mother. The Queen Mother became Sarah's godmother at her christening. Charles and Sarah were seen often in each other's company through 1977 and into 1978, but by no means exclusively. On other days at Ascot during the same season Charles showed up with Lady Camilla Fane, the striking twenty-year-old brunette daughter of the Earl and Countess of Westmoreland, other old friends of the Queen.

While Lady Camilla provoked the usual speculation, much more centered on Charles's relationship with Lady Sarah. According to one report the two were seen walking hand-in-hand in the corridors of Althorp Hall, the Spencer family home near Northampton. One weekend guest was quoted by the *Daily Express* of January, 1978, as saying, "It was quite charming to see the two of them together. They were obviously very fond of one another. One morning Charles was waiting for Sarah at the bottom of the stairs and he greeted her with a kiss. Sarah is quite besotted with Charles."

Not so, said Lady Sarah to *Woman's Own,* breaking the silence that most of Charles's girlfriends have imposed on themselves. "Our relationship is strictly platonic," she insisted. "I think of him as the big brother I never had." Not that she doesn't like Charles. "I am very fond of the Prince," she told the London *Sun.* "He makes me laugh a lot. I enjoy being with him." She also "adores" his "love of horses." In early 1978 she even joined him for a ten-day ski holiday at the Swiss resort of Klosters, along with a group of friends. But "there is no chance of my marrying him," she told *Woman's Own.* "I'm not in love with him. And I wouldn't marry anyone I didn't love whether he were the dustman or the King of England." What about Charles's feelings? Lady Sarah was cryptic: "Charles is a romantic who falls in love easily."

Lady Sarah also disclosed in *Woman's Own* that Charles makes his own dates (some people have said that he makes them through third parties). He may pick his companion up in his Aston-Martin or invite her to meet him at one of the royal residences. A mere weekend at Windsor Castle demands a suitcase full of clothes, Lady Sarah revealed. A typical day might require a riding habit for the morning, a day-dress for lunch, a skirt for tea and a long dress for dinner. Charles's dates, she said, must address him as "Sir" until, as sometimes happens, the Prince asks to be called "Charles." On the town in London, those who know Charles's habits have observed that he will sometimes make for a restaurant or his favorite private club, Annabel's (the Studio 54 of Berkeley Square), for dancing. One of his detectives always waits outside the club or restaurant and, if he escorts a companion inside her house, waits outside there as well. Even security apparently has its limits.

Charles has grown increasingly gun-shy of the press over the last few years, sometimes giving them back some of their own medicine. After Fleet Street rumored that he was camping out with a woman on a nine-day safari in Kenya in 1977, he encountered reporters at the airport as he prepared to pilot a twin-engined Andover out to the Kenyan coast. "Here's your mystery blonde bird," he said, tossing a package to one reporter. Inside the parcel was a stuffed pigeon wearing a long golden wig.

Despite such ripostes, new stories of romances persist. In September, 1978, the London tabloids were on the trail of a woman no one had ever heard of—Czech Countess Angelika Lazensky, an emigrée from the communist country said to be living and working in Paris. The story had the usual credential—the Countess had spent a weekend at Balmoral, where, it was rumored, love had bloomed. Wearily the Palace announced that the six-foot Countess was "just one of many friends" of Charles. She also happened to be Roman Catholic.

The whole revival of the Marie-Astrid story later in 1978 almost certainly ended any chance of Charles marrying a Roman Catholic—at least until some key ecumenical questions are settled, which may take decades. The volatile issue reaches back more than four centuries into British history. Since the time of Henry VIII in the early sixteenth century the monarch has been head of the Church of England; since the time of his daughter Elizabeth I that church has been uninterruptedly Protestant. But in 1685 a Roman Catholic convert—James II—came to the throne, theoretically head of a Protestant Church but owing his personal loyalty to Rome. He was tolerated. but when a son and heir was born in 1688, the prospect of another generation of Catholic monarchs was too much. In a bloodless "Glorious Revolution" Parliament forced James out and invited his daughter Mary (a Protestant) and her husband, William of Orange, to take the throne. In the 1689 Bill of Rights a provision declared that "it is inconsistent with the Safety and Welfare of this Protestant Kingdome to be governed by a Popish Prince or by any King or Queene marrying a Papist." That constitutional bar was reinforced by the Act of Settlement in 1701 insuring that the crown should pass to a Protestant heir—specifically, the German-origin House of Hanover, from which the present Royal Family is descended.

To many Britons, both Catholic and Protestant, even the language of the 1689 provision, with its references to "Papists" and "Popish," is offensive. But some militant Protestants, especially in Northern Ireland, view the cause apocalyptically. It was to them—during the most recent spate of Marie-Astrid rumors—that the demagogic Enoch Powell, MP from County Down, condemned any royal marriage to a Roman Catholic. Such an event, declared Powell, "would signal the end of the British monarchy" by bringing it under the reach of Rome.

Reaction across Britain roundly condemned Powell both for the statement and for its bigoted tone, but the message got through to Charles all the same. At an off-the-record news conference, quietly leaked to the press later, Charles told the gathered journalists: "If I were to marry a Catholic it would create problems. I wonder if it would be worth doing it." The clear answer was no. Further, Catholic Church requirements on the conscience of the Catholic partner would probably dissuade most serious Catholics from entering a marriage in which the children would have to be reared in the Church of England.

What in effect has happened to the marital choices facing Charles is that the field has grown younger. He has complained that every time he throws a dinner party, more and more of his old friends are married. A decade ago, when Charles became Prince of Wales, some of his female friends were older than he. Now, like Camilla Fane, they may be a full decade younger. As one result, like any aging bachelor, Charles finds himself more frequently in the company of married couples, and perhaps without a companion of his own. He has been a regular house guest of some couples, and may join them for an evening on the town. Columnist Nigel Dempster has even said that the single women Charles dates are smokescreens. "Prince Charles brings a pretty girl onto the polo field in front of twenty cameramen as a shield to hide his real affairs with married women." That is an easy charge to make, a difficult one to prove. Charles has been seen quite publicly at the Royal Box at Covent Garden watching the opera *La Traviata* with Charmian Stirling, the estranged wife of a Scottish landowner. When one gossip item hinted that there might be something between Charles and Rosalind Ward, wife of millionaire Gerald Ward, the Wards replied with a categorical denial in the *News of the World*. Charles was their friend and often their guest at their Berkshire mansion, the couple said, but as Rosalind put it, anything beyond that would be "highly amusing."

The troubling historical backdrop to all this is that King Edward VII in his perpetual quest for female companionship before and during his reign preferred married women precisely because they were safely married. Charles's great-uncle David, briefly Edward VIII, apparently did too, finding his ultimate solace in a woman who was married when he met her. Charles has read Frances Donaldson's revealing biography of Edward VIII and been troubled by it. There are too many converging lines that he must now try to separate.

At Blenheim Palace, the magnificent ancestral home of the Dukes of Marlborough, there exist a series of guest registers covering many years. One includes the entry:

> *Edward*
> *Wallis Simpson*
> *Ernest Simpson*

A second, almost forty years later, reads

> *Charles*
> *Rosalind Ward*
> *Gerald Ward*

An uneasy coincidence perhaps, but surely the stuff of which rumor is made. "Those foreign papers will report anything," Charles told the *Evening Standard* in 1975. "One of them said I was having an affair with someone or other the other day. They are incredibly disreputable but everyone reads them. Sometimes particularly trivial stories about me appear. I suppose I must accept that what happens to me can be newsworthy regardless of context."

Exactly so; and he acknowledged to Douglas Keay, "I have a particular responsibility to ensure that I make the right decision. A lot revolves around that decision, I believe. In many ways success or failure." The Prince's choice of a bride is obviously a crucially important matter, and as he himself admits it should not be delayed for too much longer. The Queen's subjects are eager for a royal wedding and a Princess of Wales.

CHAPTER EIGHT

A Princely Fortune
(And How It Grew)

QUEEN ELIZABETH of England is said to be the richest woman in the world, and her elder son, already affluent, will one day be one of the richest men. They are rich in money and in shares, in jewelry and in racehorses. They own priceless paintings, mansions and palaces scattered the length and breadth of the United Kingdom as well as the most expensive clothes and a fleet of Rolls-Royces. They have the use of a flight of personal helicopters and aircraft, an enormous ocean-going yacht and a new royal railway train. Even their chocolate biscuits are especially made by royal biscuit-makers, and a whole army of tradesmen boast that they are Royal Warrant Holders, singled out as provders of exclusive goods to the first family in the land.

Andrew Duncan, author of a ten-year-old bestseller, *The Reality of Monarchy,* and more recently of a study of the mideast money boom, is a unique if plain-speaking authority on the royal finances. "They have always been a racket," he says. "I remember when I wrote *The Reality of Monarchy* the Central Office of Information was going round pretending that every other member of the Royal Family except the Queen pays tax. That simply wasn't true, and after I had pointed out that Charles pays no tax they stopped pretending. Quite clearly if you believe in a monarchy then Charles should be very rich, and indeed he is. Eventually he'll be richer still because the only way the Royal Family can avoid tax successfully is by applying the system of primogeniture. In other words, when the Queen dies, he'll get everything."

Precisely how much money is involved remains a well-guarded secret, and one which no one has come near unraveling. Duncan estimates the annual cost of running the monarchy at ten million pounds, "about the same as the British National Health Service spends on tranquilizers every year." But the whole matter appears so befogged with genuine misunderstandings and deliberate obfuscation that no one really knows.

Historically the King of England was the country's greatest landowner—and land equalled wealth. He lived off the rent. In 1660, however, when the monarchy was restored after the republican interlude of the preceding dozen years, a monarchist Parliament voted Charles II an annual fixed income in addition to the rents he was collecting. In 1698 William III was given an even larger income but in 1760, when King George III succeeded, it was decided that the rent from the Crown Estates was not nearly enough to keep an English King in the manner which his status demanded. Parliament therefore voted George a stupendous £800,000 to cover all expenses not considered a State responsibility. This time, however, they exacted a price for the favor. George was compelled to surrender his hereditary estates for the whole of his lifetime in return for what was, in effect, an annual salary. This system continues. Each time a monarch succeeds he or she surrenders the crown lands for his or her lifetime *plus* six months. In return Parliament votes them a "Civil List." The Civil List, large though it now is, is nowhere near the income from the Crown Estates, which, skillfully managed by the Crown Commissioners, have risen to an estimated £7 million for the fiscal year 1978 to 1979. By comparison the Civil List, which was fixed at £475,000 per annum at the beginning of the Queen's reign, is still only about a quarter of the revenue from the Crown Estates.

In theory, at least, Charles could, when he succeeds, refuse to abide by the precedent of the last two hundred years and not surrender the Crown Estates. They include 250,000 acres of prime farmland and much of London's West End and City. Such prime properties as the Haymarket Theatre, the Strand Palace Hotel, the Royal College of Physicians and most of the Regent Street are presently owned by the Queen "in right of the Crown." This would bring Charles an income of about four times what he is likely to be voted by Parliament, but quite apart from the unlikely event of Parliament letting him get away with such an arrangement he would have to consider that the Civil List is only a small part of what the British nation pays out on the monarchy every year. Basically it includes the Privy Purse, which is the monarch's private expenditure as sovereign not as private individual, and the salaries of the royal households, the expenses of the royal household; royal bounty, alms and special services. Almost ten years ago, when the Palace made public some comprehensive figures in defense of its financial position, it was revealed that, for example, the royal yacht was costing over £800,000 a year, the Queen's Flight £700,000 and the royal train £36,000. The Department of the Environment was spending almost £1 million on maintaining the royal palaces and the Post Office was giving postal and telecommunications services to the value of £52,000. None of this was covered by the Civil List.

In practice, therefore, Charles might be better advised to give up the Crown Estates as his predecessors have done and take whatever Parliament will pay. He can always, if precedent is any guide, retain two immensely lucrative estates, which due to historical oversight are not included in the Crown Estates proper: the Duchy of Lancaster and the Duchy of Cornwall. At the moment the Duchy of Lancaster revenues go directly to the Queen, and in the first twenty-two years of her reign they amounted to a staggering £3 million tax free. As Andrew Duncan points out, under the system of primogeniture all this will pass to Charles when his mother dies.

That lies in the future, but since he was a baby Charles has been Duke of Cornwall and therefore entitled to income from the Duchy estates. In the early days it was agreed that four-fifths of the Duchy revenues should go to the government while the

149

rest should be banked for future use. By the time he was eighteen the £9,000 a year he had begun with had turned into about £20,000. At eighteen he began to draw £30,000 and at twenty-one he became entitled to all the income, though he has voluntarily surrendered half to the Exchequer. That still leaves him at least £145,000 tax free, and rising annually....

The Duchy of Cornwall has existed since 1337 and has always been based on the county of Cornwall, most westerly of British counties, a Celtic kingdom whose people regard themselves as divorced from Englishmen to the east of the River Tamar which divides Cornwall from England. On March 17, 1337, King Edward III made a charter whereby the Duchy of Cornwall was given to his elder son, Edward. Under the terms of the charter the Duchy henceforth belonged automatically to the King's elder son. If there was no son then the Duchy reverted to the Crown. The original seventeen Cornish manors were known as the *Antiqua Maneria,* then there were some *Forinseca Maneria* outside the county, and finally *Annexata Maneria* inside *and* outside the county. Because it was a Royal Duchy it was impossible to sever land from it without an Act of Parliament. In consequence it grew and grew.

The first Duke, the Black Prince who won the famous Battle of Crécy in 1346, visited his Cornish lands frequently, often with "a gallant company of knights." It was he who laid down the basis of the Duchy's administration, an administration which continued to prosper in good times and bad, giving the impression, as the great Cornish historian A.L. Rowse observes, "of an institution tenacious and conservative, one that neither relaxed its rights nor vexed its tenantry with new and unexpected impositions." After the 17th-century Civil War, the Dukes paid little attention to the Duchy. Not one of the first four Georges visited the Cornish estates, but Victoria broke that negligent precedent and since her reign every British ruler has visited the estates at least once. Revenue from the Duchy enabled Edward VII to buy Sandringham. Edward VIII, with Duchy income, bought Fort Belvedere, where he cavorted with Mrs. Simpson. At least he showed a measure of gratitude by flying the Duchy flag from the fort whenever he was there.

A Princely Fortune (And How It Grew)

Charles, however, takes a serious interest in the Duchy of Cornwall. With his good sense of history, he responds to the appeal of an ancient institution and the images it conjures up—images which A.L. Rowse evokes: "The centuries-old buildings going back to Edmund Earl of Cornwall by the quayside at Lostwithiel, lapped by the tidal waters of the River Fowey; the house at Trematon within the old walls of the castle, where Sir Richard Grenville, grandfather of the hero, took refuge in the time of the great "Commotion" of 1549, the castle to which Drake took the treasure which he brought home from his Voyage round the World, the gray walls looking down upon the broad waters of the Hamoaze; or Launceston Castle, with the ruined shell of its keep; or Tintagel, grim barbaric upon its desolate headland, the inspiration of so much poetry and legend."

But the Duchy is not merely picturesque. It is an enormously valuable piece of real estate producing a gross revenue of well over one million pounds a year. In the old days rents were different—a pair of gilt spurs here, a greyhound there, three hundred puffins from the Scilly Isles—but now with a few exceptions such as the manor of Fordington, which sends Charles a leg of lamb every St. George's Day, the money is paid in cash. It comes from golf courses (one of the few games, ironically, that Charles positively dislikes), an oysterage, two thousand acres of forestry, flower farms in the Scilly Islands, a model farm in Stoke Climsland and—most lucrative of all—sections of the 130,000 acres—the Duchy Estate in South London.

The London part of the Duchy of Cornwall lies south of the River Thames in the borough of Kennington. Once it was the site of the Black Prince's palace but for years now it has been an essentially unfashionable part of the city, mainly working class, even though one can see the Palace of Westminster from many parts of it. "South of the river" has always had an apologetic ring to it in London, and even though the Duchy now has a fair sprinkling of Members of Parliament and professional people among its tenants, it still has the unmistakeable aura of comparative poverty. The houses are mostly small and built in

151

terraces, and many of the 900 tenants live in apartment buildings of adequate but far from luxurious design. One of them is the recently deposed Labour Prime Minister James Callaghan, who rents a small apartment opposite the Kennington underground railway station.

The estate is managed from a comparatively elegant office building at 157 Kennington Lane, a busy road which runs almost parallel with the river. The sign outside the Duchy offices says "Duchy of Cornwall Estate," but that is only half the story for Mr. Hibberdine, the immaculately gray-suited Land Steward of the Estate, a partner in a firm of professional surveyors and estate managers. The Duchy is only one of his clients; he also looks after the estates of three Oxford colleges and much else besides.

Walking about the estate with Mr. Hibberdine one gets an impression of a feudal country estate in the middle of the city. A burly middle-aged man comes over, smiling, to exchange the time of day. Mr. Hibberdine asks after his newly married daughter. "He's one of the Palace footmen," says Mr. Hibberdine as the man goes on his way. Further on, he points out Woodstock Court, described in one architectural treatise as "both elegant and intimate." A plaque over the front entrance says that it was built in 1914 "to provide for old tenants of the Duchy." A caretaker lives on the ground floor just inside and the old people are in small apartments built around a neat central quadrangle with a flowering cherry in each corner. The doors of each apartment have metal knockers which gleam from constant polishing. Some are at ground level, others open onto a wide terrace at first floor level.

"They're mainly former tenants," says Mr. Hibberdine, "but some are former Palace servants, and some of them might be related to people who were tenants. We try to help out wherever possible."

Every year the inhabitants of Woodstock Court are given a Christmas box by Prince Charles and from time to time he comes down to visit them. "He's awfully good with them," says Mr. Hibberdine, "terribly natural. And he talks to everyone. I remember one occasion when there were two chaps down a manhole. Suddenly they look up and there's the Prince of Wales looking down at them." Just like that.

Woodstock Court was designed by Professor S.D. Adshead, a social realist who pioneered in low-income-dwellings design in the early twentieth century, putting up well-constructed town cottages which were fifty years ahead of their time. He is best known for his grand, very French Royal Victoria Pavilion at the seaside town of Ramsgate, but his buildings in Kennington deserve wider fame. They are small and unpretentious but Woodstock Court and the even more distinguished Courtenay Square are models of their kind.

The Duchy believes in maintaining a wide social mix of people on the estate, even to the extent of putting up six artist's studios in one of their newest developments. Although they are selling off one or two isolated properties and some five-story Georgian houses, all their other properties are to let, none of them on longer leases than seven years. In a London where private rented accommodation is disappearing fast because legislation has made life increasingly difficult for landlords, this is very unusual. Rents range from about £400 to £1200 a year, which is comparatively low, and the estate is scrupulously well kept.

Apart from houses and apartments there are some shops, mainly small newsagents and groceries, some pubs, including The Duchy Arms, and the famous Kennington Oval Cricket Ground leased to the Surrey County Cricket Club. Sadly, this lease is shortly to expire and it seems possible that the cricketers will be unable to afford its renewal. One office block is let to the NAAFI, the British equivalent of the PX, but generally the buildings are low, modest and unassuming, in stark contrast to the high concrete blocks erected nearby by Lambeth Council. Throughout the estate the name of streets and buildings are inscribed on gray slate blocks—models of subdued good taste. The London Estate appears to be a model of its kind, its landlord as beyond reproach as any private landlord will ever be. Sixty years ago the aim of the young Prince of Wales and his advisor, Sir Walter Peacock, was to clear out the disturbing slums in the area "and create a model estate." They would be pleased to see that such ideals remain those of today's Land Steward and his benevolent boss, the present Prince.

There are numerous examples of Charles's benevolence and concern. Every year a Duchy boy is sent at Duchy expense to study at Charles's old school, Gordonstoun. Charles voluntarily surrenders half of the income from the Duchy (£300,000 a year) to the British Treasury. The rest he keeps—without paying tax on it, but if the estate were taxable Charles would have to earn more than £14 million gross a year to receive that kind of net income.

Nonetheless, it is the tax exemption which lies at the root of the royal fortunes and provides the family's critics with their most potent ammunition. Not only are the family exempt from income tax, they are also free from the death duties and capital gains tax that have crippled other landowning families in Britain; there is scarcely a stately home in the country which is not now open to the paying public because the owner has been forced into it by death duties. The royal palaces remain scrupulously maintained, extravagantly manned and under no serious threat of any kind. Some parts are open to the public, but as a gesture of goodwill, certainly not from financial necessity.

Indeed the monarch has paid no tax since the days of Queen Victoria, but there are some misunderstandings about the tax position of the rest of the family. It is commonly said even by quite dispassionate observers that the other members of the family *are* liable for tax and, legally, they are. Charles does not pay tax on his income from the Duchy of Cornwall but that is not because he is exempt from income tax; it is because the *Duchy* is exempt from income tax. Any other income, such as his naval pay—which as mentioned he gave away to charity—is technically liable to income tax in the normal way. In practice other members of the Royal Family negotiate a tax-free "allowance" with the Inland Revenue. The allowance is secret but it seems certain that most royals do not pay tax.

This has led to enormous wealth and, more damagingly, to rumors of enormous wealth. When, in 1971, a parliamentary select committee was appointed to inquire into the royal finances they met with the frankest possible responses to questions about official income and expenditure and an absolutely blank refusal to say anything about private money. The Lord Chamberlain, Lord Cobbold, was disarmingly bland: "The Officers of the Household, including myself, do not handle Her Majesty's private funds and are not conversant with the details of such funds. Her Majesty handles these matters herself, as did the late King and earlier sovereigns." If the Lord Chamberlain did not know, then who did? And through the Lord Chamberlain the Queen let it be known that she was not pleased about the rumors of her private wealth. "Her Majesty has been much concerned by the astronomical figures which have been bandied about in some quarters suggesting that the value of these funds may now run into fifty to a hundred million pounds or more. She feels that these ideas can only arise from confusion about the status of the Royal Collections, which are in no sense at her private disposal. She wishes me to assure the Committee that these suggestions are wildly exaggerated. Her Majesty also wishes me to state that the income from these private funds has been used in some part to assist in meeting the expenses of other members of the Royal Family; owing to the progress of inflation, they have in many cases heavily outrun the annuities granted by Parliament to cover such expenses at the beginning of the reign."

Indeed, the Queen has subsidized poorer members of the Royal Family and this will almost certainly continue when Charles succeeds. Princess Anne, for instance, is not rich in her own right, so the Queen made her a present of Gatcombe Park, a large country house and estate in Gloucestershire. Her cousin, the Duke of Gloucester, is considered too remote from royalty to merit an official Civil List salary, and so the Queen pays his official expenses out of her private funds. Since the sovereign is excused from taxes it makes sense to keep as much money in the sovereign's hands as possible. When the Queen dies it is highly improbable that she will leave anything of great value to Anne, Andrew or Edward. Charles will probably inherit all. He will pay no taxes, but like his mother he will be expected to be generous in his subsidies to the rest of the Family.

Such practices make it difficult to distinguish between

private and public money. The Queen herself drew attention to this confusion in her references to the Royal Collections—the Queen's Picture Collection, the Crown Jewels, and the stamp collections built up by George V and George VI, "inalienable" and held in trust for the nation. However, the Queen and other members of the Family also owned pictures and jewels and perhaps even postage stamps which they clearly considered to be private property with which they could do as they liked. How they decide what is public and what is private has never been made clear. It is the same with the royal palaces. Balmoral was built by Victoria and Albert; Sandringham was bought by Edward VII. Both houses were bought by George VI as part of the settlement with the Duke of Windsor after his abdication. They seem to be regarded as private houses and yet the Queen, who, of course, is always on duty, uses both for official purposes, receiving privy councillors, visiting governor-generals and maintaining an office staff there. Public funds have been used to maintain both. On the other hand Windsor Castle and Buckingham Palace are regarded as public and official even though the Family lives in them. Until recently Buckingham Palace was exempted from the rates levied by local government, presumably on the grounds that it was an official residence of the Queen. Then Westminster City Council decided to put in a claim for a formidable £98,422. It was paid, not by the Queen but by the government.

It is all very confusing, but however it is arranged and justified the income and wealth of his family ensure that Prince Charles leads a life which may not have the ostentatious style of a Faroukh or even a Gunter Sachs but is still comfortable beyond most people's wildest dreams....

To begin with there are his homes. For the most part these are shared with his parents and his brothers and sisters. The royal palaces have had a checkered history and the present collection have not always been favored. The pattern of royal residence was changed most dramatically by George III. When in 1760 he succeeded his grandfather, George II, he refused to live in any of the palaces which his grandfather had used. That meant that the magnificent Thames-side palace of Hampton Court on the

156

outskirts of London, the small Kensington Palace near Hyde Park and the central St. James' were all virtually abandoned. George preferred Windsor, though it was too far out of London for a permanent base. Since he refused to use St. James' and since Whitehall and Westminster Palaces had both been destroyed by fire, he bought Buckingham House from the Duchess of Buckingham and set about turning that into a palace.

Windsor has been the Royal Family's regular weekend home throughout the present reign. It is also used throughout April when the annual procession of Knights of the Garter (England's oldest order of chivalry) takes place and during the famous royal race-meeting at the nearby Ascot horsetrack. It was originally built by William the Conqueror in the eleventh century but has been added to by subsequent generations, especially by George IV. That prodigal King was responsible for the great medieval round tower that dominates the skyline, and also for the great quadrangle that contains one corridor of 550 feet linking the State rooms with the Queen's private apartments. The public rooms are lavish, especially the Waterloo chamber, where the Knights of the Garter have a banquet every year. It commemorates the battle in which Napoleon was defeated and is dominated by a huge picture of the Duke of Wellington over the doorway. It also contains a carpet made for Queen Victoria in Agra, said to be the largest seamless carpet in Europe.

But Windsor is less of an office than Buckingham Palace. Though affairs of State are conducted here the private area is like a prosperous country house: dog baskets, television sets and family portraits jostle Louis XIV furniture and priceless paintings. The large park is a favorite place for weekend horse-riding. There are private gardens at Frogmore, home of the royal mausoleum, and Charles's grandmother has a home, Royal Lodge, close enough to make family visits a regular happening.

Charles keeps a set of rooms here and finds it a particularly useful weekend home in summer because it is so close to his polo grounds. In winter it is less convenient because it is some way from any good hunting.

Buckingham Palace, where the Prince's suite of rooms was designed by David Hicks, the interior decorator married to Pamela, daughter of great-uncle Dickie Mountbatten, is the family headquarters. Prince Philip jokingly refers to it as their "tied cottage." Like Windsor it is a crown property rather than a personal residence. While it might have been possible for the Duke of Windsor to have retained Sandringham or even Balmoral it would be quite unthinkable for him to have kept on Buckingham Palace. It is like the White House in Washington. It comes with the job.

Like so much of the present fabric of the monarchy it was "improved" by Queen Victoria's energetic consort, Albert. It was he who built the famous balcony, but the core of the building is the work of George IV's favorite architect, John Nash. George had been shown a number of grandiose plans by other architects but he was not impressed. "If the public wish to have a palace," he told Nash, "I have no objection to building one, but I must have a *pied-à-terre* and I will have it at Buckingham Palace." Later, when Nash's work was complete, the King sent for him. "Nash," he said, "the State Rooms you have made me are so handsome that I think I shall hold my Courts there." Nash did not agree. He considered the plan on too small a scale. After all, he had been told to build a royal *pied-à-terre* and that was what he had tried to do. "You know nothing about the matter," replied the King. "It will make an excellent palace." And a palace it has remained every since.

Charles's suite, which combines work and pleasure, is full of mementoes from his travels. One visitor described his study as "decorated with understated masculine elegance." The pale blue curtains have been bleached by the sun, the leather armchairs have taken on the patina of age. The shelves are crammed with volumes on history and archaeology and art, and there are more glossy books, including some on polo and the eighteenth century, on a coffee table. Also a box of chocolate mints; the family is inordinately fond of chocolate mints. Although Charles is an assiduous collector of phonograph records and enjoys listening to his stereo, his greatest concession to luxury at the Palace is his collection of soapstone carvings from the

Arctic. He has a special "salesroom spy" who seeks out new treasures for him, and the Palace apartment is full of walrus, seal, caribou and, best of all, a huge musk-ox, the shaggy, curly-horned bison of the far north. When Prince Charles began collecting some years ago the market for Eskimo carving and painting had hardly been touched. Now prices are sky-high.

Charles's connoisseur instincts are typical of the family. His mother has not only added some outstanding works by traditional painters such as Kneller and Samuel Cooper to the Royal Art Collection, but also displayed an intelligent foresight in commissioning a series of paintings of Windsor Castle by John Piper and also buying from such less conventional painters as L.S. Lowry and Sidney Nolan, before their popularity was as great as it is now. The Queen Mother, Charles's grandmother, has built up one of the world's most remarkable collections of early Chelsea porcelain. This tradition of patronizing the arts in an assiduous manner is a longstanding one which can be traced back at least as far as medieval days. As King, Charles seems likely to be more interested in the arts than any sovereign since Edward VII. He might even prove as knowledgeable and enthusiastic a patron as those two almost legendary benefactors of the arts—George IV and Charles II.

Both Buckingham Palace and Windsor are more official than homely, although both represent compromise. The reverse applies to Sandringham and Balmoral, both of which are in remote parts of the country and are more in the nature of holiday homes than offices. Balmoral is wonderfully secluded, a fine piece of Scottish baronial whimsy tucked into the Dee Valley in Scotland and overlooked by the wilderness of the Cairngorm Mountains. There are woods, mountains and rivers—and definitely no public. The house has never been opened to outsiders though the grounds—or "policies," as the Scots quaintly call them—are opened up when the family is away south of the border.

Late every summer the family stays at Balmoral, their visit coinciding with the beginning of the grouse-shooting season on August 12 and with the deer stalking. They fish for salmon on the river Dee and attend the Braemar Gathering, where various highland pursuits such as caber-tossing and pibroch-playing are practiced. It is probably the nearest they ever get to a retreat from official life.

Balmoral is *very* Scottish, even though to some eyes it has a hint of Prince Albert's native Thuringia. Even the carpets are tartan, and the candelabras are supported by Highland Chieftains made from Parian marble. The surrounding countryside is wild and remote, good not only for shooting, stalking and fishing but also for less predatory pursuits. The family likes to take picnics to beauty spots around the estate or to the Shiel of Altnaguisach or the Glassalt by the side of lake Muick—two retreats where Victoria indulged the terrible grief she suffered after her husband's death. It is a private place, even though ministers from London do pay occasional visits and sleep in an uncomfortable narrow bed used by British Prime Ministers ever since Disraeli and Gladstone. For official Scottish duties there is the Palace of Holyroodhouse in Edinburgh, restored by Charles's great-grandfather.

The other private home, Sandringham, in Norfolk, was built by Edward VII when he was Prince of Wales. He ripped down the old Georgian house and built a long rambling red brick mansion in its place, a rather ugly building faintly reminiscent of Tudor times. It is not a very prepossessing house inside either, though the blue, gold and white drawingroom has a surprising elegance and sophistication, a reminder that Queen Alexandra, for whom it was created, was a sister of the Czarina of Russia. But the reason Charles enjoys Sandringham is that the shooting is the best in England.

One day all these will be his, but for now he is content to share them. Unlike other Princes of Wales he is fond of his immediate family and enjoys living with them. He shows no sign of setting up his own establishment, but if and when he does he has the perfect place: a windfall, an extraordinary piece of good fortune, an ancient country house and estate, modernized at vast expense, just waiting for him to grace it with his presence.

The English countryside is incomparably rich, appropriately enough, in country houses. Most European countries have ancient palaces, sometimes royal, and sometimes the seats of old baronial families whose wealth and power would at one time have equalled that of the Crown itself. But England more than anywhere is blessed with houses which are less than palatial but far more then ordinary. There is scarcely a village in the country which does not boast its Hall or Manor or Grange, the "big" house once, and sometimes now, lived in by the local squire. Almost anyone with any pretension to social status before the 1914–18 war built himself a country house, and if that status was not based on an existing estate or village, he would buy or create one. The legacy is an architectural and historical feast, and though a depressing number have had to be destroyed or allowed to decay there are still many fine buildings either in private hands or preserved by "The National Trust," a charitable organization dedicated to the task.

Chevening House in Kent is a prime example of the English country house. It is about twenty-five miles south of London in the County of Kent, a green, friendly countryside tucked in under the south-facing escarpment of the North Downs. The villages are old, friendly places with many houses dating from before the sixteenth century, eccentric buildings with exposed beams striping their white plasterwork. General Wolfe, who won the famous victory on Quebec's Plains of Abraham in 1759, came from Westerham, just down the road from Chevening, and his defeated opponent, Montcalm, is commemorated in a smart restaurant, its windows almost blocked by credit cards. Winston Churchill's house, Chartwell, is a few miles away, now open to the public as a sort of museum.

The Stanhopes came to Chevening in 1717. James, the first Earl, was a general who had been defeated at Brihuega in Portugal and incarcerated for eighteen months in Saragossa. The defeat did not harm his reputation; he turned to politics and became King George I's favorite minister. The house he bought at Chevening had been built, almost a century before, by the celebrated architect Inigo Jones. It was "a parallelogram of five stories," built in red brick surmounted by a balustraded flat roof. But it was not big enough for the Earl, who added on two symmetrical wings, including a library, joined to the main house by curving galleries.

The Stanhopes stayed for exactly 250 years. They were all, in their different ways, distinguished. One was a historian, another a mathematician and inventor. Lady Hester Stanhope was one of England's best-known eccentrics who ended up in Lebanon, where she "went native" and became an object of universal curiosity. Each generation altered the house to suit its fancy—not always for the good. Since gentlemen wore wigs special powder rooms were built onto the main edifice, spoiling the parallelogram. A superb kitchen garden was also built. Palm trees were planted. Yellowish tiles were nailed over the bricks. The roof was changed. William Pitt, the Earl of Chatham, one of England's most brilliant statesmen and a relation by marriage, came to live at Chevening for a few months and had a road made through the parkland, driving through the high beech trees at the top of the hill in a dramatic piece of sylvan landscape that survives today and is known as "the keyhole."

The last Earl of Stanhope died in 1967. He was a sad figure in many ways. Marrying late in life, he and his wife had no children. She died in 1940 of cancer and he, in his late seventies, was run over by the private fire engine he kept on the estate and had to have a leg amputated. The sadness of his later years, though, was ameliorated by a brilliant scheme. He had always been a patriot. In the Great War he had served with the Grenadier Guards and won a Distinguished Service Order and the Military Cross for bravery. Later he became a Cabinet Minister and First Lord of the Admiralty. He was also an ardent royalist. In the 1930s, when the abdication crisis was at its height, it was Stanhope who asked the King's brother and sister-in-law, the Duke and Duchess of York, to Chevening for a quiet weekend. It was there that the Duke, deeply unhappy at the prospect of taking over the Crown, was able to relax with friends and take advice away from the glare of publicity in London. Stanhope was a Knight of the Garter—the oldest order of chivalry in Britain—and as an old man he was the senior knight, a familiar sight in his heraldic robes, limping down the aisle of St. George's Chapel, Windsor, at the annual Garter service. His funeral was attended by all the Royal Family.

Lord Stanhope was the seventh Earl and he inherited Chevening from the sixth, who inherited it from the fifth and so on, back to the first Earl. Lord Stanhope, in turn, would have liked to pass the ancestral home to an eighth Earl, but there was no such person. There was no heir. Accordingly he and his wife decided that they should offer the house to the nation so that it could be used as a private residence for a Cabinet Minister. There are precedents for this in Chequers, a country house in Buckinghamshire that is the country residence of the British Prime Ministers. "We felt," recorded Lord Stanhope, "that it would be unfortunate that such a place with such surroundings should not continue to be used as a private residence."

In the 1950s this wish began to become reality when Lord Stanhope approached the Prime Minister, Harold Macmillan, and made his offer. It was accepted, and the gift was formally made by an Act of Parliament, The Chevening Estate Act.

Before his death Lord Stanhope received a number of visits from the Royal Family. The Queen and Prince Philip came to tea; Lord Snowdon and Princess Margaret were given a tour of inspection; and Prince Charles himself, still only a teen-ager, arrived one day from Windsor. The old man and the young Prince seemed to get on well from the first. Lord Stanhope, now in his eighties, was intrigued by the teen-age Prince, enjoyed his enthusiasm and took evident pleasure in showing off the house's treasures—notably the library with its magnificent collection of manuscripts, including many of the papers of William Pitt, The Elder, Sir Robert Peel, also a British Prime Minister, and the celebrated letters of Lord Chesterfield to his son. The great 19th century historian, Lord Macaulay, considered it the best private collection he had ever seen.

From that meeting onward Lord Stanhope was set on the idea of his house going to Prince Charles. It had not been mentioned on that occasion (he was, after all, only a boy), but the prospect enchanted the old Earl.

Toward the end of his life Lord Stanhope became very frail and ill, though he occasionally rallied and was able to walk about the house and grounds as usual. One Sunday, in the summer of 1967, Prince Charles telephoned unexpectedly to say that he was going to his cousins, the Brabournes, the following day, and since Chevening was on his route he would welcome the opportunity to call. He duly arrived on the Monday, driving his Aston-Martin with only the detective for company and spent an hour or so looking round. It was one of Lord Stanhope's better days; he felt fit and well and took an obvious pleasure in showing the Prince the family papers, pointing out the portraits of all seven Earl Stanhopes in the dining room, regaling him with anecdotes of family history. As he said good-by to the Prince he felt certain that eventually he would move into Chevening and make it his home. He had been worried about it, concerned about the possibility of temporary socialist tenants, disturbed by an apparent lack of interest from the Royal Family. But after Prince Charles's visit he felt confident of Chevening's future as the home of the Prince of Wales. A week later the last Earl of Stanhope was dead. The house now became the property of the nation in fact as well as in form.

Lord Stanhope left a one-million pound estate, most of it designated for the restoration of Chevening. With those funds the house has been completely restored inside and out. The trustees also took the precaution of having each room photographed before it was altered so that it could be faithfully changed back if desired. The exterior renovations were even more drastic than the ones inside. The attic roof was beyond repair and some of the staff quarters had not been redecorated for more than a century. The exterior had to be completely restructured. The Civic Trust citation says that the work has "brought the Main House once more into scale and harmony with its supporting buildings and spaces."

And there it sits. The renovations are complete. The Trust, which has paid for all the work, is now healthier than it has ever been. But the house is empty. Charles became the Nominated Person on May 22, 1974, yet the Palace says that he has no plans to take up residence at Chevening, though he does use it on such occasions as his Jubilee Trust Appeal, which was televised there.

Of course Chevening is a large house for a bachelor, and many believe that Charles will move in as soon as he finds a bride. If the bride were Jane Wellesley that would renew an old Chevening association, for the fifth Earl Stanhope was an intimate friend of Lady Jane's most famous ancestor, the first

Duke of Wellington. He even wrote a 19th-century bestseller called *Conversations with the Duke of Wellington,* and when the last of the Stanhopes died there were still two bottles of the Duke of Wellington's port gathering dust in the cellar—though it is probably vinegar by now.

Chevening...Windsor...Balmoral...Sandringham? In Charles's case, he does not pay his money and he takes his choice.

Entitled to wear more than a score of uniforms,
Charles cuts a trim figure in all of them. Here, in
Windsor Castle in 1977, he wears his formal dress
uniform as Colonel-in-Chief of the Royal Regiment
of Wales.

THE EVENING MAIL

Encountering actress Susan
Hampshire at a gala performance in
1975,

ROLAND SCHOOR—LIAISON

Charles encounters an admirer on a
state visit to Fiji in 1974.

At Independence Day festivities in
Papua, New Guinea in 1975.

ANWAR HUSSEIN

Visiting the Ivory Coast on a 1977 trip, Charles
meets a devotee who has designed her own
Charles dress.

ANWAR HUSSEIN

Charles visits the Calgary Stampede
and finds himself surrounded by a
covey of cowgirls.

ANWAR HUSSEIN

Journeying to Alberta in 1977 to
commemorate an 1877 treaty with Blackfoot
Indians, Charles smokes a peace pipe with tribal
leaders and dons chief's regalia himself.

Backstage at the San Francisco
Opera House during a 1977 U.S.
tour, Charles exchanges kisses with
singer Pamela South.

WIDE WORLD PHOTOS

ANWAR HUSSEIN

ANWAR HUSSEIN

LEFT: Facing a poisonous snake on his 1978 visit
to Brazil, Charles keeps a wary distance, but
enthusiastically swings into a samba
(RIGHT:) with a young Brazilian dancer.

WIDE WORLD PHOTOS

For his first visit to a communist country in November, 1978, Charles chooses Yugoslavia. Through an interpreter, Charles chats with the 86-year-old Tito at the spa of Igalo.

The Prince joins the pupils of St. George's School, Maida Vale, in their presentation of a dance.

Prince Charles joins Welsh-born singer Shirley Bassey after a benefit performance for the Prince's Charities at the Club Double Diamond in Cacrphilly, Wales in December 1978.

In Yugoslavia, there are more than
political encounters. Here the Prince
is surrounded by a clutch of
Balkan beauties.

ANWAR HUSSEIN

At London's Palladium in 1978 for a
benefit performance, Charles talks
with Farrah Fawcett-Majors.

ECHAVE & ASSOCIATES

Practicing at Smith's Lawn, Windsor,
for an international polo match in 1972.

Mirroring the Gordonstoun tradition,
Charles rides full gallop down the
course at Ascot.

Chevening House in Kent, a gracious, 83-room,
17th-century mansion, may one day become
Charles' official residence as heir to the throne.

ANWAR HUSSEIN

Charles is the first member of the Royal Family to
shoot on Britain's famed Bisley rifle ranges.

ANWAR HUSSEIN

Windsurfing—sailing on a surfboard—is one of the
most recent sports to catch the Prince's attention.

Promoted to commander in the Royal Navy after leaving fulltime active duty, Charles, naval sword in hand, here wears his new rank as a "three-striper."

LEFT: At Windsor, in his uniform as Wing Commander in the Royal Air Force.

ANWAR HUSSEIN

In his tunic and bearskin as Colonel of the
Welsh Guards, Charles watches the Trooping
of the Colour.

In this 1977 photo, Charles wears a sweat shirt of his own design, with the name of the mine hunter he commanded and the three-feathered crest of the Prince of Wales with the motto Ich Dien ("I serve").

NEXT PAGE: For his 30th birthday photo, Charles poses at Balmoral Castle with Harvey, a pet retriever.

CHAPTER NINE

Noblesse Oblige

THE FOCAL POINT of the British monarchy is Buckingham Palace, an austere gray slab whose imposing facade looks down the Mall to Admiralty Arch and Trafalgar Square beyond. Outside its iron railings the London traffic swirls around on its way between fashionable Knightsbridge and Chelsea on the one hand and the City and Westminster on the other. It is poised between the London of commerce and government and what *Time* magazine once referred to as "swinging London." On the high days of royal life, after ceremonial parades or weddings down the road at Westminster Abbey, the Queen and her family will gather on the balcony to smile and wave down to the throng below. Every day at 11 A.M. the guard is changed to the sound of martial music and the click of hundreds of tourist cameras.

From the flagpole on the very center of the Palace roof the royal standard, that imperial banner of gold and scarlet and blue, flies whenever the Queen is at home, and if you happen to be passing you may talk to one of the policemen on the gate and nip in through the little door at the north end and sign the visitor's book, as thousands do every year.

Behind all that pomp and grandeur there are people at work. There may be ceremonial guards at the front but if you go round

167

the side, down the road called Buckingham Gate which leads toward Victoria railway station, you will find the back door. It doesn't look nearly as grand but it's rather busier. By the royal mews where they keep the horses, the cars are parked. Secretaries and footmen, equerries and speech writers, tradesmen and civil servants come this way, and inside the Palace they work in an atmosphere which is more like a government department across the park in Whitehall than most people's idea of a royal palace. Notice boards, for example, display in-house advertisements of cars for sale—one footman trying to sell his old Renault to another; there are announcements about the doings of the Buckingham Palace Judo Association. So despite the thick red carpets, the liveried servants, the valuable paintings hung everywhere, there is also the unmistakeable whiff of office block.

Prince Charles's suite of rooms is on the south side of the Palace, on the third floor, and it is here that he lives and works, much of the time assisted by a growing team of helpers. For many years his official life was looked after by Squadron Leader David Checketts, a former Royal Air Force officer usually credited with helping to mold the Prince's career into its present shape. Checketts was one of Prince Philip's men, and though he has hardly been a maverick he shares Prince Philip's relatively informal approach—one which is greatly at variance with the more traditional manner of the predominantly old Etonian royal servants the Queen inherited from her father. Checketts has just left the royal service and is to be replaced by a younger and more orthodox man, Edward Adeane. The Adeanes have long been courtiers. His father was an equerry and Assistant Secretary to King George VI through the whole of his reign and was the Queen's private secretary for the first nineteen years of *her* reign. The choice of young Edward is considered both sound and predictable.

With the departure of Checketts the Prince's Office will become very much his own shop. Because Checketts had been in a sense a surrogate father—he had for example been Charles's only companion on that traumatic adolescent trip to Timbertop in Australia—the relationship was never likely to survive into

Charles's majority. It was difficult for Checketts to abandon his
pseudo-paternal role and adopt the deferential attitude that
Palace convention demands. He was older, more experienced,
and he was used to being in charge. Some observers have
reported a strain between the two men, though it certainly
doesn't show most of the time. In his public appearances
throughout 1978 and early 1979, Charles was invariably
accompanied by Checketts and there were always smiles all
around. But when he goes Charles will be working with men
whom he appointed himself and who are in their thirties—not
much older than himself. There will be no doubt about who is in
charge.

At the beginning of 1979 the Palace issued Charles's program
for the first six months of the year. From the third of March
until the sixth of April he was scheduled to visit Hong Kong,
Singapore, Australia and Canada. In Hong Kong, one of the few
remaining British colonies, just off the coast of mainland China,
he was visiting King Edward VII's own Gurkhas, of which he is
Colonel-in-Chief. The Gurkhas are the only mercenaries in the
British Army. They come from the Himalayan state of Nepal.
During the rest of his trip Charles visited two more regiments of
which he is Colonel-in-Chief (The Royal Winnipeg Rifles and
the Royal Regiment of Canada). He saw two United World
Colleges—one in Singapore and one in Victoria, British
Columbia—in his capacity as president of their International
Council. Otherwise he was due to open a Prince of Wales
Museum in Yellowknife in Canada's northwest territories and to
spend no less than sixteen days in Western Australia helping the
state celebrate its 150th anniversary. All this ties in with the
Royal Family's continuing belief in the Commonwealth, the
association of former British Empire countries which still
maintain a special relationship with the Crown. Charles, a keen
supporter of the Commonwealth, recently joined the board of
the Commonwealth Development Corporation, which doles out
money to deserving Commonwealth causes (he attended four
meetings during the first six months of 1979).

Royal visits to these places are not strictly ceremonial
gestures as one might suppose. The Queen is still Queen of

Canada and of Australia. Her likeness appears on banknotes and postage stamps there, and the Governor-Generals are her appointed representatives. And despite mutterings in both countries royalty still looks to be well-established. In Canada's latest Federal-Provincial talks, for example, all eleven premiers—including the separatist René Levesque of Quebec—confirmed that the monarchy should remain in charge. So even though the Empire has been dissolved and the map is no longer pink, Charles is visiting countries which will one day be his: Canada and Australia may no longer be British, but they are still royal.

Much of the rest of Charles's program is educational. If he is to lead the nation he has to know as much as possible about how it works. On Tuesday, February 13, 1979, he went to 10 Downing Street, where Britain's then socialist premier, the avuncular "Smiling Jim" Callaghan, presided. Charles spent the day there, sitting in on a Cabinet meeting and going down to Parliament after lunch to hear Callaghan taken to task by Her Majesty's Loyal Opposition.

Charles has also been busily familiarizing himself with British industry. The National Economic Development Office has been arranging a comprehensive program: visits to trucking companies, two days with the Glacier Metal Company (a manufacturer of machine tools and engine parts), a visit to the headquarters of the Amalgamated Union of Engineering Workers, a couple of days on a trawler off northwest Scotland to see the fishing industry in action, and so on—until February 21, when Charles addressed the Parliamentary and Scientific Committee over lunch at the Savoy Hotel on the subject of labor-management relations.

At the time of Charles's speech Britain was embroiled in a continuing series of strikes by garbage collectors, hospital workers, newspaper employees and others. Charles put the blame for the situation on the shoulders of management. "I have not the slightest hesitation in making the observation that much of British management doesn't seem to understand the importance of the human factor," he said, and reporting on his recent NEDO-sponsored tour, remarked, "I discovered during

170

my recent visits that the problem of communication between management and shop floor frequently stems from a failure of communication within management." He also criticized the failure of management to discuss company performance with the workers, saying, "Open management involves a readiness to talk frankly and honestly with employees and their representatives about company performance, prospects and problems in good times as well as bad." He went on to tell his startled audience that the root of the problem lay in the British educational system. "The sort of knowledge the British attribute to high status tends to be abstract, heavily dependent upon books and textbooks, and hence somewhat divorced from the commonsense everyday world of the learners. It is little wonder, therefore, that by comparison with West Germany and France, too few of our graduates actually go into industry—and those that do tend to have an irrelevant educational discipline."

His controversial management speech brought on outspoken attacks. Sir John Methven, the sometimes sardonic Director General of the Confederation of British Industry, remarked, "We have to find solutions to our problems of productivity and inadequate profitability. I feel sure that if Prince Charles were to spend two or three years actively coping with problems like these he would come to understand that solutions are not that easy to understand." Stronger denunciations of the Prince's speech followed—from the rightwing *Daily Mail,* former socialist Cabinet Minister Richard Marsh and even a former Cambridge acquaintance of Charles who had gone into industrial management. Charles did not back off, and there were those who championed his stance. In Portsmouth, where Charles was due to receive the freedom of the City, a group of striking council workers who had been planning anti-monarchical demonstrations did an about-face, and in gratitude for Charles's support cancelled their demonstration, went back to work and cleaned up the factory so that it was spick and span for the royal visit. Charles must have been gratified by this show of support, but the overtures of other new-found allies may have been less welcome: The communist newspaper the *Morning Star* ran the Prince's remarks on the front page with editorial approval, and in Parliament leftwing socialists tried to approve Charles's criticisms of management in debate but were ruled out of order when they mentioned him by name—according to the rule of the British House of Commons it is not proper for a member of the Royal Family to be mentioned by name.

By the end of that week, Prince Charles was back in the altogether more familiar and congenial surrounds of the Royal Navy, where he is more uncritically accepted than anywhere else, and was present at the recommissioning of the aircraft carrier H.M.S. *Bulwark*. Such military and naval duties remain an essential part of the royal role, and are divided among the various members of the family. There is not one of them who does not have special links with ships or regiments or air squadrons, and as with most countries (note the example of the ex-Shah of Iran) it is in the armed forces that loyalty to hereditary monarchies tends to remain strongest.

In the first six months of 1979 Prince Charles spent much of his six weeks' foreign tour visiting service units, though these were not his only military duties. As Colonel-in-Chief of the Royal Regiment of Wales, he naturally attended their 10th anniversary celebrations on June 9; he is also Colonel-in-Chief of the Gordon Highlanders, so he also attended their Regimental Dinner on June 15; and as Colonel-in-Chief of the Parachute Regiment he was due to see them training in Denmark in early July. Most Colonels-in-Chief are reasonably orthodox, but Charles has added some distinctive touches to his colonelship. On his first visit to the regiment in Germany, for example, some of the men mentioned that they acutely felt the lack of female company. The Colonel-in-Chief listened attentively, but unlike most Colonels-in-Chief, who would have muttered something British about that being "dashed bad luck" and had they tried taking cold showers, this Colonel-in-Chief went home to his palace and compiled an Englo-German phrase book. *"Was sagen Sie zu einem kleinem Getränk?"* went one typical question, which was translated, "What about a drink, then?" In a typically humorous aside Charles added, "Don't worry if she won't, you need one anyway." Two hundred copies were printed, and the men of the Royal Regiment of Wales were duly grateful that they had a considerate young Colonel-in-Chief with a command of German and an eye for a pretty girl.

All of this may seem—and, of course, to a considerable extent is—marking time. But it is a time of preparation, and therefore, in its fashion, serious business.

"The first moment I knew I was heir to the throne is one of the most difficult questions to answer," Prince Charles told a radio interviewer, Jack de Manio. "It was something that dawns on you in the most ghastly inexorable sense. I didn't suddenly wake up in my pram one day and realize I was going to be King.

"Slowly you get the idea that you have a certain duty and responsibility, and I think it is better that way. It's a lot nicer than someone telling you suddenly you must do this or that because you are who you are."

As the present Prince of Wales and future King of England Charles takes pains to inform himself about all aspects of life in the United Kingdom. "I needn't be a figurehead," he says. "I can—and I do—participate. I believe in trying to lead from the front. I get monthly reports about what's going on. What is happening to them in Ireland, for instance. I want to be kept informed about the wounded, the widows, the families . . ." On a lighter note he adds, "And whether they are winning the Army rugby cup—which they nearly always are."

There are varied routines in Prince Charles's life. He is usually early to bed and early to rise. He likes to start the day with exercise—a swim in the indoor pool if he is at Buckingham Palace, a jog around the grounds if he is staying with friends. On a typical business day at Buckingham Palace he spends the morning in private meetings—with officers from his regiments, with delegates from organizations and societies of which he is a patron, with administrators of the Duchy of Cornwall. It is an endless procession. Business luncheons often end the morning, with more meetings, or visits to worthy institutions, consuming the afternoon. There are, of course, frequent royal occasions in which Charles is a main participant. He is equally at home in the magnificent ceremonial uniforms he's obliged to wear for such occasions as the Queen's birthday parade and in battle fatigues on the Army's German training grounds. He is also comfortable in his honorary role as Colonel-in-Chief of the Welsh regiment, and gets along well with both officers and men, who tend to be impressed by his toughness and skills as well as his evident compassion and consideration. Riding out in his scarlet and gold to review the troops is good practice for future kingly responsibilities, and a not wholly unwelcome chore.

Right now Charles sees his primary job as providing a form of leadership for his country. "I think it is trying to set an example," he explains. "To help push people along to be encouraged, to warn, advise, amuse. Everything to give people pleasure and a sense of purpose in life . . . by congratulating them and generally being seen to show interest . . ."

Since leaving the Navy at the end of 1976 Charles has greatly added to the portfolio of special interests, loosely referred to as princely "patronages." There are 170 patronages now and they indicate the rather astonishing breadth of his interests: He is patron of the Royal Anthropological Institute of Great Britain, commodore of the Royal Thames Yacht Club, patron of the Somerset County Federation of Young Farmers' Clubs, patron of the Royal Game Fair, president of the Royal Aero Club, president of the Bach Choir, and more. His memberships include such associations as the Zoological Society of London, the Melbourne Cricket Club, the Hawaii Polo Club and the Aston-Martin Owners' Club. Who else in the world could fit that eclectic portmanteau into one solitary life—and if he could, would he manage to pay more than cursory attention to each? "Not bloody likely!" as an earthy Prince Charles would—and does—say.

Charles does not take on new commitments lightly . . . "There is no point in just being a figurehead or a name at the top of a letter," he says, "which is actually what a lot of organizations want you to be and sometimes they get amazed when you do actually show interest . . . If you don't do it on that basis you never stop because I get hundreds of invitations every year, or every month, to do goodness knows how many things. . . ."

In 1974, for example, he took on the patronage of the Royal

Anthropological Institute. Since the beginning of the century the R.A.I. has had a royal patron, but for the most part they took only a formal interest in the Institute's affairs. In 1972 Charles's cousin, Prince William of Gloucester, took the job on and immediately injected a breezy note and an involvement which was quite new. Soon afterward William was killed piloting his private airplane and Charles took over. "Now what attracts me," he said in a newspaper interview, "is that the stronger and more widely influential the Anthropological Institute could be, the better contribution it could make to Britain in facing the problems of a multi-racial society [which of late have been increasingly surfacing]. The more people understand about the background of the immigrants who come to this country, the less apprehensive they would be about them. To get on neighborly terms with people of other races and countries you've got to get more familiar with them; know how they live, how they eat, how they work, what makes them laugh . . . and their history . . . you can't remove people's apprehensions in one night but you can make a start by making them more knowledgeable. If the Anthropological Institute can help to do that, I'm going to need help." Since then Charles has addressed meetings, fronted a series of BBC films and generally taken a positive and constructive interest in the Institute's work. Here as elsewhere he seems a popular and industrious patron.

The main stated reason for his leaving the Navy was that he was to take on the Queen's Silver Jubilee Appeal. Actually this was only half of the reason. After commanding the *Bronington* he would not have had another independent command for some years. Much of the point of the Navy service was to give him the chance to command men, and no one thought that five or six years tied to a desk in the Ministry of Defence in Whitehall was a useful preparation for kingship. Therefore, Charles had to be taken out of the Navy, and the Queen's Jubilee Appeal was a fine pretext for doing so.

Monarchy is peculiarly susceptible to anniversaries. Royal birthdays in Britain are celebrated with the broadcasting of the national anthem and twenty-fifth and fiftieth anniversaries are occasions for outbreaks of quite remarkable national jollity.

Queen Victoria's jubilees gave rise to amazing parties and parades, which a few very ancient Britons still claim to remember.

For Queen Elizabeth II's twenty-fifth anniversary as monarch Britain planned a splendid series of events to lighten the prevailing public gloom. The Queen and Prince Philip made visits to every part of the kingdom; there were banquets, fireworks, and a network of great bonfires or beacons such as the one that warned Britain of the Spanish Armada four hundred years earlier. At the local level every village and borough organized celebrations. In London and other cities nearly every street put on its own party and competed with other streets in trying to provide brighter decorations, noisier music, and stronger drink. London had seen nothing like it since VE Day at the end of World War II.

To give the Jubilee some extra meaning and to commemorate the event in a more permanent sense, Prince Charles was put in charge of a Jubilee Appeal. There was a precedent for this. Just over forty years earlier his predecessor as Prince of Wales had launched an appeal to mark the twenty-fifth anniversary of his father's reign. That appeal had been a tremendous success, and the money was still in existence, administered by a body called the King George V Jubilee Trust.

On April 24, 1977, Charles launched the appeal in a televised broadcast from Chevening—the first time his possible future residence had been used officially. He seemed nervous; the director hadn't told him to keep his hands still. Like his father, Charles has always had a hand problem, never seeming sure where to put them. He is constantly shifting them from deep in jacket pockets to that familiar royal "clasp-behind-the-back," or rubbing them together, or using them to jab the air for emphasis. Nevertheless, this time the ubiquitous hands obviously had an hypnotic effect, because the money immediately started to roll in, much of it simply addressed to "Prince Charles, Buckingham Palace, London."

"In the midst of all the celebration," said Charles, "I felt that it would be marvelous if there was some permanent way in which we could mark the twenty-five years of service which the Queen has given to the country and the Commonwealth. So I asked my mother what she could like us to do. After careful consideration she said she would be particularly pleased if money could be raised principally to assist and encourage the outstanding work already being done by young people in various fields."

By the time the marathon was finished 31,000 Britons had personally sent money to Prince Charles and many more had contributed in other ways. By April, 1978, when the books were closed, the Appeal had raised sixteen million pounds, a staggering sum for a country in the throes of massive inflation and rising unemployment—it represented thirteen pence (just over a quarter) for every inhabitant of the British Isles, man, woman and child.

Charles boosted the figure with constant public appearances, more appeals and a good deal of behind-the-scenes administrative work. As much of the time as possible the fund-raising was tied in with entertainment. For example, on one day that summer fund-raising on behalf of Prince Charles's appeal was going on at a musical pageant in Luton, a Victorian Evening in Oldham, a Jubilee Gala Day in Clydebank, a One-Day Horse Trail in Northern Ireland, a Carnival and Ox Roast in Holmfirth, a Real Ale Festival in Loughton, an Anglo-Latvian Evening in Leicestershire, A Navy Day in Salisbury and a *Son et Lumière* at East Linton. People tend to part with money more readily if they are enjoying themselves, a point Charles appreciated as much as anyone. He has always been keen on local involvement, on people coming up with their own ideas, so much of the year's happenings had a spontaneous, joyful feel to them.

Now that the Jubilee money had been raised, though, it had to be spent. For that the Executive Committee meets four times a year under Prince Charles's chairmanship and decides how the funds will be allocated. The motto of the Trust is "To Help Young People Help Others." Much of the day-to-day organization of the Jubilee Trust is done from Neilson-McCarthy, the public relations firm of which Squadron Leader Checketts is a director. (This firm used to work for Aristotle Onassis and continues to look after Christina's affairs.) Beth Berrington-

Haynes, who was recently made a member of the Royal Victorian Order for her work with the Trust, says that Prince Charles encourages people to think up their own ideas and put them into effect. Charles's philosophy is designed to stimulate initiative in the Trust's recipients. If they have a genuinely worthwhile scheme the Trust will help out, but the Trust's money has to be matched by the beneficiaries' effort. By the end of 1978 more than £2 million had been given to almost 2,000 projects. Most of the money is being invested and the income from what is now known as The Royal Jubilee Trusts will be used to provide grants in the future. Charles continues to pay close attention to all the applicants and the successful schemes are a good indication of his own priorities. Money has gone, for example, to help people in the Scottish county of Angus to renovate a local community hall; to provide weekend courses for youth and community leaders in Berwickshire; to renovate an ambulance used by a volunteer body in the English midlands; to help school children make tape recordings of local newspapers for blind people; to help young people provide Sunday meals for the elderly in Oxford; to enable young volunteers to restore a cottage in the troubled province of Ulster (to be shared at weekends by people of both the Protestant and Catholic faiths); to provide special equipment for a group of handicapped children who use a London adventure playground; to rebuild a village bus shelter; to support a former coal mine band of workers which ran into hard times after its north country coal mine was forced to close.

In an increasingly socialist country—Tory victories such as Macmillan's and Thatcher's only lightly modify it—much of the good works done in the country are based on charity and voluntary work. The Royal Family has traditionally encouraged this, seldom taking any part in commercial activity and then only when the proceeds go to charity or will benefit the country as a whole. Charles often tells the story of how, on a visit to Japan, he managed to persuade a Japanese company to set up a factory in Wales. Obviously that had very specific commercial benefits for particular people, but the most important aspect of the deal from his point of view was that it brought work to the people of his principality. They were poor and they were out of work and he was helping them. He could not—or would not—have taken on a paid directorship of the company, much less accepted a commission. Both might have been perfectly normal business practice, but members of the Royal Family are not permitted (by convention if not by law) to indulge in "perfectly normal business practice." Lord Snowdon, when he was married to Princess Margaret, continued his career as a photographer and Angus Ogilvy continued to have considerable business interests and directorships while married to Princess Alexandra, but both men were related to the House of Windsor by marriage rather than blood, and they were well removed from the immediate line of succession. One suspects it will be some time before Britain ever has a company director for a King.

Like his father, whose Duke of Edinburgh's Award Scheme is a leading organization in encouraging the development of young people, Charles is a great promoter of youth. "I'm intrigued with the problem of how to interest young people in a reasonably responsible type of existence," said Charles in a BBC interview. "The great difficulty is to provide younger people with adventurous opportunity, particularly in urban areas where there's limited resources for entertainment. I think this tends to bring out boredom and other things, and I believe that with their energetic impulses released in adventurous exercises, particularly in urban areas, one can do quite a lot to reduce the difficulties." One of Charles's more attractive traits is the way he translates words into action. On December 1, 1972, he invited a group of social workers and one police representative along to Buckingham Palace. Charles was twenty-four at the time, filled with a youthful idealism, conscious of his own privileged position and upbringing, anxious to provide some benefits to people of his own age who had been born into a working-class slums and whose deprived conditions might well force them into a life of total aimlessness, or even crime. The meeting was a success, the social workers going away impressed with the Prince and his ideas and determined to put their unexpected but influential ally to good use. There followed a series of consultations, conversations and meetings, and later when

Charles was in the Navy there were exchanges of letters and papers. Finally in the spring of 1976 the Queen gave her permission for the setting up of The Prince's Trust. The aim of the Trust was "to enable young people to find adventure, excitement and achievement by carrying through their own enterprises, which contribute to their own or other people's welfare and development." Echoes of Kurt Hahn, and Gordonstoun: "Adventure, excitement and achievement!"

Shortly before, Charles had spoken in the House of Lords (the first member of the Royal Family to do so in living memory) and had modestly touched on the work he wanted to do with The Prince's Trust. But it was agreed by all involved that it should remain as low-key as possible, royalty not always enjoying the affection of the young and underprivileged. As it turned out, however, Prince Charles was an exception to this rule. George Pratt, the probation officer who administers the scheme in his spare time, says that Charles's name inspired nothing but confidence among the young people he was trying to help.

The Trust has so far been a small, productive operation. Unlike other charities it has no administrative costs—everyone, including, of course, Prince Charles himself, provides his time and work free of charge. Stationery and printing have been provided for nothing and all traveling expenses have been met by an anonymous donor. To raise more money for the Trust, an Appeals and Special Resources Committee was set up which included a number of prominent British entertainment figures like Eric Morecambe and Jimmy Tarbuck, two of the country's best known stand-up comics (Charles is getting increasingly adept at cross-fertilizing different areas of his life; his celebrated sense of humor has been effective in getting professional comedians to help out with the more serious side of his responsibilities).

With The Prince's Trust, as with The Jubilee Trust, Charles was adamant that people should not merely be helped but should be helped to help themselves. The official application form states: "Projects should preferably have about them an element of adventure and personal initiative and should not require long-term financial aid." In practice this has meant that money has been undramatically, even unobtrusively, spent. When a boys' cycling club wanted some new bikes the Trust provided money for spare parts and frames. The boys built the bikes themselves and then provided a special messenger service for the old people of the neighborhood. The Trust also gave money for a sports center which was to be shared between the physically and socially disadvantaged. And equally without fanfare Charles provided money to some young people who wanted to brighten their drab street with murals and couldn't afford the paint, and to a handicapped boy who was trying to develop a talent for glass engraving. These activities did not make banner headlines in the newspapers, but they are an index to Charles's character and concerns.

That thirst for adventure and greater understanding, which seems to lie at the root of so much of Charles's activities, is even more apparent in another of his most favored patronages—the United World Colleges. Until 1978 his uncle, Lord Mountbatten, was president of the Colleges, but then he relinquished them to Charles. "[The colleges are] one of the most exciting and important experiments in international education in the world today," remarked Mountbatten, and Charles echoes his enthusiasm.

Originally the Colleges were one of Kurt Hahn's projects. That unusual and unorthodox educator, having seen Gordonstoun blossom from a hazardous experiment into a successful and prosperous school, switched his attentions to an Elizabethan Castle on the coast of South Wales. The building had once been the property of the eccentric millionaire newspaper baron William Randolph Hearst, who had installed such not so eccentric luxuries as plumbing and electric lights. Combining a certain historic grandeur with the modern comforts, it seemed to Hahn an ideal place for a school. But this was a school with a difference. First, it was international; only twenty-five percent of its pupils came from Britain. And in predictable Hahn fashion the school was dedicated to service. There was a lifeboat station and a mountain and cliff rescue station, and while some students helped with the home farm others became involved in Britain's first underwater conservation scheme on the remote island of

Lundy in the middle of the nearby Bristol Channel.

There are now two more developed colleges modeled on that first "Atlantic College" at St. Donat's Castle, one at Singapore and the other on the southern shores of Canada's Vancouver Island near the British Columbian capital of Victoria. Now the World Colleges are busily pioneering a new international exam system devised by Alec Petersen, a distinguished former don at Oxford University who has produced an International Baccalaureate which has come to be accepted by universities around the world. In addition to languages, mathematics and science, new courses have been added to the World Colleges curriculum on such subjects as the theory of knowledge and the study of man. As a product himself of the unorthodox Gordonstoun and Timbertop, Charles champions the innovations of the World Colleges. They are a project after his own heart—he loves adventure; he admires dedication; he is inspired by the idea of international understanding as exemplified by the Commonwealth.

In April, 1978, at the first Colleges committee meeting under his chairmanship, Charles unveiled a plaque in memory of Kurt Hahn. It was inscribed with some words by the great English historian, George Trevelyan: "Two passions are not likely to die in this world—love of country and love of liberty. They can be kept pure by one ideal which can tame and yet not weaken them . . . tender love of all mankind." Moved, Charles went on to say that his acceptance of the presidency was "based on a really deep and personal conviction of the intrinsic merits of the United World Colleges concept."

"He really takes a genuine personal interest," says Sir Ian Gourley. "I personally send him a monthly news letter with a report of our activities. And I'm constantly in touch with his staff at the Palace." Gourley, a dark, lean former Commandant-General of the British Royal Marine Corps, was personally recruited as UWC's chief executive by Lord Mountbatten, who had met Gourlay in the Marines. "Of course he takes his own initiatives," says Gourlay, outlining Charles's role as president. "He's got a lot of his father in him. A real enthusiast. He's often on the phone to me saying, 'Why aren't we doing this? Why don't we do that?' He'll always call me to tell me how he's got on on a foreign trip, because he's always looking after our interests when he's abroad. 'We *did it!*' he'll say. I hope that the ideals of the movement really get into his soul, and that he continues to get involved in the way he does now."

It seems certain he will, because working for the Colleges fits in so neatly with his travels. The UWC have an international network of old boys, and old girls, and in every country he visits Charles meets the national committee. Gourlay, who has been present on these occasions, comments, "They're all charmed off the twig. He does it immaculately. There was quite a lot of opposition to having a royal person when it was first suggested. People said it wasn't the mood of the seventies. But the fact is that you need someone of high elevation who can be listened to in the councils of the world. One knew he would convince the over-thirties, but the effect he's had on people of sixteen to eighteen has been remarkable. I think what really does it is that he's genuinely interested in them and he communicates with them so well."

Early in his presidency of the Colleges Charles visited St. Donat's, and on his year's tour of the world in 1979 he visited Singapore and Vancouver as well. Whenever possible he takes out a boat and puts the students through their paces, leading, as usual, from the front rather than—like W.S. Gilbert's Duke of Plazatoro—from some safe position in the rear. Whenever possible he will lobby kings or presidents or prime ministers incessantly to get them to commit funds to the Colleges (which rely heavily on scholarships from friendly countries). He is a tireless ambassador, an endless innovator, a constant reminder to those around him that he is interested. *Actively* interested.

The Colleges, though, are only one of his many jobs. There are also his various activities in Wales, such as the Prince of Wales's Committee on the Environment, the awards of which he was presenting on that overcast day in Ebbw Vale mentioned in Chapter One. There are the constant pressures of "the boxes," as the official papers are called (though Charles's are actually contained in large blue bags). Almost every day he receives a selection of cabinet and ministerial papers, nearly all classified (even his father is not supposed to see them). He does not act on them except when his mother is away, and he is left as one of the Council of Regency, not yet being part of the curious, unwritten British constitution in the way that his mother is. But he gets the papers all the same; it is part of his education just like his day in 10 Downing Street or his visit to the Industrial Truck Company.

For the moment the royal job remains almost frighteningly undefined. There are no meaningful precedents. Charles's predecessors lived in quite different worlds. Today's Prince of Wales has to contend with a critical press that does not hesitate to speak its mind, and with television coverage that scrutinizes his every gesture. Hardly a moment passes without another request for his time—to open this, to preside over that, to visit such-and-such, to dine with so-and-so. Not a decision can be taken that is not open to question and re-examination. At issue is not only his own future but also that of the institution of which he is a part: an institution that has lasted more than nine hundred years with only one break. Charles does not intend to be the second King Charles to be removed by revolution.

Being heir to the throne and a royal prince is not a job, then, but a whole series of jobs. Charles's may not have power in the way that the Prime Minister has, but he certainly has influence—and knows he must exercise it with real discretion. Those who ask him to be their president or their colonel-in-chief; who are prepared to listen avidly to his views on everything from industry to the weather; who bow deferentially to him and call him "Sir" all believe that in some mysterious way Charles is not like other people. It is a mystical belief that there is, as Shakespeare put it, "a divinity that doth hedge a king." You either believe it or you don't. At the moment enough people, at least in Britain, believe it for the Prince, like other members of the Royal Family, to have more offers of patronage than he can accept and more work than he can cope with. But the monarchy is not only a piece of mystique or mumbo-jumbo to be accepted or abandoned according to taste. It still has real power and a place in the British Constitution. Prince Charles is the heir apparent to it all. . . .

Britain does not have a written constitution, so the precise powers of the monarch are difficult to define. Much popular understanding is based on the writings of a 19th-century political journalist named Walter Bagehot, widely acknowledged to be the ultimate authority. However, since 1867, when Bagehot wrote, much has changed, and he needs bringing up to date.

Technically, the King or Queen of England is empowered to appoint or dismiss ministers, dissolve Parliament or veto legislation. The monarch rarely has occasion to exercise any of these powers, but it *can* happen. For example, in 1963 the Prime Minister, Harold Macmillan, suddenly resigned because of ill-health, leaving no obvious successor. There were several candidates, most of whom promoted themselves aggressively to their colleagues in the ruling Conservative Party. There was a party conference on at the time and the air was thick with intrigue. Ultimately the Queen gave the job to Lord Home (who resigned his title to become Sir Alec Douglas-Home), because she was advised to do so by Harold Macmillan. But Macmillan's advice was not binding because he had resigned as Prime Minister and so had no authority. There was much discontent in the Conservative Party, and a new election procedure has since been set up to prevent such an occurrence. As it happens, though he was a surprising choice, Home was an acceptable compromise, and although the documents have never been made public it seems that the palace officials consulted with several key politicians in the party. But as one expert said, it would have been better if consultation had not only taken place but "have been seen to have taken place."

The likelihood of the future King Charles ever having to make a real choice over the appointment of a Prime Minister is remote. Under the British system the Prime Minister is automatically the leader of the party which commands a majority in the House of Commons. But it could happen. If, for example, a Prime Minister resigned because he was outvoted by his Cabinet: should King Charles then call on the Leader of the Opposition? Or try to get his politicians to form a coalition? Or ask the defeated Prime Minister to hold on until his party had elected a successor? Or appoint an interim Prime Minister until a new leader was elected? Whatever the answer—and any one of them would be constitutionally possible—the choice would be King Charles's and King Charles's alone.

And, of course, if King Charles were able to appoint a new Prime Minister, he could also dismiss one. If a Prime Minister went mad or became involved in a Watergate-style scandal and then refused to resign, King Charles might be obliged to dismiss him—it is, at least theoretically, possible. In 1975 in Australia, where the constitution is different, the Queen's representative, Governor-General Sir John Kerr, dismissed the sitting Prime Minister, Gough Whitlam. The Senate, which in Australia has equal powers with the Lower House, refused to vote further monies for Whitlam unless he called an election. Whitlam refused, and Kerr fired him. There was a general uproar about this, but Whitlam was not re-elected at the next general election. Kerr, the Queen's representative, was almost certainly within his rights, but the thought of another such brouhaha diminishes the already slim chances that Prince Charles will ever become Governor-General of Australia.

The future King Charles could also, though, dissolve or refuse to dissolve Parliament. The dissolution of Parliament marks the end of the government in power and is an inevitable prelude to a general election. Normally the Prime Minister decides when to dissolve Parliament, but there have been occasions in the Commonwealth where a Governor-General has refused to grant the Prime Minister's request for a dissolution. It has happened three times this century. And after the February, 1974, British election there was much speculation that Sir Harold Wilson, the new minority Prime Minister, might be defeated at the very beginning of Parliament. If this had happened Wilson would have asked for a dissolution and a new election in which he would hope to gain an overall parliamentary majority. But would the Queen have been compelled to grant the dissolution request? Many people thought not. She could have asked the Conservative Leader Mr. Heath to try to form a minority government of his own. The Leader of the House, Mr. Edward Short, later commented: "Constitutional lawyers of the highest authority are of the clear opinion that the

Sovereign is not in all circumstances bound to grant a Prime Minister's request for a dissolution. But the exercise of the royal prerogative in this matter is not determined only by past constitutional usages and precedents: *the relevance of those usages and precedents has to be considered in relation to the actual circumstances."*

It is unlikely that King Charles will find himself caught up in the kind of crisis which would involve him in taking such far-reaching decisions, but he *could* and certainly *would* take them if the need arose. A leading Conservative political theorist, Sir Ian Gilmour, has written that "the prerogative has always contained an element of emergency power, and unquestionably some emergency power remains in the Sovereign personally as opposed to the Crown."

Or in other words, the politicians remain in charge unless or until they make a total mess of things. If, however, they go against the will of the people, then it is the sovereign's right, and duty, to safeguard the people. If a British Parliament repealed the Parliament Act and continued to sit without elections every five years—and if the House of Lords agreed to this—then the monarch would be the only person able to dissolve Parliament and force an election. The royal veto has not been used since the reign of Queen Anne more than two hundred-and-fifty years ago, but there is no constitutional reason why it could not be revived.

King Charles probably won't have to do anything quite so drastic. British politicians, including socialists, tend to be a well-mannered lot with a regard for precedent and established practice. They like Kings and Queens. Every week the Prime Minister goes to Buckingham Palace to report on the state of the nation. The sovereign, regularly apprised of government business by the daily official papers, listens and discusses. As Bagehot wrote, "The sovereign has, under a constitutional monarchy such as ours, three rights—the right to be consulted, the right to encourage, the right to warn." At these audiences the Queen, with the benefit of an experience which stretches back over a quarter of a century to the premiership of Winston Churchill, is a unique—if demanding—taskmaster. When

Harold Wilson relinquished office he said, "I shall certainly advise my successor to do his homework before his audience and to read all his telegrams and Cabinet Committee papers in time, and not leave them to the weekend, or he will feel like an unprepared schoolboy."

Prince Charles has already seen government working at close quarters; has spoken in the House of Lords; and revealed a keen interest in the political process. He already sees the official, secret papers and knows more about the day-to-day business of government than any politician outside the Cabinet. When the time comes for him to take over his mother's job, he will be very well prepared and know that though in normal times it will be enough "to be consulted, to encourage and to warn," there could be times in which he will be called upon to act as well. Times would have to be in crisis but, in the words of political commentator Peregrine Worsthorne, "On the person of no other non-elected head of state in the world, in a comparable crisis, would so much depend—for good or ill."

CHAPTER TEN

The Sporting Prince

AS A CHILD Prince Charles was less than a gifted athlete. At Cheam he captained the school soccer team, but they scored only four goals and gave up eighty-two. At that stage of his life Charles was a rather chubby, gawky boy, without the grace and poise that would come with the years. It was always his sister Anne who recklessly climbed trees while Charles stood at the bottom pondering the dangers of the ascent. Yet today Charles is transformed—fit, muscular and courageous—seemingly a born sportsman.

It is, however, the country pursuits rather than conventional sports at which Charles excels. At Gordonstoun and Timbertop outdoor pursuits and community service were emphasized at the expense of the more conventional cricket, rugby and soccer of other fee-paying establishments such as Eton, Harrow and Winchester. Then, too, the Royal Family was a country family with an eye and an aptitude for country pursuits, and in these Prince Charles was indoctrinated early. His mother was as good a horsewoman as Princess Anne is now, although unlike her daughter the Queen never took part in international three-day-event competitions. Although Charles was unable to ride at school he made up for lost time during vacations, and early in his riding career his father began to teach him the elements of his own greatest sporting love: polo. Charles is now as great a polo enthusiast as Prince Philip. "I love polo," he says. "I love the game, I love the exercise. It's my one extravagance."

Polo is not a game that is featured in the athletic curriculum of many schools for the very good reason that it is too expensive. A good polo player needs six polo ponies if he is to play the game decently, and a polo field measures 300 yards by 160 yards—few schools have such extensive grounds. Polo is the ideal game for a cavalry regiment stationed in India, and it is no accident that one of Rudyard Kipling's best animal stories, "The Maltese Cat," is the tale of an epic encounter on "the hard dusty Umballa polo ground, lined with thousands of soldiers, black and white, not counting hundreds and hundreds of carriages, and drags and dog-carts, and ladies with brilliant-colored parasols, and officers in uniform and out of it, and crowds of natives behind them, and orderlies on camels who had halted to watch the game, instead of carrying letters up and down the station, and native horse-dealers running about on thin-eared Biluchi mares, looking for a chance to sell a few first-class polo ponies." Prince Philip's uncle, Lord Mountbatten, the last Viceroy of India, was, predictably enough, a fine polo player whose book *An Introduction to Polo,* written in the thirties under the pseudonym "Marco" and recently reprinted, remains the best polo textbook ever written.

Polo is a tough game requiring great skill and is possibly the oldest organized sport in the world. It probably started in Persia some two thousand years before the birth of Christ, when it was used primarily to make the Persian cavalry fit for battle. From Persia polo moved slowly to Arabia, Tibet, China, Japan and finally became Europeanized in 1859 when it was taken up by tea planters in Assam. A few years later it was adopted by the Calcutta Club and taken home to England in 1875 by the 10th Hussars and the 9th Lancers. It crossed the Atlantic a few years later, and in 1909 an American team beat the British and established more than forty years of U.S. dominance. In 1950, however, the Argentinians became world champions and at this writing remain unquestionably the best polo players in the world—with the best horses, the most players.

Charging one's opponents is not only allowed but is an

important part of the game, provided the angle of attack is no more than 45 degrees. "Since polo ponies travel at around 30 mph," says one expert player, "the combined speed of collision is around fifty to sixty. When that happens something has to go and it's more often the jockey than the horse." Under such circumstances tempers often fray. Prince Philip was notorious for his polo field language which was—to put it mildly—salty. Clare Tomlinson, Britain's leading woman player, who shares the same handicap as Prince Charles, says, "The language gets pretty lively. But it's part of the competition and you're going very fast and want to shout out." Polo players also point out that Prince Charles takes his chances along with the rest, and is neither given nor takes any quarter . . . "When he's out there he's out as a player. If he does something wrong he'll get a bollocking same as anybody else," says one fellow player, "All we do is put the word 'Sir' on the end. Get out of my f**king, way, you imbecile . . . Sir!"

Charles first played polo in public in 1965 at Windsor, which fortuitously has one of Britain's three top polo grounds. His father, Prince Philip, has now abandoned the game because of an arthritic wrist, but it is fairly common for Charles to get home after some official engagements, change into his riding gear and do an hour's "stick and ball," as polo practice is called.

At Cambridge Charles played regularly and won a "half-blue" for representing and captaining the university team. In the Navy, though, it was difficult for him to find the time or place for polo. On the few occasions he did play it was on a strange ground with unknown ponies and players. By 1974 his game had become so rusty that his handicap was reduced from three to two (polo handicaps work in the opposite way from golf—the higher your handicap the better your game). But once he left the Royal Navy at the end of 1976 he was able to devote more time and energy to the game, his official engagements were arranged to take account of it and he was able to play a full English season from halfway through April to the first weekend in August, taking in a summer tournament at the French resort of Deauville as well.

Apart from one or two mid-week tournaments nearly all British polo takes place on weekends, which makes it possible for someone with a job to play the game. It's not easy, though. Most of the top players are either professionals or gentleman-farmers or men like Lord "Sam" Vestey who run their own companies and can organize their time to suit themselves. It also helps if, like Vestey, you have your own helicopter to whisk you from London to Circencester a hundred or so miles away, the furthest of the main polo grounds from the British capital.

Because of Charles's problems combining his work and his polo it became necessary for someone to arrange his games and coach him properly. Since Prince Philip's retirement the job has been done by Major Ronald Ferguson, a forty-seven-year-old farmer who learned his polo with the Life Guards—one of the two cavalry regiments headquartered at Windsor. Ferguson, one of Britain's better players, had been a teammate of Prince Philip. Ferguson maps out Charles's schedules and advises him on every aspect of the game. In 1973 he even traveled to Argentina to buy the Prince five ponies. In the middle of winter Ferguson gets the English polo schedule and works out where and when Charles will be competing, then tells the Prince of Wales' office where the dates are to be incorporated into the year's calendar. "The polo dates are all marked down in red," says Ferguson, "and heaven help anybody who puts anything on top of them."

This year Charles will be playing his best polo with a team called Les Diables Bleus, captained by his friend Guy Wildenstein, scion of the wealthy family of art magnates and racehorse owners. Les Diables Bleus will be Charles "High Goal" team, in which the aggregate of handicaps has to be between 17 and 22 (Medium Goal requires 13 and 16 and Low Goal 4 to 8). For the first time Charles will be moving from his former number-one position to the number-four spot. Between Wildenstein and the Prince of Wales are two high-handicapped players who give the team extra class. At two is Julian Hipwood, who with a nine-handicap is Britain's top player, and at three is a seven-handicap Mexican professional named Gracida.

Ferguson says that his charge's game is improving greatly now that he is able to concentrate on it. His handicap of three is no more than average, but Ferguson says, "I would say that a three-handicap player is probably one on the way up. He's not necessarily a good player—yet. But he's determined to succeed and that goes a long way. I don't think he's a *naturally* good games player but he's made himself into one and acquired a real game sense. He's physically very tough and now that he has had more experience of riding he genuinely enjoys it."

Until recently, Charles was a better polo player than rider, but since leaving the Navy he has ridden more often and is now a fine cross-country racer in winter. He also goes fox-hunting regularly. "Now that he has begun to spend his winters in horse activities," says Ferguson, "his riding ability has improved. He used to be just somebody sitting on a horse. Now he's part of a horse, and because he's above average as a horseman he no longer has to worry about his horse. That means his confidence is greatly increased. Since confidence is at least sixty percent of the game that obviously affects the way he plays." Ferguson adds that, unlike some, Charles never mistreats his horse, even during the roughest game. "He can do it now not by ignorance or brutality but by equitation."

Polo also has the advantage of being one of the few pastimes in which a royal prince excites hardly any notice. Royal involvement, after all, was established by Prince Philip and Lord Mountbatten, and it is traditionally a game of princes and kings and, above all, maharajahs. It is said that eighty percent of those who now play can not afford it—the price of polo ponies ranges from 3,000 to 10,000 pounds. Many players are subsidized by commercial interests or rich individuals like Wildenstein. Despite polo's increasing professionalism—17,000 spectators paid to watch the international competition at Windsor in Jubilee Year—it remains essentially a game of the monied upper classes.

One of Prince Charles's favorite informal polo events is the annual weekend in Deauville, France, where Guy Wildenstein acts as his host. Charles is there in a purely private capacity and many of those who patronize the fashionable French resort don't recognize him at all (or pretend not to). The only reminder of his status is the constant shadowing presence of the French police, which Charles sometimes tries to shake off. Nonetheless,

John MacLean, the Prince's detective, is always there and smiles through the nickname "Inspector Clouseau," after the bumbling French policeman near-immortalized by Peter Sellers.

Polo is the only team sport that Charles plays—he has represented his country on a "Young England" team and on a Commonwealth team including players from Australia, New Zealand and Nigeria—and although he is competitive, he likes to stretch *himself* rather than prove he is better than anyone else, which explains in part why he likes the vigorous pursuits of the English countryside. Of these country pursuits the most exciting to him is fox-hunting—"riding to hounds," as the British call it . . .

Neither the Queen nor Prince Philip hunts foxes. It is still a popular pastime in Britain but it is also controversial. Oscar Wilde in a memorable epithet referred to "the English country gentleman galloping after a fox—the unspeakable in full pursuit of the uneatable," but many more English writers have celebrated the sport, notably 19th-century novelist Anthony Trollope. And Charles Dickens remarked in *Oliver Twist,* "There is a passion for hunting something deeply implanted in the human breast."

When as a schoolboy Charles first attended a meet of the West Norfolk Foxhounds he incurred the outraged indignation of the National Society for the Abolition of Cruel Sports but, of course, pleased the British Field Sports Society. For years afterward he did not hunt, but then his sister, freed from strict parental control by adulthood and then marriage, began to hunt regularly, and he has followed suit. It is a controversial decision and he knows it, and so his hunting is given a resolutely low profile. He seldom attends the meet at the beginning of the hunt, preferring to join after the riders have moved into open countryside away from tarmac roads and the attentions of their opponents. Fox-hunting excites fierce passions in the English, as do its less popular sister sports—stag-hunting and beagling (the hunting of hares). Members of the anti-blood-sports organizations frequently attend meets, harass the hunters, subject them to verbal abuse and try to mislead the hounds with trails of aniseed. Princess Anne has already tangled with demonstrators, but Charles has characteristically avoided any such confrontation.

There are some two hundred "hunts" in Britain, each one with a clearly defined geographical location. The Mendip Farmers, for example, hunt across the Mendip hills in Somerset and would never venture south across the border into the land of the Blackmore and Sparkford Vale, which in turn range across pretty farmland and down into the North of Dorset—the country immortalized by the great 19th-century novelist Thomas Hardy—until they come up against the territory of the South Dorset. There are, naturally, no hunts in the cities nor in the highlands of Scotland, which are too craggy and remote to make it practical. Hunting country begins some twenty or so miles outside London, but the most popular hunt with the Royal Family is the Beaufort, a hundred miles away. The Master of the Beaufort is also the Master of the Horse, a traditional royal title belonging to the Dukes of Beaufort. The present Duke is a seventy-nine-year-old aristocrat whose estate at Badminton in Gloucestershire is the venue of the annual three-day horse trial regularly patronized by Princess Anne and Mark Philips. The presence of the entire Royal Family at this event has become almost as traditional as the event itself, and when the Philipses moved into Gatcombe Park, nearby in the Cotswold Hills, one of the contributory factors in their choice was the chance of hunting with the Beaufort. It is unique in English fox-hunting, since the pace of hounds is the personal property of the Duke and the Mastership is, like the Dukedom, hereditary. Until the late eighteenth century the Beaufort hunted stags but since then they have gone after fox. Their land extends over 760 square miles of the choicest countryside in England, and their subscribers are correspondingly well off.

Another of Prince Charles's favorite hunts is the Belvoir (pronounced "beaver"). Until 1896 the Dukes of Rutland were Masters of the Belvoir with almost the same inevitability as the Dukes of Beaufort are Masters of the Beaufort. But times have been unkind to Rutland. The county, once the smallest in England, has been abolished under local government reorganization and the Belvoir now hunts over Leicestershire and

Lincolnshire. This part of England, known as "The Shires," is the most famous hunting country of all, and it was here that Prince Charles's predecessor, Edward VIII, used to turn out regularly with his aide-de-camp, Major "Fruity" Metcalfe. Like Prince Charles, Edward was a feisty sportsman and not only performed daringly when the Quorn—most famous of all hunts—was after a fox but also rode in point-to-points, as the amateur steeplechases held at the end of the hunting season are known. Charles has not yet done this, but he is a good horseman and jumps bravely.

For its devotees fox-hunting is glamorous and exciting. From ten o'clock in the morning until mid-afternoon a hunter rides hard across beautiful countryside, which puts all his stamina and horsemanship to the test. The kill, apologists argue, is incidental. It is the chase, the getting there, that counts. Yet the successful climax *is* the kill, and the killing of a fox by hounds is offensive to many. Charles himself has said that if the pressures became too fierce he would consider giving it up. "You can't have everything you want," he says, "even if you feel it does no harm. People's sensibilities count."

As if in preparation for this he has taken up a new sport—cross-country riding which he began in the spring of 1978. It is as near as possible to hunting without the fox. The riders tear round in a circular course provided with jumps as difficult and unpredictable as those they would meet on the hunting field. It takes between five and six minutes and is exciting and demanding. Charles captains two teams, the Duke of Cornwall's Chasers and the Earl of Chester's Chasers. Each has four riders, and Charles is invariably one of the most fearless. On the hunting field he takes pride in outstripping the rest of the field and keeping up with the huntsman, whose place is with the hounds as near to the fleeing fox as possible. In the Cross-Country Team Events Charles is also recognized as a fast and fearless rider, not afraid to take a fall. "Good practice for parachuting," he says whenever he comes off his mount.

Cross-country events are organized by the local hunts and are beginning to attract crowds of about a thousand spectators, though organizers are scrupulous about not announcing Prince

Charles's participation in advance. It is more tame than fox-hunting, but also less controversial. Unlike fox-hunting it does not give Charles a chance to explore unexpected tracts of open country, nor does it have that almost mystic appeal which some seem to find in pitting one's wits against a wild animal. "The attration in hunting is that it acts on the mind as a poultice does on a sore," remarked Leon Trotsky—and for once the heir to the British throne might agree with him....

In Britain "country pursuits" mean hunting, shooting and fishing, and Prince Charles is keen on all three. Like many upper-class Englishmen he was taught to shoot when a child of no more than ten years old, and taught first by his father, a crack shot, though Charles is now generally agreed to be better still. Much of Charles's shooting is done on the holidays he takes with the rest of the family in the five weeks after Christmas at Sandringham and in August and early September at Balmoral. Shooting in Britain is governed by ancient and complex game laws, under which you can't shoot pheasant or grouse on Sundays but you may shoot geese and duck, in most English counties, though not on Christmas Day. The grouse-shooting season begins on August 12, known as "the glorious twelfth," and finishes on December 10. Balmoral encompasses some fine grouse moors, and the birds thrive there. Grouse like high, scrubby mountainous plateaus, which means that they are most numerous in Scotland or Yorkshire, though they have now been introduced to the moors of southwest England. The pheasant-shooting season begins on October 1, and partridge shooting on September 15. Both close on February 1, which means that there is opportunity for the Royal Family and their guests to shoot as often as they like during their post-Christmas holiday at Sandringham. Sandringham boasts some of the finest pheasant and partridge shooting in the world, though the day's bag, which can run to several hundred, does sometimes suggest that skill is not entirely at a premium. For most of the year the pheasants are guarded by gamekeepers expressly so that they may be hunted during the winter months. So it is one of the paradoxes of English rural life that without this ritualized killing there probably would be no pheasant or partridge in the country, since sportsmen such as Charles are the only people really interested in preserving the birds, who otherwise would die out.

Like fox-hunting, shooting has a particular mystique. The "Norfolk" jacket, heavy, tweedy, belted and, for shooting purposes, with a leather patch near the right shoulder to save the cloth from being eroded by the gun-butt, is certainly part of it. So are peaked tweed caps pulled low over the forehead and baggy plus-four trousers tucked into woollen stockings. Gun-belts containing cartridges are worn at the waist and dogs—spaniels, Labradors or retrievers—are brought along to retrieve birds and finish off those which have not been cleanly killed. The favored gun is a twelve-bore shotgun, preferably from one of the two most famous London gunsmiths, Purdey or Holland and Holland. Charles favors Purdeys.

The marksmen stand in a line, concealed from the birds, which are driven toward them by beaters. The usual cartridge is a number six, loaded with round lead pellets. Each weapon has two barrels and the crack shot will dispatch two birds each time with a well-judged shot from each barrel. It is very unlike rifle shooting, much more instinctive, a matter of conditioned reflexes rather than the slow calculating squeeze of the rifle's trigger. In shooting with a shotgun the best marksmen, like Charles, usually pull the trigger the instant the butt touches their shoulder.

The enormous "bags" of years past are now considered bad form. Shooting companions of Charles emphasize that he feels one can have a wonderful day's sport and kill hardly anything at all, while on another day one may massacre hundreds of birds and have no pleasure in doing it. At Sandringham the birds are wild and fly with all the guile, cunning and speed of their nature—Sandringham pheasant and partridges have not been artificially reared since 1910. Elsewhere, though, in what one friend of Charles disparagingly refers to as "stockbroker shooting," the birds are especially bred and reared to fly sluggishly and stupidly, providing no challenge.

Grouse, which fly at 80 mph, are often considered the best sport of all. Coming at the guns in coveys of between five and twelve, they "contour," using the wind and the slightest slopes and dips in the moors to camouflage themselves and avoid the gunfire. A really good shot will aim to bring down two birds in front of him, but in practice only exceptional marksmen can bring off two birds in front with any regularity.

The shooting seems important to Charles but the surroundings are even more so. He likes to get out into wild country with good companions—and the more rugged and challenging the better. One of his favorite pursuits is "wild-fowling," which is done at Sandringham around dawn and dusk. It is, he says, extraordinarily exciting to hear the cracking of the ice on the lakes and ponds as the wild duck emerge for the morning flight, and to hear the swoosh of their wings as they come home in the evening against a backdrop of pink sunset. It's perhaps less so to wait for them up to your waist in mud and water, though he doesn't mind. . . .

The only blood sport that Charles shares with the Queen is deer-stalking. Every summer holiday at Balmoral Queen Elizabeth goes out to shoot deer armed with a super light Rigby .275 rifle and accompanied by one of the local employees—a highly-skilled stalker who knows the rugged countryside like the back of his hand. Her fondness for stalking echoes Queen Victoria's, who loved Balmoral above all her homes and recorded her adventures there in an evocative diary:

"We scrambled up an almost perpendicular place to where there was a little box, made of hurdles and interwoven with branches of fir and heather, about five feet in height. There we seated ourselves with Bertie [her son, the Prince of Wales], Macdonald lying in the heather near us, watching and quite concealed; some had gone round to beat, and others again were at a little distance . . . Albert fancied he heard a distant sound, and, in a few minutes, Macdonald whispered that he saw stags and that Albert should wait and take a steady aim. We then heard them coming past. Albert . . . fired through the branches, and then again over the box. The deer retreated; but Albert felt certain he had hit a stag. He ran up to the keepers, and at that moment they called from below that they 'had got him,' and Albert ran on to see. I waited for a bit, but soon scrambled on with Bertie's and Macdonald's help; and Albert joined us directly and we all went down and saw a magnificent stag, a 'royal' which had dropped, soon after Albert had hit him, at one of the men's feet. The sport was successful and everyone was delighted."

Queen Victoria's enthusiasm for deer-stalking in the Scottish Highlands was soon caught by other foreigners, and today, each year about 10,000 Scottish stags and twice as many hinds are shot. This does not diminish the overall population of red deer, which is now estimated at about 270,000 and growing annually. Since the 1950s the Scots, like nearly everyone else, have become much more aware of conversation and ecology, so that the annual deer-stalking which used to be pure sport, indiscriminately pursued, is now much more in the nature of a cull—a controlled killing that actually improves the herd. In the old days Prince Albert was sufficiently un-British as to shoot tame stag from the drawingroom windows of Blair Castle. Such behavior is now out of the question. With rare exceptions, for which a hundred or more pounds are charged, the only deer shot are the old and infirm. The hunter is seen to be complementing the natural job soon to be completed by the harsh Scottish winter, which annually kills about the same number of deer humans do.

Prince Charles has taken avidly to deer-stalking. He hunts with a custom-made 7-mm rifle, built by one of the stalkers on the Balmoral estate . . . Charles found a barrel and carved and fitted the stock himself; the weight and balance and general "feel" of the weapon make it the only one Charles really likes. It's as well-fitting as a suit of clothes, he says, but the shooting of deer is only a tiny part of an exercise that normally takes all day, from 9 A.M. until after 6 P.M. and involves a rough, grueling trek across deserted and exceptionally demanding terrain. There's often very little cover, so that a good deal of time is spent scrambling about on hands and knees with only eagles, ptarmigan, grouse and deer for company. Charles goes out with a professional stalker, a local man who knows every gully and boulder, every dip and hollow—an expert in the craft he practices almost every day of his life. As soon as the deer are spotted, Charles and his stalker examine them through their telescopes and identify their quarry, then begin the stalk, going on until the Prince has a clear, unimpeded shot of between 80 and 150 yards.

Many of the great deer forests can be approached only by water and once one has begun the stalk there is no question of using anything but one's wits and strength. No little electric carts or helicopters or any of the other aids of the twentieth century. Apart from the improvement in rifles—most people now use telescopic sights to insure a clean kill—the sport is the same as it has always been, as close to recapturing his primitive past as man can get. Even the names of the forests evoke the atmosphere of peat, wet heather and impending rain: Loch Choire, Knoydart, Glenstrathfarrar, Ardnamurchan, Kildermorie and Balmoral itself. Almost one hundred and fifty years ago a gentleman named William Scrope wrote a book called *The Art of Deer-Stalking,* and his advice is as valid today as it ever was. "Your consummate deer-stalker," he says, "should not only be able to run like an antelope, and breathe like the trade winds, but should also be enriched with various other undeniable qualifications. As for instance he should be able to run in a stooping position at a greyhound pace, with his back parallel to the ground, and his face within an inch of it for miles together. He should take a singular pleasure in threading the seams of a bog, or of gliding down a burn *ventre-à-terre,* like that insinuating animal, the eel; accomplished he should be in skilfully squeezing his clothes after this operation, to make all comfortable."

A good stalker, now as then, needs the physique of a mountain goat, the stamina of a camel and the eye of a hawk. Above all, though, he needs the urge to put himself up against the elements in a near-masochistic fashion. Noel Coward used to sing "Mad dogs and Englishmen/Go out in the midday sun," which is another way of saying that some Englishmen, of whom Prince Charles is one, take their pleasures extremely seriously. For him, honorable blood, toil, tears and sweat bring their own rewards. . . .

Charles's attitude toward fishing, the third in the holy trinity of British blood sports, is very similar: his favorite fishing is in Iceland because it is remote and hard. He has been there four times and once spent two-and-a-half hours attached to one stubborn salmon that he was convinced would turn out to be a whale. To his initial chagrin, when he finally landed it, it seemed a relative minnow of seventeen pounds. A companion immediately attemtped to dispatch it with a heavy club, which shattered the instant he delivered the blow. "*That* fish was solid bone," recalls Charles, telling the story with evident relish.

On many British waters much of the work is done by ghillies—gamekeepers—who will guide the fisherman to the most likely spot, advise him on what type of fly to use, where to cast and, in short, do everything but actually catch the fish. Charles prefers to make his own mistakes and learn from them, and the isolated waters of Iceland are ideal for this. On a typical day in Iceland he may walk six miles or more, and if he has reasonable luck he will land as many as half-a-dozen ten-pound salmon. Just carrying those fish home is hardy exercise.

Charles began fishing at the age of eight in Scotland and was taught by his father, his grandmother (who is probably the best in the family after Charles) and a Balmoral ghilly named Bob Brown. Rear Admiral Sir Christopher Bonham-Carter, for years Prince Philip's treasurer and chief policy adviser, was another who helped when he began fishing the local streams for trout. Later he progressed to salmon, generally acknowledged to be the world's finest game fish.

Charles is not only adept at the technical sides, casting his wet fly adroitly into the water and letting the current carry it down to the waiting fish, he is also highly skilled at the fieldcraft, which is just as important . . . he can tell, sense, from the temperature and the strength of the current pretty much where the fish are likely to be. Of course he also makes mistakes, once spending a day on the famous Restigouche River in Canada, and catching nothing.

The biggest fish Charles has yet caught was a twenty-five-pounder he pulled from Dorset's River Frome, rated by experts one of the most difficult rivers in the world, and he once caught a twenty-four-pounder in Scotland's River Tay. Nearly all his fishing is done with a wet fly for salmon, and he is able to practice the art in some of the finest salmon rivers in Britain. The Dee near Balmoral is his home water but he also fishes the Spey, Tay, Helmsdale, Laxford and Wye. On the River Test in southern England he occasionally fishes for trout with a dry fly (in dry fly fishing the fly is cast more precisely and remains above the water line, whereas in wet fly the fly is dragged through the water). This he regards as skilled, demanding and worthy sport, but game-fishing at sea is another matter. He has tried it only once, and says he has no wish to repeat the experiment.

There is hardly a major sport in the world Charles will not or has not tried. Recently he rediscovered skiing. As a child his early endeavors on the slopes had been ruined by pressmen and photographers, but now that he has matured he is not bothered by them and in any case is now good enough to outski most journalists. He is extremely daring and not afraid to take a tumble—to the recurring alarm of his hosts and companions.

He also enjoys water-skiing and wind-surfing when he gets the chance, but is less aquatic than his naval career and background might suggest. An accomplished and stylish swimmer, he still doesn't seem to have pursued his sailing as avidly as seemed likely at one stage. On the other hand Prince Philip used to be a particularly keen sailor and was a regular participant in the renowned Cowes Regatta in the Solent between the Isle of Wight and the English coast, and several times Charles crewed for him. But since the death of his sailing companion, the bluff, sea-shanty-singing Uffa Fox, Prince Philip too seems to sail only occasionally.

Whatever, Charles keeps himself ruthlessly fit, jogging daily if he can't manage more strenuous exercise. He eats sparingly and drinks comparatively little. He is something of an anti-smoking fetishist, is a restless and complaining spectator, really happy only when he is taking part. "He would love to be able to spend more time hunting," says one of his closest friends, "but if something like this [1979 good-will] trip round the world comes up . . . there is never any question of where his duty lies."

A man for all seasons, but above all, inescapably, born to rule.

EPILOGUE

Whither Charles...?

"I DON'T ENVY YOU," one of Prince Charles's most pleasant and attractive women friends told us, sipping at her glass of chilled white burgundy. "I mean you *certainly* can't quote *me,* nor can anyone else. He wouldn't confide in anyone if he thought they were going to shoot their mouth off...."

"I had the opportunity to talk to Prince Charles about this," remarked one of his closest friends—also not for attribution—"and he is quite happy for me to have a talk with you if only because we both agree that if these books are to be written they may at least be relatively accurate...."

Prince Charles's friends, in other words, maintain the traditional stiff upper lip—buttoned down. "I trust my friends implicitly," he has said, "and they know that. The more discreet they are, the better." Conversation with them is littered with discreet silences and tight smiles. Acquaintances, however, may be garrulous and revealing—and so are never friends. Robert Lacey, writing about the Queen's friends, described them as "a small group out of the public eye and anxious to keep out of it, in a protective conspiracy extending beyond themselves." It is essentially the same with Charles.

In another sense, however, Charles's friends "betray" him,

for they are drawn almost exclusively from the upper or perhaps upper-middle classes, just as they were at Cambridge. That is not to say that Charles is stand-offish or snobbish. He gets on well with socialist politicans such as James Callaghan or with the relatively humble people who help with The Prince's Trust or his Welsh conservation interests. In one-to-one contacts with his people during ceremonial tours and public appearances Charles almost invariably makes a most favorable impression: as he moved through the wards of the eleven-million-dollar Prince Charles Hospital in Merthyr Tydfil, Wales, in December, 1977, one of the patients with whom he had been chatting exclaimed, "What a wonderful bedside manner!" And the Prince has forthrightly identified himself with the drive for racial equality in England, serving as interlocutor of the 1978 BBC anthropology series, *Face Values*, to promote his vision of racial harmony and, on a more practical basis, to insist that black as well as white social workers—and also a youth and a woman—serve among the usual establishment elders on the board of the Silver Jubilee Trust. But these contacts are all in the course of Charles's official business. For purely social life—if the heir to the throne can be said to have a purely social life—he chooses friends such as Lord and Lady Tollemache. Lord Tollemache, "Tim" to his friends, inherited a family brewing business in East Anglia. He is a few years older than Charles, an old Etonian who hunts, shoots and fishes and owns two country houses, one in Cheshire, the other in Suffolk. Others in Charles's set include Norton Knatchbull, son of Lord Mountbatten's daughter Pamela (she is married to Lord Brabourne, the film producer who made *Sink the Bismarck*). Knatchbull was at Gordonstoun, one of the few surviving friends from schooldays, though he is a family rather than childhood friend. Another is Nicholas Soames, son of Britain's former Ambassador to France and a grandson, through his mother Mary, of Sir Winston Churchill. Charles is also close to Richard Beckett, a barrister whose father is a baronet (the least of the hereditary titles in Britain), to Hugh van Cutsem, son of the late Newmarket racehorse owner Bernard van Cutsem and formerly an officer in the Brigade of Guards, and to Lord and Lady Tryon, who have accompanied him on fishing trips to Iceland in August. Tryon is an old Etonian merchant banker. His father was the Queen's treasurer, and he himself was once her page. (It is often suggested that of the two, Charles actually prefers Tryon's Australian born wife, Dale; just as it is often hinted that he prefers Rosalind Ward to her husband, Gerald.)

Such as those he describes as his "few but very good friends." When discussing friendship in an interview with a London evening paper, he added, "I always rather fought shy at school and elsewhere of group or gang behavior. I've always been happier with one or two people. I do have some marvelous friends; I'm very lucky. I've made them since I left school." Elsewhere, of course, he has said that "I enjoy shooting; and therefore I see a lot of people who shoot." Clearly he enjoys the company of those who have similar tastes and interests—not so remarkable—and since those tastes and interests tend to be those of the landed aristocracy, his friends tend to be landed aristocrats. Not exclusively, but mainly.

Apart from the fairly exclusive company he keeps, another factor that might alienate the populace from a monarch of less than Charles's considerable charm and tact is the undeniable luxury in which he lives. Charles is not a conspicuous spendthrift in the playboy manner, and yet he does have the best of everything: foreign holidays, private aircraft, private trains, opulent castles, the most expensive clothing, (even his famous "T"-shirts are personalized). However sympathetic Charles may be to the concerns of his less fortunate subjects—and he has said that "the first function of any monarchy is the human concern for people"—he can't know firsthand what it is like to struggle to work every morning on the subway; or to live in a one-room tenement; or to be burdened with heavy mortgage payments on a house; or to wonder where the next meal is coming from or how to vote in the next general election (he has reminded reporters "that in company with convicts, lunatics and peers of the realm I am ineligible to vote").

Margot Asquith, wife of the former Liberal Prime Minister, observed: "Royal Persons are necessarily divorced from the true opinions of people that count, and are almost always obliged to take safe and commonplace views. To them, clever men are 'prigs'; clever women 'too advanced'; Liberals are 'Socialists'; the uninteresting 'pleasant'; the interesting 'intriguers' and the dreamers 'mad.'" That verdict is more than fifty years old, and since it was delivered the British monarchy has, in many respects, been streamlined and democratized. Prince Charles is without question nearer to the average Briton than any previous heir to the throne. His upbringing was designed to make him so, with concessions such as his boarding school education or his service career.

Moreover, it is a personal triumph for Charles that his privileged status is not more widely resented. He is seen—and accurately—to work hard as well as play hard, to be concerned about the nation's problems and to have a sense of humor and perspective. All this will go a long distance to protect him during the years to come. Obviously he believes in his motto *Ich Dien* ("I serve") and is prepared to work hard at serving his people. "If people respect you," he has said, "think you are worthwhile, then they'll want to be associated with you. They'll want you to help them with their activities, with their ventures; and if you choose to go in with them you can reasonably hope to try to influence them to do what you think is good and useful."

At the moment all the evidence is that most Britons do indeed think him "worthwhile," to say the least. In 1978 *Life* magazine reported that a recent poll showed no less than one third of them would like to see Queen Elizabeth step down and Charles assume the throne. Marge Davies, an Oxford cleaning woman, told *Time* magazine, "Charlie would really be good for the country. We need someone like him." And porter Jack Diment seems to voice the consensus of the country in the judgment, "He is a thoroughly good bloke."

Tact and modesty, though, may not be enough to overcome a number of more immediate problems—the first of which is his marriage. By now he must surely regret that casual remark—"I personally feel that a good age for a man to get married is around thirty." He will be "around thirty" for a few years, but the pressure is on, and every time he is seen with a woman, there are fresh and pervasive rumors...a visit to the Duke of

Wellington's estates in Spain, and the usual "authoritative" stories about an imminent marriage to Lady Jane Wellesely begin to fly once again. And most recently, in March, 1979, a rendezvous with Davina Sheffield in Perth, Australia, set off press predictions of an immediate bethrothal. All very irritating to Charles, but it is four years now since he said, "When you get to my extraordinary stage of decrepitude one begins ... to look at a girl and think, 'I wonder if one could every marry her,' or something like that. And obviously there are certain people I've thought of on those lines."

Just who those "certain people" are is anyone's (everyone's) guess, though Lady Jane Wellesley would seem to place—or have placed—high in the sweepstakes.

Lord Mountbatten was fond of telling reporters that the eventual bride will come as a complete surprise to all. In view of the way that the press and public attempt to monitor Prince Charles's every move, that would be a considerable achievement. As of this writing the offical line put out by the Palace in public and by Charles in private is that the next and future Queen is as much a mystery to the next and future King as she is to his future subjects. As he has always said, she will have to be a very particular person because she will be marrying into the firm as well as the family, and she will be taking on a role as well as a husband—a role and the success she makes of it to be of crucial importance to the future of the monarchy. In recent years the wise, or fortuitous, royal marriages to Elizabeth Bowes-Lyon, now the Queen Mother, and to Prince Philip, have done much to enhance the prestige of the monarchy. By the same token it was the unwise matrimonial aspirations of Edward VIII which almost toppled it. For Charles and the monarchy it is the single most important question to be answered, and it is a matter of concern to everyone. No one could relish so public a courtship, but then being a crown prince, for all its undeniable advantages and privileges, does have drawbacks and being public property is, of course, one of them. It is possible that by the time this book is published Charles may have announced an engagement. He has already made it clear that he will be as pragmatic about it as possible, for his marriage must be "forever." As he told Kenneth

Harris of the *Observer*, "If I'm deciding on whom I want to live with for fifty years—well, that's the last decision in which I would want to be ruled by my heart. It's nothing to do with class—it's to do with compatibility.... Marriage isn't an 'up' or 'down' issue anyway. It's a side-by-side issue."

On the basis of what we know it seems certain that the Princess of Wales will be a young, attractive Englishwoman of aristocratic if not noble birth. She will not be a Roman Catholic, nor a foreigner. And she is likely to be an old friend. On *that* basis Lady Jane Wellesley would seem to do very nicely indeed.

All this, of course, supposes that Charles is as keen to marry as he says he is. He does obviously enjoy taking out pretty girls whom he has no intention of marrying. On January 10, 1979, for example, he escorted Susan George to the Piccadilly Theatre to see the Australian comic Barry Humphries do his celebrated impersonation of "Dame Edna Everage." Miss George, a former beauty queen and good friend of tennis star Jimmy Connors and singer Jack Jones, is an admirable dinner date for a dashing bachelor crown prince, but she is no more appropriate or likely as a future Queen than, say, Margaret Trudeau or Shirley Bassey. As Charles told Douglas Keay of *Woman's Own,* "I have to be careful I don't get too involved . . . falling madly in love with someone is not necessarily the starting point to getting married."

Today he may be conscious of the ever-increasing pressure on him to marry (from his immediate family as well as from newspaper columnists and politicians), but he is not noticeably averse to bachelor life. He enjoys sowing a few wild oats and is not unaware of the advantages in that activity of his rank and title: gentlemen may prefer blondes, but ladies are clearly drawn to future kings.

Meanwhile, the prospect of an aging bachelor Prince of Wales is disquieting for many, and not only because it conjures up the ghost of the ill-fated Duke of Windsor. Much of the Royal Family's current success is founded on the picture of family fidelity that they present to the world. In an age of promiscuity, high divorce rate, agnosticism and a general disinterest in the moral precepts of earlier times, the House of

Windsor stands for the solid virtues of family life. Support for the monarchy comes from a silent majority which may not always practice such virtues itself but at least still respects them in others and demands something—someone—to look up to.

Similarly, there is concern about a prince who is *permanently* in waiting. Victoria's son waited until he was fifty-nine, and by then he was debauched and long past his best. Edward, Charles's predecessor as Prince of Wales, was in his early forties when he took over the throne, with such disruptive consequences. If Elizabeth lives as long as Victoria, her son, like Victoria's, will be nearing sixty—taking on his role just when many people are contemplating their slippers and rocking chair.

One solution would be abdication. Not likely. Charles himself has said, "I don't believe it's a good idea for a monarch to abdicate before time," a remark which seemed to leave the door marginally open. The Queen herself has never mentioned it and appears to hold the official line which Charles has also expressed: "I believe the monarch is of even more assistance to the whole country and the government, the older he or she is. I think you gain so much in experience in understanding events and problems, prime ministers and personalities that you are of infinitely more help." Queen Elizabeth's experience already stretches back more than a quarter of a century and her weekly prime-ministerial audiences began with Sir Winston Churchill. A premature retirement would only be likely if her health began to fail badly, and even then a formal abdication seems improbable. It is much more likely that Prince Charles would then act as Regent for the duration of the crisis rather than take over the title as well as the duties of kingship.

If abdication is ruled out, Charles has to find something to do with the thirty-odd years which probably remain to him before he becomes King. Part of the reason for the failure and disenchantment of his two immediate predecessors is now said to be that they were dangerously unfilfilled, that they had nothing meaningful to do. Charles, as we have seen, has been better educated than any heir to the throne so far and is also fully occupied. His schedule is crowded, his dedication enormous, his energy near-uncontrollable, and he divides his time and energy between work and purposeful recreation. Nor does he seem to think of his present duties simply as a preparation for kingship. "I'm not much conscious of being a monarch-to-be," he told the *Observer's* Kenneth Harris. "I'm much more conscious of being a Prince of Wales-as-is." A fair and realistic point. Yet for all his apparent sense of purpose and place, he also said to students of his old university, "My great problem is that I do not really know what my role in life is. *At the moment* [italics ours] I do not have one, but somehow I must find one for myself."

A popular solution has long been the Governor-Generalship of Australia, but the Australians have for years now insisted that the Queen's official representative be a native Australian. Besides, Governor-Generalships are too likely to be politically sensitive posts these days—the new Canadian incumbent, Ed Schreyer, a young and active politician, is a case in point; and a Governor-General would almost certainly need to be married. Moreover, such an appointment would require an invitation from Australia.

Charles could have stayed on in the Navy, but once he had achieved his own command there would have been an inevitable period of shore-bound staff work. Neither he nor his advisers thought this sensible. Lord Butler wanted him to go into the Foreign Office like his cousin Prince William of Gloucester (killed piloting his own plane), but members of his family thought this was political.

So for the foreseeable future Charles will continue to throw himself into the work of the United World Colleges and The Prince's Trust and the Committee for the Environment in Wales; he will continue to tour the British Isles and the world outside, learning on the one hand, advising on the other; constantly changing from one uniform into another, wearing any number of literal and figurative hats and, in each one, trying to be as gracious and well-informed and interested and useful as he is decorative. He will continue to visit industrial companies and Trade Union offices; to attend degree ceremonies and dinners; to open new buildings and railway lines and leisure centers; to accept honorary memberships in ancient companies; to inspect troops; to give away prizes, address annual general meetings and conferences, listen to the English Chamber Orchestra (of which he is patron) and the Bach Choir (of which he is president), receive the freedom of cities, and smile and wave and shake hands and altogether put on a very good show indeed... "Life is what I make it," says Charles, who is clearly determined to make the most of the present while preparing for the future. "In these times the monarchy is called into question," he adds. "It is not to be taken for granted. One has to be far more professional than one ever used to be." Says one American journalist who has traveled with Prince Charles, "The guy works so hard you'd think he was running for office."

Through it all, he is, in the British idiom, a nice chap. The breadth of his duties and interests may preclude depth, but the British have always especially prized the all-rounder, the generalist, and they tend to distrust intellectuals as "too clever by half." Charles is keen enough on the arts to satisfy the culturally inclined but he combines this with enough of his father's down-to-earth common sense to appeal to the average Briton.

After the often depressing days of childhood when he seemed dull and lacking in self-confidence Charles has emerged into a debonair, ebullient and assured adulthood. After a slow start he has reached maturity, he has acquired a man's estate. And now there is the future. Will he really be content with being colonel of this and president of that, with launching well-intentioned if somewhat peripheral schemes to help young people and improve aspects of the environment? If so he will have done better than many of his predecessors; but it is scarcely enough. The position he enjoys has, maddeningly, nearly as many constraints as it has opportunities. How uniquely irritating to know that when you speak the world listens but that you are not allowed, in many areas, to speak your mind. It is that sense of frustration which so characterizes his father—an able man whose cherished naval career was cut off in its prime and who has been condemned to a secondary position ever since. For Charles Philip Arthur George the prospect of a lifetime in his mother's shadow is, one suspects, more disconcerting than he acknowledges. He has abilities and gifts and extraordinary

213

opportunities to use them, and at the back of his mind must echo the tortured words of the last Prince of Wales: "Something must be done."

Without question Charles is already doing much more than any previous Prince of Wales and he plans to continue adding on to his workload. "I am planning," he said, "to find out all I can about British life, including the government, the civil service, business, agriculture, the unions—everything."

An ambitious outlook, perhaps, but surely one right and fitting for the man who will be King.